Eating Well
for People with Learning Disabilities

Eating Well
for People with Learning Disabilities

NUTRITIONAL AND PRACTICAL GUIDELINES

SECOND EDITION

Edited by Carly Atkinson RD

www.cwt.org.uk

© The Caroline Walker Trust, 2025
ISBN 978-1-897820-49-0

Published by The Caroline Walker Trust, 2025.
First Edition published 2007

www.cwt.org.uk
E: info@cwt.org.uk
Registered charity number: 328580

Typeset by Chris Sims
Printed in Great Britain

This report is provided for information only, and individual advice on diet and health should always be sought from appropriate health professionals.

The Caroline Walker Trust
The Caroline Walker Trust (CWT) is dedicated to the improvement of public health by means of good food. It was established in 1989 to continue the work of the campaigning nutritionist Caroline Walker, who passionately believed that everyone deserves access to good-quality food. The CWT has produced a series of publications which provide practical guidance on eating well for those who care for vulnerable people in our society.

The aim of CWT reports is to provide a summary of current knowledge about the eating and drinking issues for specific population groups and to provide nutrient-based standards, practical guidelines and recommendations which people can use as the basis for improving practice and developing policy both nationally and locally.

© 2025 The Caroline Walker Trust, (print and electronic)
All rights reserved.

This book is copyright material and must not be copied, reproduced, transferred, transmitted, distributed, leased, licensed, stored in a retrieval system, used in AI-Generated content, or publicly performed or used in any way except as specifically permitted in writing by the publishers, as allowed under the terms and conditions under which it was purchased or as strictly permitted by applicable copyright law. Any unauthorised distribution or use of this text may be a direct infringement of the author's and publisher's rights, and those responsible may be liable in law accordingly.

For permission requests, write to the publisher, address
"Attention: Permissions for EWLD", at the email address below:
The Caroline Walker Trust
info@cwt.org.uk

Other publications by The Caroline Walker Trust
Eating Well: First Year of Life – Practical Guide
Eating Well for 1-4 Year Olds – Practical Guide
Eating Well for 12-18 Year Olds – Practical Guide
Eating Well for Looked After Children and Young People
Eating Well: Supporting Older People and Older People with Dementia
Supplementary Guides on Balanced Meal Pictures

Contents

Chapter 1 **Summary and Recommendations**
Summary 13
What is the scope of this report? 14
Recommendations 15
Practical Guidelines 17

Chapter 2 **About Learning Disabilities**
What is a learning disability? 26
Care and support for people with learning disabilities 27
Causes of learning disabilities and their
impact on health 28
Other health difficulties associated
with learning disabilities 31
The impact of learning disabilities on eating and drinking . . 34
The effects of drugs on nutritional status 37
Can diet be used to prevent or treat learning disabilities? . . 39
Can diet be used to treat specific conditions found among
people with learning disabilities? 40

Chapter 3 **Principles of Good Nutrition**
The Eatwell Guide 49
Energy (calories) 50
Fat 51
Carbohydrates 52
Fibre 53
Protein 54
Vitamins 54
Minerals 57
Water 59
Alcohol 60
Improving health outcomes: heart disease,
bone disorders, cancer and infections 60

Chapter 4 **Nutrition through the Lifespan for People
with Learning Disabilities**
Infants 66
Children 67
Teenagers 68
Pregnancy 69
Parenthood 70
The Menopause 70
Older Age 70
End-of-Life 71

Chapter 5	**Monitoring Nutritional Status and Supporting People with Healthy Weight**
	Monitoring Nutritional Status 74
	Underweight and Malnutrition Risks 76
	Nutrition Support 78
	Managing Overweight 79
	Type 2 Diabetes 81
	Physical Activity 85

Chapter 6	**Gastrointestinal Disorders, Swallowing Difficulties and Oral Health**
	Gastrointestinal Disorders 92
	Constipation 92
	Diarrhoea 96
	Coeliac Disease 96
	Swallowing Difficulties (Dysphagia) 97
	Oral Health 98

Chapter 7	**Encouraging Eating Well**
	Philosophy of Care: Rights and Responsibilities 105
	The Eating Environment 106
	Helping People Make Good Choices 108
	Organisational Culture 110
	Staff Training and Support 110
	Involving and listening to family and friends 111
	Food as a treat or reward 111
	Engaging with health and other professionals 112
	Health action plans and annual health checks 113
	Food knowledge and skills of people with learning disabilities 114

Chapter 8	**Supporting People with Eating Difficulties**
	Maintaining independence in eating 117
	Helping people to eat 117
	Positioning when people need help with eating and drinking 118
	Strategies to deal with eating and drinking difficulties 119
	• Extreme faddy or selective eating 119
	• Food refusal 120
	• Nausea and vomiting 121
	• Mouth sensitivity 121
	• Drooling or dribbling 122
	• Bruxism (teeth grinding) 122
	Other problem behaviours around food and drink 122

Chapter 9 **Food-based Guidance**

Food Labels 128
Food Groups 129
- Starchy Carbohydrates 129
- Fruit and Vegetables 130
- Beans, pulses, fish, eggs, meat and
  other protein foods 131
- Dairy or dairy alternatives 133
- Oils and spreads 134

Sugar 134
Salt 135
Vitamin, mineral and herbal supplements 136

Chapter 10 **Menu Planning**

Eating patterns and timing of meals and snacks 139
- Breakfast 139
- Packed Lunches 139
- School Lunches 140
- Snacks 140
- Eating Out and Takeaways 142
- Drinks 143

Example meal ideas 146
- 1 – 4 years 146
- 5 – 11 years 147
- 12 – 18 years 148
- Adults 149

The cost of a good diet 151
Sustainability 151
Why encourage people to cook 151
Meeting Nutrient Based Standards' 152

Chapter 11 **Special Diets**

Vegetarian Diets 155
Vegan Diets 155
Traditional Ethnic and Religious Diets 156
Food Allergy and Intolerance 158
Finger Foods 159
Changing Food and Drink Textures 162

Appendix 1	**Good Sources of Nutrients**	167
Appendix 2	**Resources**	169
Appendix 3	**Weight Monitoring Chart**	178
Appendix 4	**Food, Fluid, Bowel and Symptom Chart**	179
Appendix 5	**Health and Social Care Regulations**	180
Appendix 6	**An example of a Mental Capacity Assessment**	183
Appendix 7	**Example Food/Nutrition Policy**	185
Appendix 8	**Height Conversion Chart**	186
Appendix 9	**Weight Conversion Chart**	187
Index		188

Preface

In recent years, there have been continued developments in the way people with learning disabilities are supported, including better nutrition advice and a greater recognition of their individual needs and rights to lead fulfilling and healthy lives. We are delighted to introduce this revised edition, which brings together the latest evidence, expert insights, and practical guidance. This publication continues our commitment to supporting those who care for vulnerable individuals, providing a trusted resource to help improve nutrition and enhance the quality of care.

The Caroline Walker Trust is dedicated to improving public health by encouraging the provision of good food. Since 1989, the trust has continued the work of Caroline Walker, who passionately believed that everyone deserves access to good-quality food. Our approach has always been to produce publications which provide practical guidance on eating well. We take pride in delivering expertise in the form of clear, evidence-based guidance to those who care for vulnerable individuals, supporting their efforts to enhance the quality of care and improve the well-being of those in their care.

Our first edition was published in 2007, and since then, numerous changes have taken place in the way we support people with learning disabilities. Originally written by a multidisciplinary team of experts in the field, our guide has remained unrivalled by other publications. However, as time has passed, new challenges and approaches have emerged.

To meet these developments and incorporate the latest evidence-based recommendations, the Trust was fortunate to benefit from the enthusiasm and dedication of one of our Trustees and Specialist Dietitians, Carly Atkinson. Working in the NHS as a Specialist Learning Disabilities Dietitian, Carly understands first-hand the challenges faced by carers and other health professionals. Collaborating with other learning disability specialists, she has devoted countless hours to coordinating the updated guidance, ensuring it reflects both current research and practical experience.

The revised publication explores food choice and eating well for individuals with learning disabilities, bringing together the latest evidence and practical guidance. It introduces new information on restrictive eating, creating supportive mealtime environments, understanding eating behaviours and encouraging healthier habits. It also addresses a range of nutritional needs, from diverse diets and swallowing difficulties to weight management and common health conditions, providing practical advice that caregivers and healthcare professionals can apply daily.

Building on the foundations of the previous edition, this guide continues to provide evidence-based advice on supplements, oral health, and meal planning, along with introducing age-appropriate meal ideas tailored to different age groups. Updates to the text have made it more accessible, featuring a cleaner layout, illustrative tables, additional photography of meals, and tips from health organisations, as well as the experiences of parents.

While many of our colleagues, including health and social care professionals, dietetics, nutrition and nursing students, will see the value of having this comprehensive resource, this guide reaches far beyond a health professional audience. For carers, care managers, residential managers, family members and friends who have first-hand experience but may not have received formal training, this guide unravels the science behind eating well when supporting people with learning disabilities. It is indeed a much-needed, comprehensive, and expert-led resource that not only deepens understanding but also offers practical advice to anyone supporting individuals with learning disabilities in achieving good eating habits, thereby improving this aspect of their health.

The Trust would like to thank all those who supported the timely publication of this guide. We are hugely grateful to members of the various working groups who contributed to its revision. We would also like to thank the volunteers who kindly assisted with editing and those behind the scenes who generously gave their valuable time to review the publication during its final stages. Most importantly, we would like to thank Carly Atkinson for taking on the enormous task of revising this publication and transforming it into the superb publication we are now proud to offer to all who care for and support people with learning disabilities.

Kathy Lewis
Chair of the Board of Trustees
The Caroline Walker Trust

Acknowledgements

The Caroline Walker Trust would like to thank the Anton Jurgens Charitable Trust for funding the revision and publication of the second edition of this resource. In addition, we would like to thank Kia Ora! – Healthy Living for People with Special Needs, for additional funding to support this book, and all those who contributed via our JustGiving pre-order appeal.

We would like to acknowledge the team at Artbox London for their design skills in creating our new cover and Chris Sims for his expertise in design and typesetting.

We would like to thank the Learning Disabilities Specialist Subgroup of the British Dietetic Association for their expert contributions and support in the revision of the content of this resource, with special mention to Briony Caffrey, Laura Clark, Victoria Dagnan, Holly Shotton, Jane Varghese and Rachael Colley.

We would like to acknowledge the Expert Working Group who were involved in the production of the first edition.

Many thanks to the student interns who worked on various sections and contributed recipes, menu planning information and photography: Luke Maher, Alice Cullinane, Karen Bailey, Sarah Penny, Emma Bryant, and Amy Clark.

Thanks are due to all those who have helped in the production of this updated version, with particular thanks to Kathy Lewis, Shona Nolan and Clara Stancombe Postigo for subediting, parent carers Zöe Heath and Nicola Swaffield, and subject matter experts Rana Conway, Kathryn Styles, Kathy Lewis, Cathy Zephir, Rebecca Stevens, Samuel Lucking, and the GHC Speech and Language Therapy Team.

Introduction

Eating Well is essential for those with a learning disability but poses a challenge for many. Food forms a central role in people's lives; in their wellbeing; in their activities of daily living; in their routines; in their behaviours; in their health.

In the 18 years since this report was first published progress has been made. The accessibility of annual health checks has improved, as has our understanding of existing health inequalities through targeted initiatives such as the Learning Disability Mortality Reviews (LeDeR). What we continue to learn is that action is needed to ensure good nutritional health for people with learning disabilities and their families. Only by giving this issue higher priority in national and local initiatives will we seek to address the issues of premature, avoidable death from conditions such as constipation, dysphagia and cardiovascular disease.

Reviewing the evidence for this resource one could be forgiven for feeling disheartened that we appear to have achieved very little in improving this area of people's lives. However, in the 5 years I spent training carers on this subject I only ever experienced people keen to learn and to make a difference for the people they support. I have visited homes where the smell of homemade meals fills the air as you arrive, and I have reviewed menu plans put together with creativity, personalisation and love. Every day I see examples of the guidelines in this resource being implemented as an everyday part of life, with passionate carers passing on their interest in good food to the people they work with. It can be done well and where it isn't done well we need to understand why and try harder to educate, upskill, support and signpost to ensure everyone has the opportunity to eat good food that keeps them well.

We hope that this updated report stimulates discussion, upskilling and policy development among all those who support children, young people or adults with learning disabilities throughout the UK. We also hope others will now take up the challenge to put the nutritional and practical guidelines in this report into action.

CWT is extremely grateful for the support of the Learning Disabilities Specialist Interest Group of the British Dietetic Association who steered this report and provided advice and useful discussions throughout. The publication of this revision is testament to the dedication of a small group of very passionate people who want better for the people they support.

Carly Atkinson MSc RD
Editor, Specialist Learning Disabilities Dietitian and Trustee at CWT

CHAPTER 1

Summary and Recommendations

Summary and Recommendations

Summary

Food and drink bring enormous pleasure to our lives. Eating and drinking well play an essential part in the health and wellbeing of people of all ages in the UK. Simple changes to what we eat and how much we eat can contribute to a better quality of life, and enabling people to eat well is one of the most positive things we can do as part of providing support and good care.

People with learning disabilities have greater health needs when compared with the general population, and their health needs are frequently unrecognised and unmet in both health and social care settings. This includes providing the right environment to support eating safely and well. Supporting people to manage their health through diet appropriately can be complex. It will be specific to the individual and dependent on a number of factors related to health needs, levels of independence, communication, medications and capacity. It is a skill, and it is essential that all those who are involved at any level in supporting the care of someone with a learning disability invest time in upskilling themselves in this area.

Why nutritional guidelines are needed for people with learning disabilities

There is considerable evidence that people with learning disabilities are more likely than those in the general population to have nutrition-related ill health. Importantly, support staff and professionals are less likely to recognise dietary problems in people with learning disabilities than in the general population. Issues relating to body weight (both overweight and underweight), swallowing difficulties, gastro-oesophageal reflux disorder, diabetes, bowel disorders and oral health are frequently reported among people with learning disabilities. The prevalence of other common age-related disorders which might be linked to poor diet – such as hypertension (high blood pressure), stroke and coronary heart disease – among people with learning disabilities may be similar to the prevalence in the general population. However, many of these conditions and related ill health are avoidable. People with learning disabilities are also frequently on low incomes, live in more challenging circumstances and may be socially excluded, all factors which can contribute to poorer eating patterns.

The evidence presented in this report suggests that there is an urgent need for awareness on how to enable people with learning disabilities to eat well and to provide healthy eating choices for their families if they become parents.

Despite evidence of excellent practice in some areas of the UK and considerable innovative work promoting better health, the nutritional health status of many people with learning disabilities remains poor.

Evidence suggests the median age of death for people with a learning disability in 2021 was 62. The median age for the general population (2018-2020) was 82.7. Six out of ten people with a learning disability died before they were 65. This compares to around one in ten of the general population. It is highly likely that poor nutritional status throughout life contributes to this reduced lifespan, as well as contributing to ill health and poorer quality of life. It is also acknowledged that there is insufficient attention paid to the health needs of people with learning disabilities, a lack of basic health promotion, insufficient support to achieve a healthy lifestyle, and under- identification of particular health conditions, all of which require specific action.

In this report, we outline why people with learning disabilities may be more vulnerable to poor nutrition, and how positive changes to eating and drinking can improve their health and wellbeing. We also provide practical guidelines to explain what good nutrition means and the steps that can be taken to make positive changes. From the evidence reviewed, a series of recommendations and a summary of some

> **Despite evidence of excellent practice in some areas of the UK and considerable innovative work promoting better health, the nutritional health status of many people with learning disabilities remains poor.**

important practical guidelines have also been compiled with the purpose of improving good nutrition for this population group and these are given on pages 15-22.

What is the scope of this report?

This is an evidence-based report which summarises available information on the nutritional needs of people with learning disabilities. It also examines issues around food choice and eating well, and provides practical information to support these groups and those caring for or supporting them.

This report is one of a series of expert reports from the **Caroline Walker Trust**, which has produced nutritional and practical guidelines for under-5s, school-aged children and young people, older people in residential care, and older people with dementia. These publications are available on the **Caroline Walker Trust** website www.cwt.org.uk.

The aims of this report are to:

- Provide clear, evidence-based information about the importance of good nutrition to the health of people with learning disabilities.
- Offer practical and nutritional guidelines to enable all those with a responsibility for providing food for people with learning disabilities to develop suitable menus and make good food choices.
- Offer practical and nutritional guidelines to enable people with learning disabilities to make good food and drink choices for themselves and their families.
- Highlight some of the important practical issues which need to be considered for people with learning disabilities to eat and drink safely and wel.
- Provide examples of good practice in encouraging eating well for people with learning disabilities.
- To make recommendations about the training and support needed to ensure that people with learning disabilities are enabled to eat and drink well, and can provide good food choices for their families if they become parents.
- Act as a reference document for all those working for better standards of care for people with learning disabilities.
- Raise public and political awareness of the importance of eating well for people with learning disabilities.

Who the report is for

- Policy makers, health care providers, inspectors and regulators, health and safety authorities, healthcare and social services staff, teachers, community workers, Children and Family Court Advisory and Support Service (CAFCASS) advisors, legal representatives, Independent Mental Capacity Advocates, and others who are responsible for ensuring that people with learning disabilities receive the best possible care and support throughout their lifetime.
- Commissioners and contractors of services for people with learning disabilities.
- Managers, catering staff, support staff and others in care settings (including residential and day care settings) who support people with learning disabilities.
- MPs, civil servants, journalists, researchers, writers and others who may wish to know more about the importance of eating well for people with learning disabilities.
- Parents and Foster Parents who are navigating the complex care needs of their child(ren) at different stages of life.
- Relatives and friends of people with learning disabilities who would like to know more about eating well and who want to promote better nutrition in environments where food is provided for the people they care for and support.

Recommendations

These recommendations are addressed to:

- All those who make, implement and enforce policy and legislation – specifically the UK government, health and social care commissioners, local authorities, and the Judiciary.
- All those who regulate, inspect and manage services that support people of any age with a learning disability.
- All those who devise and deliver training and development for families, professionals and care teams who support people of any age with a learning disability.

Policy development

- Government departments should refer to the guidelines in this report in all guidance and legislation affecting residential, day care, respite and domiciliary support for people with learning disabilities.
- Those responsible for legislative change to national minimum care standards for residential, day care, respite and domiciliary care should make sure these include clear standards which ensure service users are supported by staff and managers who are competent in enabling them to eat well.
- Local authorities, relevant NHS bodies and primary care networks should work in partnership to ensure continuity of nutritional care for individuals with learning disabilities throughout their lifespan. General practice should be proactive in identifying and working with patients with learning disabilities to coordinate, monitor and manage their nutritional health.
- Appropriate health promotion agencies should ensure that the practical guidelines in this report are made accessible to family, friends and support staff of individuals with learning disabilities.
- Agencies that provide practical information and advice on healthy eating to the UK population – for example the Department of Health and Social Care, Public Health Scotland, the Public Health Agency Northern Ireland, Public Health Wales, the Office for Health Improvement and Disparities, and relevant voluntary organisations – should ensure that all their existing and new advice is provided in formats that are appropriate for people with learning disabilities and their family, friends and supporters.
- Agencies which provide information for health professionals – such as with NHS England and the Scottish Intercollegiate Guidelines Network (SIGN) – and relevant voluntary organisations, should ensure professionals involved in the support of individuals with learning disabilities receive appropriate information about promoting good nutrition.
- Nutrition should be identified nationally as a priority in the support and care of individuals with learning disabilities and those responsible for implementation of the NHS Long Term Plan should make sure that support to eat well is prioritised.
- Those regulating services for people with learning disabilities should ensure that inspection reports include specific and detailed comments on food service and the management of nutritional issues in that setting, based on the information in this report.

Commissioning services

- Local authorities should ensure that detailed nutritional guidelines/policies and staff training frameworks are included in their specifications when commissioning catering and other services for the support of people with learning disabilities in residential, day care, respite or domiciliary settings. Local authorities who provide such services 'in-house' should similarly adopt, implement and monitor nutritional standards in these settings.
- Nutrition should feature in the commissioning guidelines for services which will be directed to people with learning disabilities. Integrated Care Boards and other organisations commissioning healthcare interventions should make nutrition a priority in any relevant services they commission.

Coordinated healthcare planning

- Primary care settings should be involved in promoting the nutritional health of people with learning disabilities throughout their lives.
- Primary care settings should proactively offer people with learning disabilities an annual health check. This should look at a range of indicators related to nutritional health, such as body weight, weight change, bowel health, oral health, specific medical conditions, difficulties around eating and drinking, and medication reviews.

- Everyone with a learning disability should be encouraged to be involved in developing their own health action plan, with support from a health facilitator, and to include personalised nutritional information within it.

Education and training

- Managers and contractors for residential, day care, respite and domiciliary services supporting people with learning disabilities should ensure staff, including agency staff, have suitable ongoing training about eating well. This should include food safety and hygiene, allergen awareness, and how to implement the nutritional and practical guidelines in this report.
- The guidelines in this report should be used as part of training and guidance for all those who regulate residential, day care, respite or domiciliary services for children, young people and adults with learning disabilities.
- NVQs, SVQs and other appropriate social care qualifications are essential training opportunities for support workers and other staff. Qualifications at all levels should contain appropriate content on nutrition and eating well, which allows students to understand the information in this report.
- Professional validation courses for doctors, dentists, nurses, allied health professionals and other health and social care workers should provide information about monitoring and supporting good nutritional health for individuals with learning disabilities.
- Training in the provision of dental care for people with learning disabilities and the importance of advising people with learning disabilities and their families, friends and support staff on food and drink choices which impact on oral health should be included in the curriculum for dentists and in training for dental nurses and oral health promoters.
- The Education and Skills Funding Agency (ESFA) should accredit courses in nutrition and health, and basic cookery, for all people with learning disabilities, and make courses or training accessible for supporters where appropriate. Courses should be culturally appropriate and take into account the special diets people may be following for their health.
- All those who support people with learning disabilities should have specialist training in:
  - recognising and managing swallowing difficulties (dysphagia).
  - recognising and managing constipation.
  - first aid – to ensure that they know how to deal with choking among ambulatory, chairbound or bedbound people as appropriate.

Legal representation and advocacy

- Judges, magistrates and magistrates' clerks, legal representatives (barristers, solicitors and legal executives), guardians ad litem, Independent Mental Capacity Advocates, and other advocates should use the information in this report when dealing with issues around good nutrition for people with learning disabilities.
- The Judicial Studies Board, the Court of Protection, the Office of the Public Guardian, the Official Solicitor and the Ministry of Justice should be aware that there are nutritional and practical guidelines which can help those who are responsible for supporting people with learning disabilities and their families to eat well in all settings.
- Social workers, court-appointed guardians and Children and Family Court Advisory and Support Service (CAFCASS) advisors who work with families of children with learning disabilities or with learning-disabled parents should be aware that practical guidelines on eating well are available to help them support their clients to eat well. They should also ensure that learning-disabled parents have access to information and support, giving them the best possible opportunity to learn how to care for the nutritional health of their children.
- Staff undertaking child or adult protection investigations should be aware of the recommendations and the nutritional and practical guidelines in this report. It is essential that staff are well informed about the signs and consequences of poor nutrition and its relevance in cases of neglect.

Practical Guidelines

A summary of practical guidelines to help children, young people and adults with learning disabilities to eat well is provided below. For more details about these guidelines, see the relevant chapters of this report.

Eating well

- People with learning disabilities should be encouraged by family, friends and support staff to eat a varied diet. They should eat foods from each of the four main food groups every day to ensure they get all the nutrients they need. The four main food groups are:
    - fruit and vegetables,
    - bread, pasta, other cereals (such as rice), and potatoes and other starchy roots such as yams (wholegrain and higher fibre versions recommended),
    - beans, lentils and peas, nuts, eggs, fish, tofu, meat and meat alternatives such as Quorn,
    - milk and dairy foods, and alternatives such as soya and oat milks
- Fruit and vegetables are particularly important for good health. Everyone should be encouraged to eat at least 5 portions of a variety of different fruits and vegetables every day.
- Most people in the UK consume more energy than they need. Foods which are high in fat and sugar can contribute to being overweight and obesity. Many people with learning disabilities, in particular those who are overweight or have obesity, should be supported to replace foods high in unsaturated fat, sugary drinks and snacks with more fruit, vegetables and higher fibre alternatives.
- Most people in the UK eat too much salt, and this can contribute to high blood pressure, which is a risk factor for coronary heart disease and stroke. Most people are encouraged to reduce the amount of high-salt foods and snacks they eat and to reduce the amount of salt they use in cooking and at the table.
- Adults are encouraged to eat 2 portions of fish per week. One of these should be oily fish – for example, salmon, trout, mackerel, herring or sardines – since the long-chain fats in oil-rich fish have been shown to help with heart health. There is no equivalent food suitable for vegetarians, but a diet which includes walnuts, flaxseeds, flaxseed oil and is rich in wholegrain cereals, peas, beans, lentils, vegetables and fruit will contribute to a diet low in saturated fat and high in and fibre, which is recommended to prevent heart disease.

For more information on eating well, see Chapter 3.

Drinks

- It is important that everyone is encouraged to drink a sufficient, but not excessive, amount of fluid each day. It should not be assumed that people will necessarily drink enough fluid without encouragement. From the age of 14, women should be drinking at least 1.6 litres (1600 ml) and men at least 2 litres (2000 ml).
- Excessive fluid intake (more than 5 litres a day) can be very dangerous, and advice should be sought from a medical practitioner if there is concern that someone is drinking excessively.
- Free, fresh, chilled tap water should always be offered with meals and regularly throughout the day and should be widely available in places where people with learning disabilities may live, work or visit.
- The amount of soft drinks given to children with learning disabilities should be limited since these offer little nutritional benefit and may suppress appetite and prevent children from eating more nutritious foods.
- If sugary, fruit-based or fizzy drinks are consumed by people with learning disabilities, they should be kept to mealtimes since frequent consumption of soft drinks is related to tooth decay and tooth erosion. Drinks other than milk or water should not be given at bedtime or during the night.

For more information on drinks, see page 143.

Physical activity

- Everyone should be as active as possible. Physical activity builds muscle strength and overall fitness, improves mobility and balance, increases appetite and can help maintain a healthy weight. Activity also helps prevent constipation, coronary heart disease, dementia and osteoporosis, and is associated with better mental health.

- Where practical, children and young people should be encouraged to do moderate-intensity activity – for example, playing with their friends in a playground, swimming or playing football – for at least an hour a day. Adults should aim to do, or build up to, at least 150 minutes of moderate-intensity activity a week and muscle-strengthening exercises at least twice a week.
- Where people with learning disabilities also have physical disabilities which make movement difficult, it is important that they are given as much help as possible to be as active as they can be, even if this involves only limited chair-based movement.
- People with learning disabilities may find taking part in activities more enjoyable if they do this with others, and support staff should consider taking part in activities with service users wherever possible. Staff involvement and interest in activities helps motivate and improve connections between individuals with a learning disability and their care staff, helping to build relationships.

For more information, see Physical activity on page 85.

Monitoring nutritional status

- All support staff should be able to make simple nutritional assessments that might alert them to changes in the nutritional status of those they care for.

For more information, see page 74.

Healthy body weight

- Support staff should be able to monitor weight change easily and act on weight changes appropriately. All residential settings should have appropriate weighing scales for monthly weight checks. The scales should be checked and calibrated appropriately. Support staff should be shown how to act on the recorded weight data, and an appropriate chart should be included in each person's care plan that highlights when action is needed due to significant weight changes.
- Challenging the perception of what normal body weights and shapes for children, young people and adults with learning disabilities is essential. It is vital that health professionals are given clear information on the growth and development that should be expected among people with learning disabilities and the importance of intervention if an individual is below or above a healthy body weight for their height.
- Where weight gain is rapid and avoidable, where someone is very heavy for their height, or where waist circumference is measured as a risk to health, and where an assessment has been made by a dietitian or medical practitioner that weight maintenance or weight loss would be beneficial, individuals with learning disabilities should be supported to reduce the amount of calories they eat and to be more active.

For more information on healthy body weight, see Chapter 5.

Undernutrition

When people with learning disabilities have small appetites or eating difficulties, it may be difficult for them to eat enough food to obtain all the nutrients they need. Carers should be aware of the importance of adopting strategies to encourage sufficient food intake and seeking advice where needed.

For more information on undernutrition, see page 76.

Nutrition support

- People who receive some or all of their nutrients through a naso-gastric or gastrostomy tube will often rely on family or support staff to help manage this, with back-up from a dietitian or nutrition support nurse. Training should always be provided so that supporters know how to manage tube feeding and resolve any practical issues that people may encounter.

For more information on nutrition support, see page 78.

Helping people make good choices

- A variety of foods and drinks should be made available, including healthy options. Support staff should be trained and supported to help people with learning disabilities make informed choices. Where there are communication difficulties around food and drink choices and eating, support staff should be enabled to develop skills in interpreting people's wishes.
- Courses on nutrition and health and basic cookery for people with learning disabilities, and for their supporters, should be made available. Special courses for parents with learning disabilities should

also be made available. Courses should ensure that they meet the cultural and religious dietary needs of those attending and cater for those following special diets for health.

For more information on making choices, see page 108.

The eating environment and timing of meals and snacks

- Children, young people and adults with learning disabilities should be respected as individuals and their food preferences considered alongside any religious and cultural requirements around food.
- Food should be appetising and attractively served, to ensure that people enjoy their food. This is particularly important if the food has its form or texture changed for people with swallowing difficulties.
- The timing of meals and snacks throughout the day should be organised to fit around the needs of the individual being supported. Some people may need frequent small meals and snacks throughout the day.
- It is vital to ensure that everyone has enough time to eat and drink and that, where necessary, food is kept warm safely during the meal for those who eat and drink slowly.
- It is essential to ensure that people arrive ready at mealtimes, e.g. having had the opportunity to go to the toilet and wash their hands, or collect their hearing aid, glasses or dentures.
- To make mealtimes pleasant and sociable, it is good practice for staff to sit with the people they support during meals and snacks, and where appropriate share the same foods and drinks.
- Mealtimes offer an opportunity for support staff to model eating skills and to encourage social interaction and conversation. To encourage this, distractions such as television are best avoided during mealtimes.

For more information on the eating environment and timing of meals and snacks, see pages 107 and 139.

Involving and listening to family and friends

- A genuine partnership between individuals and their families, friends and support staff is essential so that everyone works together to ensure that each individual eats and drinks in a manner they prefer and which is appropriate, safe and health-promoting. In residential and day care settings, it is important that adequate notice of, and the reasons for, changes to meals and snacks are given to everyone so that people can comment on and discuss the changes before they are introduced.

For more information on involving and listening to family and friends, see page 111.

Maintaining independence in eating, and helping people to eat

- Those who can eat independently, even if this is by hand only, should be encouraged to do so to maximise independence and dignity. If independent eating skills are not encouraged, there may be a rapid decline to dependence.
- The use of finger foods – foods which are presented in a form that can be eaten easily by hand without the need for cutlery – should be used as a way of preserving eating skills and promoting independence for those who have difficulty using utensils or who do not recognise the purpose of cutlery.
- Where people need help with eating, it is essential for staff to be trained in assisting them to eat in a sensitive and safe manner.

For more information, see page 117.

Philosophy of care – rights and responsibilities

- All those working in care should be aware of the fundamental duty of care that they have to the individual they support. The Health and Social Care Act 2008 (Regulated Activities) Regulations 2014, outline the responsibilities of care providers in meeting the nutritional and hydration needs of people using their services, and the care certificate dedicates Standard 8 to fluids and nutrition.
- Managers and support staff should be aware of the Mental Capacity Act 2005 Codes of Practice which presumes that anyone over the age of 16 has the right to make his or her own decisions and must be assumed to have the capacity to do so unless proved otherwise, and that people should be supported to make their own decisions and choices, including in relation to food.

- Where a person's capacity to make decisions around their food choices and health is uncertain, a capacity assessment should be completed. Where someone is found not to have capacity in this aspect of their daily life, a best-interest nutrition plan should be developed with support from health and social care professionals, family and carers. The significant risks to health from poor diet, as outlined in this report, need to be considered when undertaking best-interest discussions, alongside approaches which minimise restrictions to the freedom of the individual.
- All individuals, regardless of capacity, should be encouraged to partake in a healthy lifestyle and be provided with information accessible to them in order that they can make informed decisions about their health.

For more on the Mental Capacity Act, see page 105.

Organisational culture

- In all settings, it is essential that there is a commitment to good nutrition and an awareness of the broader role of food and drink in contributing to wellbeing and quality of life. Managers and staff at all levels need to demonstrate their commitment to good nutrition by ensuring everyone receives adequate training and support. The production of a setting-specific food policy, outlining this commitment, is recommended.
- Efforts should be made to find out about the food preferences and eating patterns of people with learning disabilities – including those who move into new settings, regardless of how long they will stay there. This information should be recorded, shared with all support staff, and regularly updated.
- People with learning disabilities should be encouraged to include information about food and nutritional health in their health action plan, which is compiled to explain their health needs.

For more information on organisational culture, see page 110.

Food allergy and food intolerance

- If an individual has a medically diagnosed food allergy, this needs to be taken extremely seriously. Everyone must understand the importance of avoiding contact with foods that may trigger a serious reaction. Full information on the food allergy should be carefully recorded in care plans and be communicated to schools, day centres, respite settings and any other places that the person may visit regularly, with all supporters being fully trained in the handling of food allergens.
- It is vital that food allergies should be medically diagnosed. People with learning disabilities and their supporters should be discouraged from attempting to restrict a person's diet due to a perceived allergy or intolerance, as this may make it difficult for the person to get all the nutrients they need and cause unnecessary anxiety. Ensure advice on allergies and intolerances is sought from a qualified health professional. Many home tests are inaccurate resulting in unnecessary food restrictions.

For more information on food allergy and food intolerance, see page 158.

Food hygiene and safety

- It is important to remind individuals with learning disabilities, and those who support them, about the importance of washing their hands with soap and water before eating meals or snacks and after going to the toilet.
- Support staff need to ensure they know how to store and prepare food safely, handle leftover food, and cook and heat food appropriately. They should educate the people they support to do the same where able.
- Children under 5 and anyone who has any form of eating difficulty should never be left unattended when eating or drinking, as they may choke.

For more information on food hygiene and safety, see page 111.

> "Since it is difficult for people to get enough vitamin D from food alone, everyone should consider taking a daily supplement containing 10 mcg of vitamin D during the autumn and winter months."

Vitamin, mineral and herbal supplements

- Advice should always be sought from a dietitian, medical practitioner or pharmacist before any dietary supplements are taken. High doses of certain vitamins and minerals and some herbal supplements can cause adverse reactions and may interfere with the absorption of other nutrients or the action of medicines.

For more detailed information on vitamins, minerals and herbal supplements, see page 136.

See also: page 69 for information on supplements for pregnant women and on vitamin drops for children; and page 62 for information on vitamin D supplements.

Bone health

- To minimise the possibility of low bone density, people with learning disabilities should be as mobile as possible, spend time outside in the summer sunshine safely, and have adequate vitamin D and calcium intakes.
- Anyone who has little regular exposure to summer sunshine, children under 5 years, pregnant and breastfeeding women, those who live in residential care, all adults aged 65 years or more and those taking certain anti-epileptic medications, should be considered for year-round vitamin D supplementation. If you are unsure, seek advice from a dietitian or medical practitioner.
- Since it is difficult for people to get enough vitamin D from food alone, everyone should consider taking a daily supplement containing 10 mcg of vitamin D during the autumn and winter months.
- People who are at increased risk of falling and fracturing their bones should be assessed by a multi-disciplinary team to ensure that sufficient preventative strategies are put in place to prevent falls and that adequate calcium and vitamin D intakes are ensured.

For more information on both Vitamin D and Bone Health, see Bone Disorders on page 61.

Constipation

- Constipation is common in people with learning disabilities and is a preventable cause of death and discomfort. Anyone with constipation should seek advice from a healthcare professional on how best to reestablish a healthy bowel pattern.
- All those who support people with learning disabilities should be alert to signs which may indicate constipation, such as a reluctance to go to the toilet, obvious discomfort, swelling or hardening of the abdomen, long periods spent in the toilet, a change in eating habits, unexplained diarrhoea, food refusal, or an unexplained change in behaviour.
- To avoid constipation, it is important that individuals are as mobile as possible, and have sufficient fluid and fibre in their diet.
- Those who toilet independently should be educated on the symptoms of constipation and encouraged to share information about any changes in their toileting patterns as soon as possible.
- A bowel management plan should be in place for those who are at high risk of constipation. Bowel monitoring charts should be used routinely. Medications should be reviewed regularly to avoid overuse of laxatives.

For more information on constipation, see page 92.

Dysphagia (swallowing difficulties)

- Dysphagia should always be considered when there are unexplained eating, drinking, or breathing difficulties, changes in eating patterns, distress associated with eating, or recurrent chest infections.
- Those who are at high risk of dysphagia should be assessed for vulnerability and their care plans updated accordingly. The involvement of a speech and language therapist with specialist knowledge of swallowing disorders is critical in creating a management strategy and for training the person themselves and all those supporting them.
- Where a modified texture diet is recommended, the person, family or support staff should ensure they are confident in their ability to provide a nutritionally balanced, varied and palatable diet, acknowledging the higher risk of low energy, fibre and micronutrient intake. The advice of a dietitian should be sought where this is proving challenging.
- Where extra support is needed to ensure safe eating and drinking, a review of funded care packages may be required.

For more information on dysphagia, see page 97.

Oral health

- All children, young people and adults with learning disabilities should visit the dentist twice a year.
- Cutting down on the amount of sugar eaten, and on how frequently sugary foods and drinks are consumed throughout the day, will help to prevent dental decay.
- Good daily oral hygiene is essential, including brushing teeth twice a day with fluoride toothpaste. Children under the age of 8 years and anyone who may have difficulty in brushing their teeth independently should be helped when brushing their teeth.
- Support staff should be offered training on the importance of oral health and how to help someone clean their teeth.
- All those who support people with learning disabilities should be alert to signs of discomfort or changes in behaviour such as food refusal, unwillingness to participate in activities, sleeplessness, irritability or self-harm, and should explore if mouth or tooth pain is a possible cause.

For more information on oral health, see page 98.

References

1. Mencap (2012). *Death by indifference 74 deaths and counting.* Available at: https://www.mencap.org.uk/sites/default/files/2016-08/Death%20by%20Indifference%20-%2074%20deaths%20and%20counting.pdf

2. Parliamentary and Health Service Ombudsman (2009). *Six lives: the provision of public services to people with learning disabilities.* Available at: https://assets.publishing.service.gov.uk/media/5a7c845fed915d6969f456ea/0203.pdf

3. CIPOLD (2011). *The Confidential Inquiry into the deaths of people with learning disabilities.* 16(5), pp.18–25. doi:https://doi.org/10.1108/13595471111185729

4. LeDeR (2022). *Learning from Lives and Deaths - people with a learning disability and autistic people (LeDeR) Annual Reports.* Available at: https://leder.nhs.uk/resources/annual-reports

5. NHS England (2023). *Safe and wellbeing reviews: thematic review and lessons learned.* Available at: https://www.england.nhs.uk/publication/safe-and-wellbeing-reviews-thematic-review-and-lessons-learned/

6. Suffolk Safeguarding Partnership (2015). *A Serious Case Review: James.* Available at: https://static1.squarespace.com/static/62ea37b2f412d231ae2c2f35/t/676e9f611db1d7674b22ecb2/1735303010236/nf_SCR-Case-James.pdf

7. Suffolk Safeguarding Partnership (2015). *A Serious Case Review: Amy.* Available at: https://static1.squarespace.com/static/62ea37b2f412d231ae2c2f35/t/6398714cb742183a08b72983/1670934862128/SCR-Case-Amy.pdf

8. Batra A, Marino LV, Beattie RM (2022). Feeding children with neurodisability: challenges and practicalities. *Archives of Disease in Childhood,* 107(11):967-972 doi:https://doi.org/10.1136/archdischild-2021-322102

9. Ullian K, Caffrey B (2022). Identifying and managing malnutrition in people with learning disabilities. *Learning Disability Practice.* http://doi.org/10.7748/ldp.2022.e2181

10. McAllister A, Sjöstrand E, Rodby–Bousquet E (2022). Eating and drinking ability and nutritional status in adults with cerebral palsy. *Developmental Medicine & Child Neurology,* 64(8). doi:https://doi.org/10.1111/dmcn.15196

11. Gast DAA, Wi GLC, Hoof A, Vries JHM et al. (2021). Diet quality among people with intellectual disabilities and borderline intellectual functioning. *Journal of Applied Research in Intellectual Disabilities,* 35(2), pp.488–494. doi:https://doi.org/10.1111/jar.12958

12. Maslen C, Hodge R, Tie K, Laugharne R et al. (2022). Constipation in autistic people and people with learning disabilities. *British Journal of General Practice,* 72(720), pp.348–351. doi:https://doi.org/10.3399/bjgp22x720077

13. MacRae S, Brown M, Karatzias T et al. (2015). Diabetes in people with intellectual disabilities: A systematic review of the literature. Research in Developmental Disabilities, 47, pp.352–374. doi:https://doi.org/10.1016/j.ridd.2015.10.003

14. NHS Digital (2022). *Health and Care of People with Learning Disabilities, Experimental Statistics 2021 to 2022.* Available at: https://digital.nhs.uk/data-and-information/publications/statistical/health-and-care-of-people-with-learning-disabilities/experimental-statistics-2021-to-2022

15. Draheim CC (2006). Cardiovascular disease prevalence and risk factors of persons with mental retardation. *Mental Retardation and Developmental Disabilities Research Reviews,* 12(1), pp.3–12. doi:https://doi.org/10.1002/mrdd.20095

16. Public Health England (2019). *Health matters: preventing cardiovascular disease.* Available at: https://www.gov.uk/government/publications/health-matters-preventing-cardiovascular-disease/health-matters-preventing-cardiovascular-disease

17. Cooper SA, Hughes-McCormack L, Greenlaw N et al. (2017). *Management and prevalence of long-term conditions in primary health care for adults with intellectual disabilities compared with the general population: A population-based cohort study. Journal of Applied Research in Intellectual Disabilities,* 31(S1), pp.68–81. doi:https://doi.org/10.1111/jar.12386

18. Humphries K, Traci MA, Seekins T.(2009). Nutrition and Adults with Intellectual or Developmental Disabilities: Systematic Literature Review Results*. *Intellectual and Developmental Disabilities,* 47(3), pp.163–185. doi:https://doi.org/10.1352/1934-9556-47.3.163

19. Harris L, Melville C, Murray H, Hankey C (2018). The effects of multi-component weight management interventions on weight loss in adults with intellectual disabilities and obesity: A systematic review and meta-analysis of randomised controlled trials. *Research in Developmental Disabilities,* 72, pp.42–55. doi:https://doi.org/10.1016/j.ridd.2017.10.021

20. Melville CA, McGarty A, Harris L et al. (2017). A population-based, cross-sectional study of the prevalence and correlates of sedentary behaviour of adults with intellectual disabilities. *Journal of Intellectual Disability Research,* 62(1), pp.60–71.
doi:https://doi.org/10.1111/jir.12454

21. Dairo YM, Collett J, Dawes H et al. (2016). Physical activity levels in adults with intellectual disabilities: A systematic review. *Preventive Medicine Reports,* 4(4), pp.209–219.
doi:https://doi.org/10.1016/j.pmedr.2016.06.008

22. Emerson E, Hatton C (2023). Health Inequalities and People with Intellectual Disabilities. *Cambridge University Press.* Available at:
https://www.cambridge.org/core/books/health-inequalities-and-people-with-intellectual-disabilities/ECA88C01BFEB94B0746C22E4F483DE51

23. Worsfold J, Kew J (2017). Outcomes from a quality improvement initiative in an eating and drinking difficulties service for people with learning disabilities. *Learning Disability Practice,* 20(6), pp.24–28.
doi:https://doi.org/10.7748/ldp.2017.e1815

24. Morgan S, Luxon E, Soomro A at al. (2018). Use of mealtime advice mats in special schools for children with learning disabilities. *Learning Disability Practice,* 21(2), pp.20–26.
doi:https://doi.org/10.7748/ldp.2018.e1856

25. Shovlin A, Flynn M, Louw J et al. (2020). Implementing blended feeding for children with intellectual disabilities in a school environment. *Learning Disability Practice,* 23(6), pp.17–23.
doi:https://doi.org/10.7748/ldp.2020.e2093

26. NHS England (2023). *Constipation resources for people with a learning disability.* Available at:
https://www.england.nhs.uk/publication/constipation-resources-for-people-with-a-learning-disability/

CHAPTER 2

About Learning Disabilities

About Learning Disabilities

What is a learning disability?

Learning disability is a term used to describe the presence of a significantly reduced ability to understand new or complex information or to learn new skills (impaired intelligence), along with a reduced ability to cope independently (impaired social functioning), which started before adulthood, and has a lasting effect on development. The classification of a learning disability as mild, moderate or severe is often related to the amount of support a person might require. In all cases a learning disability is lifelong.

A person with a mild learning disability may manage well in social interactions and be able to cope with most everyday tasks. However, they may need support in certain areas of their lives, such as filling out forms, menu planning or budgeting.

People with a severe learning disability, or profound and multiple learning disability (PMLD), will need more care and support with areas such as mobility, personal care and communication. People with a moderate learning disability may also need support in some of these areas, but not always.

Many people with learning disabilities also have sensory and/or physical impairments, which make them more in need of assistance, and some people have very complex health needs which require significant intervention. In these guidelines, the term severe learning disabilities is used to describe individuals who have significant support needs that might be considered severe or profound.

It has been estimated that around 1.5 million people in the UK (over 2% of the population) have some form of learning disability. Of these, approximately 870,000 are adults of working age, and 353,000 are children aged 0-17 years. Differences in the definitions of learning disability make it challenging to compare prevalence figures further afield. Standard terminology varies internationally, with the term 'Intellectual disability' being used in some countries. The term 'learning disabilities' is used in this document.

Who has learning disabilities in the UK?

People with learning disabilities are born into families from all walks of life and ethnic backgrounds. Some of the primary causes of learning disabilities are genetic and include Down's syndrome, Fragile X syndrome, Phenylketonuria, Prader-Willi syndrome, and congenital abnormalities such as congenital hypothyroidism.

Secondary disorders, which can occur during or after birth, may result from external factors such as oxygen deprivation, or alcohol or drug abuse. They may also occur as a result of a traumatic birth, meningitis or head injury, or as a result of a child being undernourished, abused or neglected. Low birthweight and prematurity are strongly correlated with the later development of learning disabilities. There are, however, incidences in which no reason for the learning disability can be identified.

Severe learning disabilities are more common in males, young people, and people of South Asian origin, but are uniformly spread among all socioeconomic groups. Mild learning disabilities are more common among males, young people and those from families living in poverty or with other mental health and social difficulties. More boys are born with

learning disabilities than girls because some causes are genetically determined and associated with males. Approximately 60% of children and young adults with learning disabilities are male. This ratio decreases with age as women typically live longer than men.

Parents with learning disabilities

It is estimated that around 7% of people with a learning disability are parents. Parents with a learning disability are often affected by poverty, social isolation, communication difficulties and the negative attitudes and perceptions of others. They may have significant physical or mental health challenges and often struggle to access the support they need. Parents with learning disabilities are far more likely than other parents to have their children removed from them and permanently placed outside the family home, with around 40% of parents with a learning disability not living with their children.

Care and support for people with learning disabilities

People with learning disabilities may live in a variety of settings including their own homes, family homes, group residential accommodation, nursing homes, sheltered housing, hostels, with landlords, in private shared arrangements supported by home carers or others, or in other forms of supported lodgings.

The most common living situation for children with a learning disability is with family. The number of children looked after (CLA) by local authorities in England in 2023 was 83,630, and it is likely that around 4% (3200) of looked after children may have a learning disability.

In 2017 to 2018, the most common living situation for working-age adults in England with learning disabilities getting long-term support from the council was 'living with family or friends' (36.7% of all working-age adults with learning disabilities receiving long-term social care). The next most common living situation was living in supported accommodation, supported lodgings or supported group homes. This applied to 22.2%, followed by 16.1% living in residential care homes.

Respite Care

Some people with learning disabilities will also spend some time away from their own home in respite care, either overnight or for short breaks.

Day services

Day care enables adults who have care needs to engage in social and organised activities. Well-led day care opportunities can support people to reduce social isolation, access healthcare services, promote independence and develop important routines, relationships and occupations outside the home. They can also provide a regular break for carers.

Day care settings often include the provision of meals, snacks and drinks and can be important opportunities for education around healthy lifestyles.

It is recognised that the closure of many of these facilities during the Covid-19 pandemic had a significant negative impact on the health and wellbeing of attendees and their carers.

How does having a learning disability impact everyday life?

Learning disabilities can affect many aspects of a person's life, and individuals will be affected differently.

Some of the aspects of daily life frequently affected include:

- **Reasoning** (sometimes called cognition) – the person may not be able to organise and put thoughts together, use thinking and learning strategies, or learn from mistakes.
- **Memory** – difficulties remembering facts and instructions.
- **Social behaviour** – difficulties with social judgement, tolerating frustration and making friends.
- **Physical coordination** – difficulty with handwriting, manipulating small objects, running and jumping.
- **Physical and mental health** – people with learning disabilities are more likely to have additional health conditions.
- **Organisation** – managing time and belongings, or carrying out a plan.

- **Communication** – difficulties with expressive and receptive communication.
- **Reading** – difficulties decoding, recognising and understanding words.
- **Written language** – may not find it easy to write, spell and organise ideas.
- **Mathematical skills** – may not find it easy to understand arithmetic.

People with severe learning disabilities may find tasks associated with daily living impossible to carry out without assistance. They may have a number of additional health difficulties which impact their quality of life.

People with severe learning disabilities may have additional difficulties with:

- **Communication** – Communicating thoughts and feelings can be difficult and frustrating for people with severe learning disabilities. The person may not be able to talk clearly and communication may be by signing (e.g. Makaton) or through other forms of non-verbal communication such as gestures, body language, facial expressions or by using resources such as Talking Mats. In addition the person may not be able to understand speech unless very simple language and short sentences are used.
- **Behaviours that challenge** – aggressive, disruptive or socially unacceptable behaviours and/or little or no sense of danger. Such behaviour may be an expression of an underlying problem, such as pain or distress.
- **Physical difficulties** – restricted mobility, poor motor skills, posture, swallowing, chewing and eating difficulties may make simple tasks of daily living difficult.
- **Ill health** – other physical and mental health difficulties which impact daily life may coexist, such as epilepsy, autism, sensory impairments, gastrointestinal disorders (problems with the digestive system) and respiratory problems.

Causes of learning disabilities and their impact on health

Some of the causes of learning disabilities and their impacts on health are outlined below. While support staff may feel uncomfortable about labelling people, it is important for people's health to understand the implications of certain conditions. This list is not exhaustive since there are many conditions that can lead to some level of learning disability, for example, a stroke or an accident.

Cerebral Palsy

In resource-rich countries, one child in every 285 - 500 is born with cerebral palsy (CP). Rates in resource-poor countries may be around three times higher, due to differences in antenatal care, nutrition, and facilities for delivery and perinatal care. Learning disabilities are not inevitable but can occur as a result of the brain damage that has caused the CP. In about 1 in 50 cases of CP, learning disabilities are a result of poor brain development, and in about 1 in 10 cases, they are due to damage to the brain during birth. Other causes of CP include brain cell damage caused by a lack of oxygen resulting from infections such as meningitis or encephalitis in early childhood, when the brain is still developing.

CP can cause difficulties with speech, hearing, balance, coordination and sight. It can also cause limbs to stick rigidly in abnormal positions, and epilepsy. People with CP often have specific difficulties with swallowing, gastrointestinal difficulties, low body weight, and a greater risk of heart disease. Children with CP may also be at greater risk of vitamin and mineral deficiencies.

Congenital Hypothyroidism

One child in every 2000-3000 is born with congenital hypothyroidism (CHT) in the UK. It is a general term for a collection of genetic disorders of the thyroid or pituitary glands that result in too little, or very rarely the total absence of, thyroid hormone production. The vast majority of children with CHT in the UK will have been screened at birth and treated with thyroxine from an early age and will grow up unaffected. However, if diagnosed late or left untreated, CHT can result in impaired brain development and irreversible damage to the nervous system.

Down's Syndrome

Also known as Trisomy 21, Down's Syndrome is one of the most commonly diagnosed chromosomal conditions in the UK, affecting one in every 800 - 900 live births. It is caused by an extra chromosome at position 21. In most cases, Down's syndrome is not inherited and does not run in families. The chance of having a child with Down's syndrome increases with maternal age. There are approximately 41,700 people living in England and Wales with Down's syndrome.

The life expectancy and life chances for people with Down's syndrome have dramatically improved in recent years. Typical life expectancy in the UK for people with Down's syndrome is now approaching 60 years, a dramatic increase from just 12 years in the 1940s. People with Down's syndrome are increasingly able to live rich and varied lives, which may include becoming parents.

However, there are a number of health difficulties which may be more common among people with Down's syndrome, including an increased incidence of obstructed gastrointestinal tract, respiratory difficulties, thyroid disorders and congenital heart problems. Compared with the general population, people with Down's syndrome are more likely to have diabetes, obesity, depression, and difficulties with hearing and vision. It is suggested that 50% or more of people with Down's Syndrome will also develop dementia, similar to Alzheimer's disease, as they age.

Fetal Alcohol Syndrome (FASD)

Fetal alcohol syndrome is the most common non-genetic cause of intellectual disability in the Western world. Alcohol consumed during pregnancy can pass to the foetus, resulting in negative effects on development that persist throughout life. These may include pervasive and long-standing central nervous system dysfunction in motor skills, cognition, impulse control and hyperactivity, affective regulation, and social and communication skills. Children with FASD are also at increased risk of additional structural defects, including congenital heart defects, growth problems and orofacial clefts, as well as learning disabilities.

Individuals can experience a wide range of problems with varying degrees of severity, depending on the timing, frequency and level of alcohol exposure. The Department of Health recommends pregnant women or those trying to conceive not to drink alcohol.

> Typical life expectancy in the UK for people with Down's syndrome is now approaching 60 years, a dramatic increase from just 12 years in the 1940s.

Fragile X Syndrome

This occurs in approximately 1 in 4,000 people of both sexes, although females are usually less severely affected. It is caused by abnormal expansion of the DNA at the top of one arm of the X chromosome and results in learning disabilities that can range from mild to severe. People with Fragile X syndrome can also have behavioural and social difficulties, a characteristic appearance in boys, and distorted or delayed language or speech skills.

Klinefelter's Syndrome

Klinefelter's Syndrome (sometimes called KS or XXY) is a common genetic condition. It is found in around 1 in 600 live male births and is caused by the presence of one or more additional sex chromosomes. Males typically have one X and one Y chromosome (XY) and females have two X chromosomes (XX). Boys and men with KS have two X chromosomes and one Y chromosome (XXY). Common characteristics include small testes, sparse facial and body hair, enlarged breasts, and tall stature with disproportionately long legs and arms. Many people remain unaware of the condition until experiencing fertility problems in adulthood.

Individuals with Klinefelter's Syndrome are at increased risk of having a learning disability, as well as anxiety, depression and difficulties with communication and social skills. The syndrome also results in a slight increase in risk of developing other health problems such as autoimmune conditions (including diabetes and hypothyroidism), cardiovascular disease and osteoporosis.

Neurofibromatosis

Neurofibromatosis is a genetic disorder of the nerve tissue. There are two types (I and II) depending on the affected gene. The disorder can be inherited or occur

> **People with learning disabilities are more likely to experience traumatic life events that make them vulnerable to mental ill health**

spontaneously. It can cause tumours, and affect the nerves, bones or organs.

Between 30% and 60% of those with Neurofibromatosis 1 also have learning disabilities. Features may include a lack of fine motor skills, failure to understand non-verbal communication, poor spatial awareness, poor short-term memory, and impulsive or unpredictable behaviour. The symptoms vary and are often overlooked or mistaken for laziness or misbehaviour.

Phenylketonuria (PKU)

PKU is a rare inherited disorder that affects the metabolism of the amino acid phenylalanine found in protein-containing foods. Approximately 1 in every 10,000 babies in the UK is born with PKU. Diagnosis is made by the 'heel prick' blood test, given to babies shortly after birth as part of a national screening programme. Treatment requires a strict lifelong diet using protein food substitutes which are low in phenylalanine. Untreated or poorly managed PKU can result in cognitive defects, including severe brain damage, increased hyperactivity and learning disabilities.

Prader-Willi Syndrome (PWS)

PWS is caused by a defect in chromosome 15. The incidence of PWS is estimated at about 1 in 20,000 – 25,000 live births. PWS causes weak muscle tone, varying degrees of learning disability, and delayed emotional and social development, and it is associated with increased risk of affective psychosis (mood-altered state). Hyperphagia (abnormally increased or excessive appetite) results in the consumption of excessive amounts of food if given the opportunity. Stealing or hoarding food, binge eating, and pica (eating non-food items) are common and food is often a trigger for behaviours that challenge. In the past, life expectancy for those with PWS was short, mainly due to health problems associated with extreme obesity, but better dietary management and understanding of the syndrome are improving life expectancy.

Prematurity

A preterm birth is one that happens before 37 weeks of pregnancy. Across the UK, there were around 53,000 babies born prematurely in 2021. This accounted for 7.6% of births in England and Wales that year. One in ten of all premature babies will have a permanent disability such as lung disease, cerebral palsy, blindness or deafness. The risk of severe disability increases with increasing prematurity, with 22% of children born before 26 weeks' gestation found to have a severe disability (including low cognitive scores), and a further 24% having a moderate disability.

Rett syndrome

Rett syndrome is a rare genetic disorder estimated to affect around 1 in 10,000 live births each year. It affects mainly girls. Although present at birth, it becomes more evident during the second year of life when a range of neurological symptoms may start to present. People with Rett syndrome have severe learning disabilities and are highly dependent on others for their needs, including eating and drinking, throughout their lives.

Tuberous Sclerosis

Tuberous sclerosis is a rare genetic disorder in which non-cancerous (benign) tumours develop in different parts of the body. The tumours most often affect the brain, skin, kidneys, heart, eyes and lungs. Common health issues that result from these tumours include epilepsy, autism, learning difficulties and kidney problems. However, the way that tuberous sclerosis impacts a person's life varies considerably. It is estimated to affect between 3,700 and 11,000 people in the UK.

Turner Syndrome

Turner syndrome affects females and is caused by absence of all or part of the second X chromosome. It occurs in 1 in 2,000 to 4,000 live female births. Turner syndrome occurs in 1-2% of conceptions, but many of these pregnancies are miscarried with only 1% being carried to term. The primary characteristics are short stature and early ovarian failure, resulting in failure to produce eggs and the hormones necessary for development into puberty.

People with Turner syndrome may also experience heart, bone, thyroid and hearing problems, are more likely to have coeliac disease and thyroid disorders, and have varying degrees of severity of non-verbal memory and attention span. Around 10% of people with Turner syndrome will also have a learning disability.

Other health difficulties associated with learning disabilities

People with learning disabilities may also have a physical disability or another health problem such as; epilepsy, thyroid disorder, osteoporosis, sight or hearing problems, mental ill health, including dementia, or congenital heart disease, some of which are discussed below. Other conditions are included in the sections on improving health outcomes (Chapter 3) and in Chapter 6.

Epilepsy

About 30% of people who have a mild to moderate learning disability also have epilepsy, increasing in incidence with increasing severity of learning disability. Around 1 in 5 people with epilepsy also have a learning disability. Some types of epileptic seizures are hard to recognise and include strange, repetitive or unusual behaviour and confusion. In some people with a learning disability, it may be difficult to distinguish a seizure from usual behaviour, and the person may be unable to communicate how they are feeling. Drugs are normally used to control seizures, but this may prove more difficult in people with learning disabilities because of the underlying cause. The side effects of anti-seizure drugs – such as nausea, drowsiness, disturbed vision, inflamed gums, tremor and dizziness – may result in changes to a person' behaviour, including their eating patterns. Drugs frequently given to control epilepsy may also impact nutritional status since they may interfere with vitamin D and folate metabolism.

Most people will successfully have their symptoms managed with medication, but for others, there is increasing interest in the use of the ketogenic diet. The ketogenic diet is a high fat, low carbohydrate, controlled protein diet which can reduce seizures in children and adults with hard-to-control epilepsy. This is a restrictive and challenging diet to follow and must only be followed with the support of an experienced epilepsy specialist and dietitian. More information on the use of the ketogenic diet in epilepsy is available at www.matthewsfriends.org

Thyroid Disorders

Thyroid disease can occur at any age but is more common among older people and is particularly common in people with Down's syndrome. Thyroid disease can be difficult to diagnose and should be suspected if changes in behaviour are reported or there is an unexplained increase in appetite and/or weight loss (hyperthyroidism), or a decreased appetite and/or weight gain (hypothyroidism). Other symptoms of thyroid disorder include dry skin, constipation, tiredness, irregular menstruation and depression.

Mental Health

Learning disabilities and mental illness are two separate diagnoses. However, as those with learning disabilities are often unable to express themselves, mental illness can fail to receive proper attention or diagnosis. This is called 'diagnostic overshadowing'. Some studies suggest the rate of mental health problems in people with a learning disability is double that of the general population.

Many learning disability syndromes of genetic origin are associated with psychiatric disorders, and people with learning disabilities are more likely to experience traumatic life events that make them vulnerable to mental ill health. One study reported that having a learning disability increased the risk of schizophrenia by three times that of the general population.

Poverty and social exclusion may also contribute to the development of mental health disorders for some people with a learning disability.

The most common types of mental health problems experienced by people with a learning disability are depression and anxiety disorders.

Eating Disorders/Disordered Eating

Eating disorders are serious mental illnesses which significantly affect a person's physical and mental health and can be fatal. People with eating disorders use disordered eating behaviour to cope with difficult situations or feelings. This can include:

- Limiting the amount of food eaten (restriction).
- Eating very large quantities of food at once (bingeing).
- Getting rid of food eaten through unhealthy means, known as 'purging'. This could be through making themselves sick, misusing laxatives, fasting, or excessive exercise.
- A combination of all of the above.

Types of Eating Disorders include:
- Anorexia Nervosa.
- Bulimia Nervosa.
- Binge Eating Disorder.
- Avoidant Restrictive Food Intake Disorder (ARFID).
- Other Specified Eating or Feeding Disorder (OFSED) e.g. night eating syndrome.
- Other eating and feeding problems which may affect people with a learning disability include pica and rumination disorder, which are discussed on page 35 and page 36, respectively.

A recent study suggests that over 20% of adults with learning disabilities meet the diagnostic criteria for binge eating disorder, with 4.3% of the sample meeting criteria for anorexia nervosa and 6.7% for bulimia nervosa. Those with a learning disability who are also autistic are more likely to experience feeding and eating disorders than those who are not autistic.

As a more recent addition to the Eating Disorders Diagnosis, ARFID is less commonly known than anorexia nervosa (AN) and bulimia nervosa (BN), and those with ARFID do not display the same concerns around body weight and shape that are present in AN and BN.

> **The driver behind food avoidance/refusal for those with ARFID is related to:**
> - Avoidance based on sensory characteristics of food, e.g. texture, smell, taste.
> - Concern about adverse consequences related to eating e.g. fear of choking or vomiting.
> - Lack of interest in eating or food, e.g. lack of hunger drive or easily distracted from eating.
> - Any combination of these drivers acting together.

Getting help as early as possible in the onset of disordered eating is widely regarded as an important factor in improving outcomes for people with eating disorders. People with eating disorders should be offered assessment and support from a multidisciplinary team (MDT) consisting of mental and physical health care professionals. Traditional treatment models may need to be adapted to suit the cognitive abilities, trauma history, and sensory needs of those with a learning disability.

More information in relation to recognising and treating eating disorders is available at **beateatingdisorders.org.uk**

Dementia

Dementia is defined as the 'The Deterioration of intellectual faculties, such as memory, concentration, and judgement, resulting from an organic disease or a disorder of the brain. It is sometimes accompanied by emotional disturbance and personality changes.' The term dementia encompasses a number of physical disorders of the brain arising from a variety of causes. It is a progressive condition that can impact a person's ability to communicate, to swallow, and to live an independent life. People with dementia may fail to recognise food or know what to do with it. The physical and psychological changes associated with dementia place an added burden on family, friends and support staff. People with dementia have a reduced life expectancy and quality of life.

A person with a learning disability is more likely to develop dementia, and the condition may get worse more quickly than in someone without a learning disability.

The estimated prevalence of dementia in adults with Down's syndrome aged 40-49 years is 9% rising to 32% among those aged 50-59 years. This is significantly earlier than the typical onset in the non-learning disabilities population.

> For more detailed information on eating well among with dementia, see the The Caroline Walker Trust publication *Eating well: Supporting Older People and Older People with Dementia*.

Attention deficit hyperactivity disorder (ADHD) and autism

These conditions are not just specific to learning disabilities. However, someone who has one of these conditions is more likely than other people to have a learning disability.

ADHD

Attention deficit hyperactivity disorder (ADHD) refers to a range of difficulties associated with poor attention span, with or without hyperactivity. Symptoms can include restlessness, impulsivity, talkativeness, indecisiveness and procrastination. It is estimated that ADHD affects 2.5-5% of the population, and boys are more likely to be affected than girls. People with ADHD are more likely to have a learning disability, and people with learning disabilities are also more likely to be diagnosed with ADHD. In 2023-2024, 9% of people in England known to have a learning disability also had a diagnosis of ADHD.

Failure to recognise ADHD means appropriate specialist support may not be put in place, which may contribute to the overuse of non-ADHD psychotropic medication in people with learning disabilities and behaviours that challenge

For information on the effect of artificial food colours on behaviour and concentration, see page 40.

Autism

Autism is a lifelong condition. It affects how a person communicates with, and relates to, other people and how they experience the world around them. Approximately 1% of the population is autistic, with a much higher incidence in the learning disability population. The number of people with a learning disability diagnosed with autism has increased in recent years, from 19.8% in 2016-17 to 33.3% in 2023-24. Autistic people have a higher incidence of obsessive compulsive disorder, ADHD and mental health conditions such as depression and anxiety.

Autistic people have difficulties with verbal or non-verbal communication, and understanding social behaviour, which can affect their ability to form relationships. Autistic people often exhibit restrictive, obsessional or repetitive patterns of behaviour, activities or interests, to the extent that these limit and impair everyday functioning.

There are no differences in the nutritional requirements of autistic people compared to people who are not autistic. However, adaptations and support may be required to enable an autistic person to access a balanced dietary intake for a number of different reasons. This includes ensuring the individual's specific needs are understood and met. Examples of common adaptations include offering a structured routine around mealtimes, using specific seating or plates/cutlery, and adaptations due to an individual's sensory preferences. Common sensory sensitivities within the autistic population include hyper- or hyposensitivity to sights, sounds, smells, lighting or textures, which all impact upon dietary intake. It is important to take these into consideration during mealtimes and to make appropriate adaptations to the environment to minimise anxiety or distraction.

Expert nutritional advice and guidance should be sought for children, young people and adults with autism who present with significant food selectivity or restriction. A highly restricted diet may adversely impact growth in children and young adults and/or result in physical symptoms due to nutritional deficiencies. Advice should be sought from qualified healthcare professionals such as a registered specialist dietitian (see *Who can give appropriate nutrition advice?* on page 113).

For more information on diet and autism, see the websites of the **British Dietetic Association** at **www.bda.uk.com** and the **National Autism Society** at **autism.org.uk**.

TOP TIPS REGARDING AUTISM AND DIET

- Ensure a consistent routine around activities and mealtimes. This can be reassuring and help to reduce anxiety around mealtimes.
- Some autistic people may have special interests and these can be used to help engage with any dietary interventions.
- Being aware of sensory needs can be helpful in creating a calmer mealtime. This may include managing noise and smells at mealtimes.
- Watching others eat can be off-putting for some people, who may prefer to have their own space at mealtimes.
- Environmental distractions such as iPads, television or gaming can be difficult to 'move on' from and cues to help people with processing this may be helpful, given that hunger is not always a strong driver for people.
- Only change one thing at a time. Trying or offering similar foods to those already eaten can help increase the food range. Small changes, one at a time, are usually best.
- Increase the visibility of different foods. Being more aware of a food means it becomes more familiar. Get people involved in food shopping or chopping vegetables if they are happy to, even if they are not expected to eat what they prepare.
- Do not be tempted to add new foods to the diet covertly. This can lead to distrust and to previously enjoyed foods being discarded.
- Be patient. Taking small steps is important and can take time. If you are supporting someone who is autistic, offering lots of support and praise along the way helps.

The impact of learning disabilities on eating and drinking

Learning disabilities are likely to impact on a person's ability to eat and drink well in a number of ways:

- Lack of understanding among learning disabled individuals and their family, friends and support staff about the need for a balanced diet may lead to poor food choices.
- Physical and dental health problems and difficulties with eating, chewing or swallowing may directly impact food choice and the ability to eat well unaided.
- Lack of appropriately skilled staff, specialist eating and drinking equipment or insufficient support at mealtimes to help slow eaters or those who require modified texture foods and drinks may cause difficulties and frustrations.
- Digestive problems such as gastro-oesophageal reflux disorder may deter people from eating.
- Bowel function problems such as constipation and diarrhoea may deter people from eating because of the unpleasant consequences.
- Poor communication skills may mean that food choices are overlooked, the temperature of food is wrong, and portion sizes are misjudged.
- Sensory impairments, the need for assistance with eating, and loss of eating independence may reduce enjoyment at mealtimes.
- Sensory processing issues, such as being hypersensitive or hyposensitive to the environment, can impact how an individual responds to foods and mealtimes and hence the amount and types of foods eaten.
- Some medicines may have side effects which play a part in abnormal eating behaviour, appetite changes or food refusal. There may also be interactions between particular drugs and nutrients.
- Structural brain damage or dysfunction, seen in some people with learning disabilities, has been linked to hyperphagia (abnormally increased or excessive appetite), and episodes of binge eating.
- Some people with learning disabilities have abnormal eating behaviours or disorders (such as pica), and eating disorders and restrictive eating are more common among people with learning disabilities.
- Poverty, poor housing and social isolation may mean that food choice is restricted, and that affordable, good-quality food cannot be accessed easily.
- Studies suggest that many adults with learning disabilities eat diets low in vegetables and micronutrients (vitamins and minerals) and high in fat and sugar. Information on the nutritional intake of children with learning disabilities is discussed on page 67.

Factors which may contribute to problematic eating and drinking

Dysphagia

Dysphagia is the term used to describe eating and drinking disorders, including difficulties with movements of the mouth such as sucking and chewing that prepare food for swallowing, as well as the process of swallowing itself. There is no reliable data on the prevalence of dysphagia in people with learning disabilities, but we know it occurs more frequently than it does in the general population and is a significant problem for those with the most complex needs. Estimates range from 36% (based on speech and language therapy caseloads) to over 70% (based on inpatient populations). More recent studies have shown that about 15% of adults with learning disabilities require support with eating and drinking, and 8% of those known to learning disability services have dysphagia. Dysphagia is more common among adults with learning disabilities who have a physical disability such as cerebral palsy, disability of the palate, teeth or tongue, and those with the greatest health needs. It is also seen (as with the non-learning population) in acquired conditions such as Stroke and Parkinson's disease.

In infants and children, dysphagia can present very early on as a failure to develop expected eating and drinking skills, e.g. abilities around sucking, chewing and sipping from a cup. If, despite support, these difficulties are unable to be resolved in childhood, it is highly unlikely that any change in ability can be achieved in adulthood.

Dysphagia can lead to aspiration of food or fluid into the lungs, which causes coughing and gagging. It can also cause choking and death through asphyxiation. Aspiration is also related to respiratory tract infections and pneumonia, which are leading causes of death among people with learning disabilities. Dysphagia is frequently under-diagnosed and often poorly managed in people with learning disabilities despite its potential life-threatening implications in terms of undernutrition, dehydration, choking and aspiration. For information on how to recognise and manage swallowing difficulties, see page 97.

Information on how to modify the consistency of solids and liquids to support those with swallowing difficulties can be found on page 162.

Dyspepsia (indigestion)

This is very common in children with complex neurological difficulties and in adults with similar difficulties. There are three types of dyspepsia: gastro-oesophageal reflux disease (GORD); functional (dysmotility) dyspepsia;, and structural (organic) dyspepsia.

Gastro-oesophageal reflux disease (GORD)

GORD is a major clinical problem in people with learning disabilities and is frequently under-diagnosed. It is estimated to occur in 48% of people with learning disabilities, more frequently among those with cerebral palsy, severe learning disabilities, those with an IQ less than 35, and those with a history of rumination. It also occurs in up to 75% of neurologically impaired children. The risk of GORD is increased for those taking anti-convulsant drugs, drugs which slow gastric emptying, and benzodiazepines. GORD is caused by acid from the stomach entering the oesophagus, causing pain and symptoms including heartburn, painful swallowing, vomiting, vomiting blood, regurgitation and re-chewing of food. The very severe pain that can be caused by GORD can lead to behaviours that challenge, particularly among individuals with learning disabilities who are unable to express themselves. If symptoms go unnoticed or unreported and the condition is untreated, the oesophagus can be permanently damaged, and oesophageal cancer can develop. GORD is a highly treatable condition, so it is essential that it is recognised and treated.

Laryngopharyngeal Reflux (LPR)

Often referred to as 'Silent Reflux', this is a condition where stomach acid enters the back of the throat, affecting the throat lining and voice box (larynx) and causing irritation and hoarseness. It usually occurs at night and can cause coughing, sore throat, difficulty swallowing and a change in voice. The condition usually responds well to non-prescription antacids/alginate preparations (e.g. Gaviscon Advance).

Pica

Pica is the term used for eating non-food items such as plaster, hair, faeces, soil, paper or chalk. Pica, which is not normally seen in the general population (except occasionally among pregnant women and young children), has been associated with severe learning disabilities and those taking antipsychotic medications or experiencing a psychotic illness. Eating non-food items can prevent the absorption of vital nutrients, cause nicotine or lead toxicity, block the colon, or produce medical problems if the ingested item is toxic or harmful. There has been debate as to whether pica may be associated with mineral deficiencies, and there is some evidence that pica is more common among those with low iron, zinc and calcium status. Whether this is the cause of pica or a consequence of the pica itself has not been established, but diagnosing and treating any underlying nutritional deficiencies is a sensible first step in managing the condition. Additional strategies for dealing with problem eating behaviours among people with pica are considered on page 123.

Polydipsia

Polydipsia is the excessive drinking of non-alcoholic drinks in the absence of a physiological stimulus to drink or a physiological condition such as diabetes. Acute excessive fluid consumption (which has been defined as more than 5 litres of fluid a day) can result in restlessness, confusion, lethargy, nausea, diarrhoea, vomiting, convulsions, seizures, coma and even death. Chronic polydipsia may result in long-term physical complications such as incontinence, renal failure, cardiac failure and dementia. This disorder has been noted in particular among autistic people and those with schizophrenia, anorexia nervosa and obsessive compulsive disorder, with a suggested prevalence rate of 14.5% among those with learning disabilities. There are likely to be behavioural aspects to polydipsia: it has been suggested that excessive drinking of fluid might be associated with agitation, stress or pre-menstrual stress, or might be a reaction to conditions such as a toothache or constipation. Polydipsia may also be linked to lifestyle factors such as smoking, experiencing limited availability of fluids, or to the side effects of some medications. The potentially fatal consequences of polydipsia mean it is essential that excessive fluid intake is recognised and actions put in place to support people in managing their fluid intake at a safe level. A blood test for low sodium levels (hyponatraemia) can be helpful to indicate if someone's fluid intake is a health risk.

Hyperphagia

Hyperphagia, also known as polyphagia, is an abnormally increased or excessive appetite which is insatiable. The person is continually seeking food and may binge eat or eat inappropriate things such as frozen or uncooked food or food waste. This is often to the point of gastric pain or vomiting. It is generally linked to damage to the hypothalamus. This condition is frequently seen in people with Prader-Willi syndrome and can lead to excessive weight gain.

Rumination

Rumination involves the continuous regurgitation, re-chewing and sometimes re-swallowing of food. The condition often presents in childhood but can occur in adults and may emerge at times of stress. Rumination disorder is particularly high among those with developmental disabilities and other neurodevelopmental disorders, and in these cases, it may be a tool for self-soothing or self-stimulation. Rumination disorder can lead to malnutrition, weight loss, dental erosions, and electrolyte disturbances if left untreated.

Drooling

The escape of saliva from the mouth as drooling can result from problems with the facial and palate muscles and from a head-forward posture. Drooling can cause chronic irritation of the facial skin, infections around the mouth area, halitosis (bad breath), and dehydration due to fluid loss, and can be undignified and unpleasant. Many management techniques – surgical, non-surgical and pharmacological – have been used, but none appear to be universally successful, and many of the drugs have problematic side effects. Management is mainly aimed at alleviating the symptoms and maintaining the head in an upright position. Some strategies to support those who have difficulties with drooling are outlined on page 122.

Bruxism

Bruxism, or the grinding of teeth, can lead to tooth wear and, in severe cases, can lead to tooth pain, infections and oral wounds when it is also associated with cheek chewing. Bruxism has been reported among people with learning disabilities, particularly among people with cerebral palsy, where it is suggested it may be linked to anxiety and communication problems. Bruxism is also associated with Rett syndrome and Down's syndrome, as well as gastro- oesophageal reflux and with long-term use of some drugs, including some used for treating

depression or behavioural problems. The possibility of tooth grinding as a non-verbal means of communicating tooth or gum pain should also be explored. Teeth-grinding requires careful individual assessment to prevent damage to teeth and oral tissues and to treat any pain that might interfere with eating and drinking.

Posture and mobility

There are high rates of mobility difficulties among people with learning disabilities that increase with age and contribute to nutrition ill-health, such as chronic constipation, gastro-oesophageal reflux disease and osteoporosis. People may also have postural difficulties and be unable to sit up straight or hold their head up, making eating and drinking more difficult. For advice on positioning for eating and drinking, see page 118.

Sensory disabilities

Among adults with learning disabilities, almost 50% have some degree of visual impairment. There will also be age-related deterioration of vision. People with Down's syndrome have a higher prevalence of sight problems than other people with learning disabilities.

People who cannot see well are likely to find daily living tasks more challenging. They may find it harder to prepare food, may not see if food is unfit to eat, or may be unable to read food labels, or cooking and preparation instructions. It is essential to ensure that people with learning disabilities have their sight tested regularly, that corrective glasses are available and that these are worn. For those with poor vision, consider using high-contrast place settings to help identify tableware and food. For example, use a dark place mat with a light plate and cup. If serving darker foods, use a light-coloured plate.

The RNIB provides helpful advice on adapting cooking methods for those who are blind or partially sighted https://www.rnib.org.uk/living-with-sight-loss/independent-living/cooking/

Restrictive eating or selective eating

People with a learning disability and autistic people may present with restrictive or selective patterns of eating. These can be attributed to a number of factors, such as sensory sensitivity to specific foods and preference for routine or familiarity.

Sensory sensitivities involving foods can include sensitivities to specific textures, preferences regarding colour, temperature and taste. This may include strong affiliations with particular brands of foods, particularly where the appearance or taste of these are highly predictable on serving. It is also important to consider the person's past experiences relating to food and fluids and any trauma which may have occurred, which may impact dietary intake and result in distressed behaviours involving certain foods. Caregivers should be aware of the individual's food preferences and tolerances, and any routines required when providing food. Where there are concerns around people accepting only a very restricted diet, advice should be sought from health care professionals to develop a personalised, holistic plan to expand the variety of accepted foods and identify areas where specific supplementation may be required.

The effects of drugs on nutritional status

Many people with learning disabilities take a number of different drugs, both those prescribed by medical practitioners as well as over-the-counter medicines. Many drugs influence appetite, food intake, and ultimately nutritional status. Some drugs can cause side effects such as nausea, dry mouth, changes or loss in taste. Some drugs may also alter bowel function, causing constipation or diarrhoea. If drugs cause drowsiness, people may miss meals and snacks. It is also important to recognise that poor nutritional status can impair drug metabolism, and people who are dehydrated or who have recently lost weight may experience greater side effects.

COMMONLY USED MEDICINES WHICH CAN IMPACT ON EATING AND DRINKING

Drug	Possible side effects
Psychotropic medicines (e.g. Olanzapine, clozapine, risperidone, aripiprazole)	Weight gain, craving for sugary foods, dry mouth, constipation, can affect swallowing function
SSRI Drugs (antidepressants) (e.g. Citalopram, fluoxetine, sertraline)	Nausea, vomiting, diarrhoea and constipation, can affect swallowing function
Lithium	Nausea, vomiting, diarrhoea, weight gain, excessive thirst
Drugs for epilepsy (anticonvulsants) (e.g. Sodium valproate, carbamazepine, lamotrigine)	Constipation, diarrhoea, nausea, weight loss or weight gain, and can affect swallowing function
Drugs for ADHD (e.g. Methylphenidate, lisdexamfetamine)	Reduced appetite, nausea, vomiting, diarrhoea
Drugs for Dementia (e.g. Aricept, rivastigmine)	Nausea, diarrhoea, vomiting, loss of appetite, weight loss, abdominal pain

Psychotropic medicines

A disproportionate number of people with learning disabilities in community settings are prescribed antipsychotics and antidepressants. Public Health England (2018) reported that 17.5% of people known to have a learning disability were prescribed antipsychotics, compared to 0.9% of people without a learning disability. In 2023-2024, 13.9% of people known to have a learning disability in England were prescribed antipsychotics, compared to 0.9% of people without a learning disability. The number has been reducing due to the work of the high-profile campaigns STOMP (stopping the over-prescribing of people with intellectual disability, autism or both) and STAMP (supporting treatment and appropriate medication in paediatrics).

These medications may be given for treating mental illness (antipsychotic medication), helping with challenging behaviour (anxiolytic medication) and reducing anxiety and depression (antidepressants). The side effects of many antipsychotics and antidepressants include weight gain, a craving for sugary foods, raised blood cholesterol levels, dry mouth and an increased incidence of diabetes.

All antipsychotics and some antidepressants cause constipation. The risk of constipation is particularly raised with the use of the antipsychotic clozapine, and if left untreated this can have fatal side effects. As such it is extremely important to monitor for constipation in people taking clozapine.

Newer SSRI drugs (selective serotonin reuptake inhibitors), which may be given for depression or other psychological difficulties, may cause nausea, vomiting, dry mouth, diarrhoea and constipation, and the mood stabiliser lithium can cause nausea, vomiting, diarrhoea, and polydipsia (increased thirst).

Drugs for epilepsy

Drugs which may be given to control epilepsy (particularly phenytoin) can lead to vitamin D deficiency and may put people with limited exposure to sunlight at risk of osteoporosis (see page 61). Some drugs given to control epilepsy may also interfere with blood levels of folic acid and vitamin B12 and may cause constipation, diarrhoea, nausea, weight loss or weight gain.

Drug-nutrient interactions

As well as drugs having an impact on nutritional status, certain foods and fluids can have an impact on the way the drug is absorbed or used in the body and hence its effectiveness. Examples include grapefruit affecting some statins, and cranberry juice increasing the blood-thinning effect of warfarin. It is important to read the information leaflets which come with any new medication to ensure you are aware of any changes to diet that are required.

Drugs which affect swallowing function

Medication which alters levels of alertness (e.g. some anti-psychotics and drugs used for managing epilepsy), those which alter muscle tone or coordination (e.g. some antidepressants), and medicines which delay the swallowing process or increase salivation (e.g. some antipsychotics) can impact swallowing function.

> Specific weight management care plans may be needed on initiating or changing a person's antipsychotic medications, and a referral to a dietitian should be considered to improve outcomes.

Managing medication among people with swallowing difficulties

There are also particular problems in managing medication among those with swallowing difficulties and some side effects of the drugs themselves, such as having a dry mouth, can make taking medication more difficult.

Guidance on managing medication among adults with swallowing difficulties has been produced.

Medication reviews

It is essential that there are regular reviews of medication among people with learning disabilities and that side effects which may impact eating, drinking and nutritional status are considered carefully when medication is prescribed.

Can diet be used to prevent or treat learning disabilities?

The brain is an organ of the body that requires a steady supply of nutrients, and it is affected by what we eat and drink, but the links between diet and the brain are complex. We know that diet can affect development in the womb: the role of folic acid, for example, in preventing neural tube defect births is well established. However, to what extent diet and dietary manipulation can impact the brain and its function after it has developed remains speculative. We know that learning disabilities associated with specific inborn errors of metabolism (for example, phenylketonuria) can be prevented when a person consumes, from birth, a diet that manages the levels of amino acids in the blood, which may damage the nervous system, but these are very specific metabolic diseases. The evidence so far accumulated for other conditions, or for the population as a whole, does not show that diet can prevent or cure brain-related disorders. There is, however, increasing interest in the role of polyunsaturated fats and some minerals and vitamins in potentially relieving the symptoms of certain mental illnesses, improving the effectiveness of medication for some conditions, and reducing the side effects of some medications.

Eating and drinking well during pregnancy, breastfeeding for at least six months, and weaning infants onto a varied, nutrient-dense diet are all recommended to ensure that children have an optimum start in life. Encouraging individuals with learning disabilities to eat well is a sensible approach and is particularly important for those who have both learning disabilities and mental ill health, and those who may have had poor nutritional experiences in early life.

CAN DIET IMPACT ON BEHAVIOUR AND LEARNING IN CHILDREN?

There has been a longstanding interest in whether dietary components can influence the behaviour and learning of children, but it is a difficult area to research and there remains insufficient evidence to reach clear conclusions. Overall, research shows that a regular, varied diet is the best way to ensure optimal mental and behavioural performance in children. Ensuring the diet has sufficient energy, fibre, omega-3 fatty acids, and vitamins and minerals will support mood, attention and learning. Providing regular meals based on complex carbohydrates and varied protein sources is also important.

Supplementation with individual nutrients tends not to show promising results in the majority of studies, but children who struggle to eat a balanced diet may benefit from taking a multi-nutrient supplement, or from a vitamin D or omega-3 supplement when sun exposure or oily fish intake is limited. The opportunity should be taken during annual health checks to discuss any nutritional concerns.

For information on the effect of artificial food colours on behaviour and concentration in children, see the following page.

Can diet be used to treat specific conditions found among people with learning disabilities?

Autism

The use of gluten-free and casein-free (GFCF) diets is one of the most researched dietary therapies in the autistic population. This is in part due to the theory that proteins found in these foods (wheat, barley, rye and dairy products) may exacerbate certain features of autism. However, the evidence regarding dietary restriction is mixed. Some research studies suggest potential benefits, while others raise concerns that such diets may lead to malnutrition and specific vitamin and mineral deficiencies.

There is also mixed evidence in the scientific literature regarding supplementation with specific vitamins in relation to the management of autistic characteristics. Current NICE guidelines published in 2012 and updated in 2021 recommend that exclusion diets (such as gluten- or casein-free and ketogenic diets) or the use of vitamins, minerals and dietary supplements (such as vitamin B6 or iron) should not be used in the management of autism in adults. However, specific vitamin and mineral supplements may be required where the diet is severely restricted.

Expert nutritional advice and guidance should be sought for autistic children, young people and adults who present with significant food selectivity or restriction. A highly restricted diet may impact growth in children and young adults and/or result in (potentially irreversible) physical symptoms due to nutrient deficiencies. Advice should be sought from qualified healthcare professionals such as a registered specialist dietitian (see *Who can give nutrition advice?* on page 113).

For more information on diet and autism, see the websites of the **British Dietetic Association** at www.bda.uk.com and the **National Autism Society** at www.autism.org.uk.

Attention deficit hyperactivity disorder (ADHD)

The role of diet in ADHD is controversial. A review of studies that have attempted to link ADHD to various

nutritional disorders found some evidence among some children of links with deficiencies of essential fatty acids, iron and zinc. However, there remains a need for clinical trials of longer duration before conclusions can be reached. Permanently eliminating groups of foods and using high-dose supplements may be harmful. Professional advice should be obtained from a registered dietitian before significant dietary changes are attempted.

There is some anecdotal evidence that certain vitamins, minerals, or omega-3 supplements can help treat ADHD. Again, the evidence is inconclusive and the safety of high-dose supplements is of concern. It would seem prudent to ensure that those with ADHD are given a varied and balanced diet, including oily fish rich in omega-3 fats once a week (e.g. mackerel, herring, trout or salmon) if fish is eaten.

New evidence suggests that some artificial food colours may negatively impact behaviour and concentration for some children. Current advice from the Food Standards Agency is that if a child shows signs of attention-deficit hyperactivity disorder (ADHD), eliminating the colours sunset yellow (E110), quinoline yellow (E104), carmoisine (E122), and allura red (E129) from their diet might be beneficial.

References

1. Department of Health and Social Care (2001). *Valuing People - A New Strategy for Learning Disability for the 21st Century.* Available at: **https://www.gov.uk/government/publications/valuing-people-a-new-strategy-for-learning-disability-for-the-21st-century**
2. ICD-11 for Mortality and Morbidity Statistics (2024). 6A00 Disorders of intellectual development *ICD-11*. Available at: **https://icd.who.int/browse/2024-01/mms/en#605267007**
3. Mencap (2019). *How common is a learning disability?* Available at: **https://www.mencap.org.uk/learning-disability-explained/research-and-statistics/how-common-learning-disability**
4. Child Protection Resource (2014). *Parents with Learning Disabilities/Difficulties* Available at: **https://childprotectionresource.online/parents-with-learning-difficulties/**
5. Department for Education (2021). *Children looked after in England including adoption: 2020 to 2021.* Available at: **https://www.gov.uk/government/statistics/children-looked-after-in-england-including-adoption-2020-to-2021**
6. Public Health England (2020). *Chapter 5: adult social care.* Available at: **https://www.gov.uk/government/publications/people-with-learning-disabilities-in-england/chapter-5-adult-social-care**
7. Public Health England (2020). *People with learning disabilities in England.* Available at: **https://www.gov.uk/government/publications/people-with-learning-disabilities-in-england**
8. NHS Health Scotland (2017). *People with Learning Disabilities in Scotland: 2017 Health Needs Assessment Update Report.* Available at: **https://www.csp.org.uk/system/files/people-with-learning-disabilities-in-scotland.pdf**
9. Coram Voice (2024). *Disability, disparity and demand: an analysis of the numbers and experiences of children in care and care leavers with a disability or long-term health conditions.* Available at: **https://coramvoice.org.uk/wp-content/uploads/sites/2/2024/10/FINAL-Disability-full-report.pdf**
10. Department for Education (2024). *Children Looked after in England Including adoptions, Reporting Year 2024.* Available at: **https://explore-education-statistics.service.gov.uk/find-statistics/children-looked-after-in-england-including-adoptions**

11. Social Care Institute for Excellence (2023). *Delivering safe, face-to-face adult day care.* Available at: https://www.scie.org.uk/providing-care/safe-delivery/
12. NICE (2019). *Clinical knowledge summaries Cerebral Palsy: How Common Is It?* [online] Available at: https://cks.nice.org.uk/topics/cerebral-palsy/background-information/prevalence/
13. Zhu H, Mao S, Li W. (2023). Association between Cu/Zn/Iron/Ca/Mg levels and cerebral palsy: a pooled-analysis. *Scientific Reports,* 13(1). doi:https://doi.org/10.1038/s41598-023-45697-w
14. British Thyroid Foundation (2018). *Congenital Hypothyroidism.* Available at: https://www.btf-thyroid.org/congenital-hypothyroidism
15. The Down Syndrome Medical Interest Group (2020). *Demography.* Available at: https://www.dsmig.org.uk/information-resources/by-topic/demography/.
16. Department of Health and Social Care (2021). *Fetal alcohol spectrum disorder: health needs assessment.* Available at: https://www.gov.uk/government/publications/fetal-alcohol-spectrum-disorder-health-needs-assessment/fetal-alcohol-spectrum-disorder-health-needs-assessment
17. National Genomics Education Programme (2023). *Fragile X syndrome - Knowledge Hub.* Available at: https://www.genomicseducation.hee.nhs.uk/genotes/knowledge-hub/fragile-x-syndrome/
18. NHS (2019). *Symptoms – Neurofibromatosis type 1.* Available at: https://www.nhs.uk/conditions/neurofibromatosis-type-1/symptoms/
19. Van Wegberg AMJ, MacDonald A, Ahring K et al. (2017). The complete European guidelines on phenylketonuria: Diagnosis and treatment. *Orphanet Journal of Rare Diseases,* 12(1). https://doi.org/10.1186/s13023-017-0685-2.
20. Public Health England (2023). *Newborn blood spot screening: data collection and performance analysis reports.* Available at: https://www.gov.uk/government/publications/newborn-blood-spot-screening-data-collection-and-performance-analysis-report
21. Further Information Neurogenetic Disorders (2019). *History and Prevalence of Prader-Willi Syndrome.* Available at: https://findresources.co.uk/the-syndromes/prader-willi/history-prevalence
22. Prader-Willi Syndrome Association (2024). *What is PWS?* Available at: https://www.pwsa.co.uk/what-is-pws
23. Tommy's (2022). *Premature birth statistics.* Available at: https://www.tommys.org/pregnancy-information/premature-birth/premature-birth-statistics
24. World Health Organization (2023). *Preterm birth.* Available at: https://www.who.int/news-room/fact-sheets/detail/preterm-birth
25. NHS (2023). *Rett Syndrome.* Available at: https://www.nhs.uk/conditions/rett-syndrome
26. Tuberous Sclerosis Association (2023). *What is TSC?* Available at: https://tuberous-sclerosis.org/information-and-support/what-is-tsc/
27. Turner Syndrome Society (2023) *About Turner Syndrome* Available at: https://www.turnersyndrome.org/turner-syndrome-overview
28. Epilepsy Society (2024). *Learning disabilities* Available at: https://epilepsysociety.org.uk/about-epilepsy/what-epilepsy/learning-disabilities
29. Epilepsy Society (2024). *Ketogenic diet* Available at: https://epilepsysociety.org.uk/about-epilepsy/treatment/ketogenic-diet
30. Amr NH (2018). Thyroid disorders in subjects with Down syndrome: an update. *Acta Bio Medica* 89(1), pp.132–139. https://doi.org/10.23750/abm.v89i1.7120
31. NHS (2021). *Underactive thyroid (hypothyroidism) – Symptoms.* Available at: https://www.nhs.uk/conditions/underactive-thyroid-hypothyroidism/symptoms/.
32. NICE (2016). *Mental health problems in people with learning disabilities: prevention, assessment and management.* Available at: https://www.nice.org.uk/guidance/ng54
33. Mencap (2018). *Learning Disability Explained – Mental health.* Available at: https://www.mencap.org.uk/learning-disability-explained/research-and-statistics/health/mental-health
34. Cooper SA, Smiley E, Morrison J et al. (2007). Mental ill-health in adults with intellectual disabilities: prevalence and associated factors. *British Journal of Psychiatry,* 190(01), pp.27–35. https://doi.org/10.1192/bjp.bp.106.022483.
35. Emerson E, Hatton C. (2007). Mental health of children and adolescents with intellectual disabilities in Britain. *British Journal of Psychiatry,* 191(6), pp.493–499. https://doi.org/10.1192/bjp.bp.107.038729

36. Reid KA, Smiley E, Cooper SA. (2011). Prevalence and associations of anxiety disorders in adults with intellectual disabilities. *Journal of Intellectual Disability Research,* 55(2), pp.172–181. https://doi.org/10.1111/j.1365-2788.2010.01360.x

37. Bertelli MO, Paletti F, Merli MP et al.. (2025). Eating and feeding disorders in adults with intellectual developmental disorder with and without autism spectrum disorder. *Journal of Intellectual Disability Research,* 69(2). https://doi.org/10.1111/jir.13195

38. American Psychiatric Association (2024). *Diagnostic and statistical manual of mental disorders (DSM-5-TR).* Available at: https://www.psychiatry.org/psychiatrists/ practice/dsm

39. Alzheimer's Society (2019). *Learning disabilities and dementia.* www.alzheimers.org.uk. Available at: https://www.alzheimers.org.uk/about-dementia/types-dementia/learning-disabilities-dementia#content-start

40. Phipps L (2019). *Does Down's syndrome hold the key to cracking Alzheimer's?* Available at: https://www.alzheimersresearchuk.org/news/does-downs-syndrome-hold-the-key-to-cracking-alzheimers/

41. Wu J, Morris JK (2013). The population prevalence of Down's syndrome in England and Wales in 2011. *European Journal of Human Genetics,* 21(9), pp.1016–1019. doi:https://doi.org/10.1038/ejhg.2012.294

42. Coppus A, Evenhuis H, Verberne G et al. (2006). Dementia and mortality in persons with Down's syndrome. *Journal of Intellectual Disability Research,* 50(10), pp.768–777. https://doi.org/10.1111/j.1365-2788.2006.00842.x

43. Song P, Zha M, Yang Q et al. (2021). The prevalence of adult attention-deficit hyperactivity disorder: A global systematic review and meta-analysis. *Journal of Global Health,* 11(04009). https://doi.org/10.7189/jogh.11.04009

44. Simon V, Czobor P, Bálint S et al. (2009). Prevalence and correlates of adult attention-deficit hyperactivity disorder: meta-analysis. *British Journal of Psychiatry,* 194(3), pp.204–211. https://doi.org/10.1192/bjp.bp.107.048827

45. Royal College of Psychiatrists. (2021). *Attention deficit hyperactivity disorder (ADHD) in adults with intellectual disability* (CR230). Available at: https://www.rcpsych.ac.uk/improving-care/campaigning-for-better-mental-health-policy/college-reports/2021-college-reports/ADHD-in-adults-with-intellectual-disability-CR230

46. Royal College of Psychiatrists. (2015). *ADHD and hyperkinetic disorder for parents and carers.* Available at: https://www.rcpsych.ac.uk/mental-health/parents-and-young-people/information-for-parents-and-carers/ADHD-and-hyperkinetic-disorder-information-for-parents

47. Sahoo MK, Biswas H, Padhy SK. (2015). Psychological co-morbidity in children with specific learning disorders. *Journal of Family Medicine and Primary Care,* 4(1), p.21. https://doi.org/10.4103/2249-4863.152243

48. La Malfa G, Lassi S, Bertelli M et al.. (2008). Detecting attention-deficit/hyperactivity disorder (ADHD) in adults with intellectual disability: The use of Conners' Adult ADHD Rating Scales (CAARS). *Research in Developmental Disabilities,* 29(2), pp.158–164. https://doi.org/10.1016/j.ridd.2007.02.002

49. NHS Digital. (2024). *Health and Care of People with Learning Disabilities Experimental Statistics 2023 to 2024.* Available at: https://digital.nhs.uk/data-and-information/publications/statistical/health-and-care-of-people-with-learning-disabilities.

50. NHS England and NHS Improvement (2019). *People with a Learning disability, Autism or Both: Liaison and Diversion Managers and Practitioner Resources.* Available at: https://www.england.nhs.uk/wp-content/uploads/2020/01/Learning-disability-and-autism.pdf

51. Royal College of Psychiatrists (2020). *The psychiatric management of autism in adults.* Available at: https://www.rcpsych.ac.uk/docs/default-source/improving-care/better-mh-policy/college-reports/college-report-cr228.pdf?sfvrsn=c64e10e3_2

52. Hamzaid NH, O'Connor HT, Flood VM. (2019). Observed Dietary Intake in Adults with Intellectual Disability Living in Group Homes. *Nutrients,* 12(1). https://doi.org/10.3390/nu12010037

53. Hoey E, Staines A, Walsh D et al. (2017). An examination of the nutritional intake and anthropometric status of individuals with intellectual disabilities: Results from the SOPHIE study. *Journal of Intellectual Disabilities,* 21(4), pp.346–365. https://doi.org/10.1177/1744629516657946.

54. Public Health England (2018). *Dysphagia in people with learning difficulties: reasonable adjustments guidance.* Available at: https://www.gov.uk/government/publications/dysphagia-and-people-with-learning-disabilities/dysphagia-in-people-with-learning-difficulties-reasonable-adjustments-guidance

55. Griffiths C, Fleming S, Horan P et al. (2018). Supporting safe eating and drinking for people with severe and profound intellectual and multiple disabilities. *Learning Disability Practice,* 21(1), pp.26–31. https://doi.org/10.7748/ldp.2018.e1817.

56. Truesdale M, Melville C, Barlow F et al.. (2021). Respiratory-associated deaths in people with intellectual disabilities: a systematic review and meta-analysis. *BMJ Open,* 11(7), p.e043658. https://doi.org/10.1136/bmjopen-2020-043658.

57. Down's Syndrome Association. (2018). *Health Series: Gastrointestinal Conditions in adults.* Available at: https://www.downs-syndrome.org.uk/wp-content/uploads/2020/06/Gastrointestinal-conditions-in-adults-Final-25th-Oct-DSMIG.pdf

58. Romano C, van Wynckel M, Hulst J et al. (2017). European Society for Paediatric Gastroenterology, Hepatology and Nutrition: Guidelines for the Evaluation and Treatment of Gastrointestinal and Nutritional Complications in Children With Neurological Impairment. *Journal of Pediatric Gastroenterology & Nutrition,* 65(2), pp.242–264. https://doi.org/10.1097/mpg.0000000000001646

59. Harding C, Wright J (2010). Dysphagia: the challenge of managing eating and drinking difficulties in children and adults who have learning disabilities. *Tizard Learning Disability Review,* 15(1), pp.4–13. https://doi.org/10.5042/tldr.2010.0024.

60. Howseman T. (2013) Dysphagia in people with learning disabilities. *Learning Disability Practice,* 16(9), pp.14-22. http://doi.org/10.7748/ldp2013.11.16.9.14.e1477

61. Public Health England (2016). *Making reasonable adjustments to dysphagia services for people with learning disabilities.* Available at: https://www.ndti.org.uk/assets/files/Dysphagia_RA_report_FINAL.pdf

62. Glover G, Ayub M. (2010). *How People With Learning Disabilities Die.* Available at: https://www.researchgate.net/publication/257984926_How_People_With_Learning_Disabilities_Die

63. Barton J, Blinder MD, Salama C (2008). An Update on Pica: Prevalence, Contributing Causes, and Treatment. *Psychiatric Times* 25(6). Available at: https://www.psychiatrictimes.com/view/update-pica-prevalence-contributing-causes-and-treatment

64. Mills R, Wing L. (2015). Excessive drinking of fluids in children and adults on the autism spectrum: a brief report. *Advances in Autism,* 1(2), pp.51–60. https://doi.org/10.1108/aia-08-2015-0014

65. Ahmadi L, Goldman MB. (2020). Primary polydipsia: Update. *Best Practice & Research Clinical Endocrinology & Metabolism,* 34(5), p.101469. https://doi.org/10.1016/j.beem.2020.101469

66. Halland M. (2019). Rumination syndrome: when to suspect and how to treat. *Current Opinion in Gastroenterology,* 35(4), pp.387–393. https://doi.org/10.1097/mog.0000000000000549

67. Murray HB, Juarascio AS, Lorenzo CD et al. (2019). Diagnosis and Treatment of Rumination Syndrome: A Critical Review. *The American journal of gastroenterology,* 114(4), pp.562–578. https://doi.org/10.14309/ajg.0000000000000060

68. Rajindrajith S, Devanarayana NM, Crispus Perera BJ. (2012). Rumination syndrome in children and adolescents: a school survey assessing prevalence and symptomatology. *BMC Gastroenterology,* 12(1). https://doi.org/10.1186/1471-230x-12-163

69. Soykan I, Chen J, Kendall BJ et al.. (1997). The rumination syndrome: clinical and manometric profile, therapy, and long-term outcome. *Digestive Diseases and Sciences,* 42(9), pp.1866–1872. https://doi.org/10.1023/a:1018854925196

70. Psychology Today (2021). *Rumination Disorder.* Available at: https://www.psychologytoday.com/us/conditions/rumination-disorder

71. Beat Eating Disorders (2019). *Rumination Disorder.* Available at: https://www.beateatingdisorders.org.uk/get-information-and-support/about-eating-disorders/types/other-eating-feeding-problems/rumination-disorder/

72. Sehrawat N, Marwaha M, Bansal K. et al.. (2014). Cerebral Palsy: A Dental Update. *International Journal of Clinical Pediatric Dentistry,* 7(2), pp.109–118. https://doi.org/10.5005/jp-journals-10005-1247

73. Mahdi SS, Jafri HA, Allana R at al.. (2021). Oral Manifestations of Rett Syndrome – A Systematic Review. *International Journal of Environmental Research and Public Health,* 18(3), p.1162. https://doi.org/10.3390/ijerph18031162

74. Alam MK, Aksharari AHL, Shayeb MAL et al. (2023). Prevalence of bruxism in down syndrome patients: A systematic review and meta-analysis. *Journal of Oral Rehabilitation,* 50(12), pp.1498–1507. https://doi.org/10.1111/joor.13563

75. Emerson E, Robertson J. (2011). *The Estimated Prevalence of Visual Impairment among People with Learning Disabilities in the UK.* Available at: https://media.rnib.org.uk/documents/Estimated_prevalence_of_VI_among_people_with_LD_in_UK_-_Research_report.pdf
76. Krinsky-McHale SJ, Jenkins EC et al.. (2012). Ophthalmic Disorders in Adults with Down Syndrome. *Current Gerontology and Geriatrics Research,* 2012, p.e974253. https://doi.org/10.1155/2012/974253
77. Bandini LG, Anderson SE, Curtin C et al.. (2010). Food Selectivity in Children with Autism Spectrum Disorders and Typically Developing Children. *The Journal of Pediatrics,* 157(2), pp.259–264. https://doi.org/10.1016/j.jpeds.2010.02.013
78. White, R. (2010). Drugs and nutrition: how side effects can influence nutritional intake. *Proceedings of the Nutrition Society,* [online] 69(4), pp.558–564. https://doi.org/10.1017/S0029665110001989
79. Genser, D. (2008). Food and Drug Interaction: Consequences for the Nutrition/Health Status. *Annals of Nutrition and Metabolism,* 52(1), pp.29–32. https://doi.org/10.1159/000115345
80. Mason, P. (2010). Important drug–nutrient interactions. *Proceedings of the Nutrition Society,* 69(4), pp.551–557. https://doi.org/10.1017/S0029665110001576
81. Bak M, Fransen A, Janssen J et al.. (2014). Almost All Antipsychotics Result in Weight Gain: A Meta-Analysis. *PLoS ONE,* 9(4), p.e94112. https://doi.org/10.1371/journal.pone.0094112
82. Rummel-Kluge C, Komossa K, Schwarz S et al (2010). Head-to-head comparisons of metabolic side effects of second generation antipsychotics in the treatment of schizophrenia: A systematic review and meta-analysis. *Schizophrenia Research,* 123(2-3), pp.225–233. https://doi.org/10.1016/j.schres.2010.07.012
83. Xu Y, Amdanee N, Zhang X. (2021). Antipsychotic-Induced Constipation: A Review of the Pathogenesis, Clinical Diagnosis, and Treatment. *CNS Drugs,* 35(12), pp.1265–1274. https://doi.org/10.1007/s40263-021-00859-0
84. NHS (2021). *Side effects – Selective serotonin reuptake inhibitors (SSRIs).* Available at: https://www.nhs.uk/mental-health/talking-therapies-medicine-treatments/medicines-and-psychiatry/ssri-antidepressants/side-effects/
85. NHS (2023). *Side effects of lithium.* Available at: https://www.nhs.uk/medicines/lithium/side-effects-of-lithium/
86. Teasdale, S.B., Ward, P.B., Rosenbaum, S., Samaras, K. and Stubbs, B. (2017). Solving a weighty problem: Systematic review and meta-analysis of nutrition interventions in severe mental illness. *British Journal of Psychiatry,* 210(2), pp.110–118. https://doi.org/10.1192/bjp.bp.115.177139
87. Jahromi SR, Togha M, Fesharaki SH et al. (2011). Gastrointestinal adverse effects of antiepileptic drugs in intractable epileptic patients. *Seizure,* 20(4), pp.343–346. https://doi.org/10.1016/j.seizure.2010.12.011
88. Ben-Menachem E. (2007). Weight issues for people with epilepsy-A review. *Epilepsia,* 48, pp.42–45. https://doi.org/10.1111/j.1528-1167.2007.01402.x
89. Siniscalchi A, De Arro G, Michniewicz A et al. (2016). Conventional and New Antiepileptic Drugs on Vitamin D and Bone Health: What We Know to Date? *Current Clinical Pharmacology,* 11(1), pp.69–70. https://doi.org/10.2174/1574884711101160204121835
90. Huang HL, Zhou H, Wang N et al.. (2016). Effects of antiepileptic drugs on the serum folate and vitamin B12 in various epileptic patients. *Biomedical Reports,* 5(4), pp.413–416. https://doi.org/10.3892/br.2016.737
91. Linnebank M, Moskau S, Semmler A et al.. (2011). Antiepileptic drugs interact with folate and vitamin B12 serum levels. *Annals of Neurology,* 69(2), pp.352–359. https://doi.org/10.1002/ana.22229
92. Scully C (2003). Drug effects on salivary glands: dry mouth. *Oral Diseases,* 9(4), pp.165–176. https://doi.org/10.1034/j.1601-0825.2003.03967.x
93. Prasher VP (2004). Review of donepezil, rivastigmine, galantamine and memantine for the treatment of dementia in Alzheimer's disease in adults with Down syndrome: implications for the intellectual disability population. *International Journal of Geriatric Psychiatry,* 19(6), pp.509–515. https://doi.org/10.1002/gps.1077
94. Gallagher L, Naidoo P. (2008). Prescription Drugs and Their Effects on Swallowing. *Dysphagia,* 24(2), pp.159–166. https://doi.org/10.1007/s00455-008-9187-7
95. Stoschus B, Allescher HD. (1993). Drug-induced dysphagia. *Dysphagia,* 8(2), pp.154–159. https://doi.org/10.1007/BF02266997
96. Wright D, Begent D, Crawford H et al.. (2017) *Guideline on the Medication Management of Adults with Swallowing Difficulties.* Available at: https://www.rosemontpharma.com/wp-content/uploads/2023/11/Guideline-on-the-medication-management-of-adults-with-swallowing-difficulties-Ref-1.pdf

97. Mental Health Foundation Policy Briefing (2017) *Food for thought: Mental health and nutrition briefing.* Available at: https://www.mentalhealth.org.uk/sites/default/files/2022-09/MHF-food-for-thought-mental-health-nutrition-briefing-march-2017.pdf

98. Langley-Evans SC. (2015). Nutrition in early life and the programming of adult disease: a review. *Journal of Human Nutrition and Dietetics,* 28(1), pp.1-14. https://doi.org/10.1111/jhn.12212

99. Burrows T, Teasdale S, Rocks T et al. (2022). Effectiveness of dietary interventions in mental health treatment: A rapid review of reviews. *Nutrition & Dietetics,* 79(3), pp.279-290. https://doi.org/10.1111/1747-0080.12754

100. Van de Weyer C. (2005). *Changing Diets, Changing Minds - how food affects mental health and behaviour.* Available at: https://www.sustainweb.org/reports/changing_diets_changing_minds/

101. Adams PB, Lawson S, Sanigorski A et al.. (1996). Arachidonic acid to eicosapentaenoic acid ratio in blood correlates positively with clinical symptoms of depression. *Lipids,* 31(1), pp.S157–S161. https://doi.org/10.1007/bf02637069.

102. Amminger GP, Berger GE, Schäfer MR et al. (2007). Omega-3 Fatty Acids Supplementation in Children with Autism: a Double-blind Randomized, Placebo-controlled Pilot Study. *Biological Psychiatry,* 61(4), pp.551–553. https://doi.org/10.1016/j.biopsych.2006.05.007

103. Arnold LE, Bozzolo H, Hollway J et al. (2005). Serum Zinc Correlates with Parent- and Teacher- Rated Inattention in Children with Attention-Deficit/Hyperactivity Disorder. *Journal of Child and Adolescent Psychopharmacology,* 15(4), pp.628–636. https://doi.org/10.1089/cap.2005.15.628

104. Barragán E, Breuer D, Döpfner M. (2016). Efficacy and Safety of Omega-3/6 Fatty Acids, Methylphenidate, and a Combined Treatment in Children with ADHD. *Journal of Attention Disorders,* 21(5), pp.433–441. doi:https://doi.org/10.1177/1087054713518239

105. Bell JG, MacKinlay EE, Dick JR et al.. (2004). Essential Fatty Acids and Phospholipase A2 in Autistic Spectrum Disorders. *Prostaglandins, Leukotrienes and Essential Fatty Acids,* 71(4), pp.201–204. https://doi.org/10.1016/j.plefa.2004.03.008

106. Bilici M, Yıldırım F, Kandil S, et al. (2004). Double-blind, placebo-controlled study of zinc sulfate in the treatment of attention deficit hyperactivity disorder. *Progress in Neuro-Psychopharmacology and Biological Psychiatry,* 28(1), pp.181–190. https://doi.org/10.1016/j.pnpbp.2003.09.034

107. Bloch MH, Qawasmi A. (2011). Omega-3 Fatty Acid Supplementation for the Treatment of Children with Attention-Deficit/Hyperactivity Disorder Symptomatology: Systematic Review and Meta-Analysis. *Journal of the American Academy of Child & Adolescent Psychiatry,* 50(10), pp.991–1000. https://doi.org/10.1016/j.jaac.2011.06.008

108. Burgess JR, Stevens L, Zhang W et al.. (2000). Long-chain polyunsaturated fatty acids in children with attention-deficit hyperactivity disorder. *The American Journal of Clinical Nutrition,* 71(1), pp.327S330S. https://doi.org/10.1093/ajcn/71.1.327s

109. Coppen A, Bolander-Gouaille C. (2005). Treatment of depression: time to consider folic acid and vitamin B12. *Journal of psychopharmacology* 19(1), pp.59–65. https://doi.org/10.1177/0269881105048899

110. Bos DJ, Oranje B, Veerhoek ES et al. (2015). Reduced Symptoms of Inattention after Dietary Omega-3 Fatty Acid Supplementation in Boys with and without Attention Deficit/Hyperactivity Disorder. *Neuropsychopharmacology,* 40(10), pp.2298–2306. https://doi.org/10.1038/npp.2015.73

111. Food Standards Agency (2024). *Food Additives – Food colours and hyperactivity.* Available at: https://www.food.gov.uk/safety-hygiene/food-additives

112. Freeman MP, Hibbeln JR, Wisner KL et al. (2006). Omega-3 fatty acids: evidence basis for treatment and future research in psychiatry. *The Journal of Clinical Psychiatry,* 67(12), pp.1954–1967. https://doi.org/10.4088/jcp.v67n1217

113. Gillie O (2008) *Scotland's Health Deficit – An explanation and a plan.* Health Research Forum Occasional Reports: No 3. Health Research Forum. London

114. Hibbeln JR, Davis JM, Steer C et al. (2007). Maternal seafood consumption in pregnancy and neurodevelopmental outcomes in childhood (ALSPAC study): an observational cohort study. *The Lancet,* 369(9561), pp.578–585. https://doi.org/10.1016/s0140-6736(07)60277-3

115. SACN & COT (2004). *Advice on fish consumption: benefits & risks.* Available at: https://assets.publishing.service.gov.uk/media/5a7dbedc40f0b65d88634277/SACN_Advice_on_Fish_Consumption.pdf

116. Johnson M, Östlund S, Fransson G et al.. (2009). Omega-3/Omega-6 Fatty Acids for Attention Deficit Hyperactivity Disorder. *Journal of Attention Disorders,* 12(5), pp.394–401. https://doi.org/10.1177/1087054708316261.

117. Kesby JP, Eyles DW, Burne THJ et al.. (2011). The effects of vitamin D on brain development and adult brain function. *Molecular and Cellular Endocrinology,* 347(1-2), pp.121–127. **https://doi.org/10.1016/j.mce.2011.05.014**

118. Mahoney CR, Taylor HA, Kanarek RB et al. (2005). Effect of breakfast composition on cognitive processes in elementary school children. *Physiology & Behavior,* 85(5), pp.635–645. **https://doi.org/10.1016/j.physbeh.2005.06.023**

119. Mocking RJT, Harmsen I, Assies J et al.. (2016). Meta-analysis and meta-regression of omega-3 polyunsaturated fatty acid supplementation for major depressive disorder. *Translational Psychiatry,* 6(3), pp.e756–e756. **https://doi.org/10.1038/tp.2016.29**

120. Montgomery P, Burton JR, Sewell RP et al.. (2014). Fatty acids and sleep in UK children: subjective and pilot objective sleep results from the DOLAB study – a randomized controlled trial. *Journal of Sleep Research,* 23(4), pp.364–388. **https://doi.org/10.1111/jsr.12135**

121. Pelsser LM, Frankena K, Toorman J et al. (2011). Effects of a restricted elimination diet on the behaviour of children with attention-deficit hyperactivity disorder (INCA study): a randomised controlled trial. *The Lancet,* 377(9764), pp.494–503. **https://doi.org/10.1016/s0140-6736(10)62227-1**

122. Richardson AJ, Montgomery P. (2005). The Oxford-Durham Study: A Randomized, Controlled Trial of Dietary Supplementation With Fatty Acids in Children With Developmental Coordination Disorder. *Pediatrics,* 115(5), pp.1360–1366. **doi:https://doi.org/10.1542/peds.2004-2164**

123. Schab DW, Trinh NHT. (2004). Do Artificial Food Colors Promote Hyperactivity in Children with Hyperactive Syndromes? A Meta-Analysis of Double-Blind Placebo-Controlled Trials. *Journal of Developmental & Behavioral Pediatrics,* 25(6), pp.423–434. **https://doi.org/10.1097/00004703-200412000-00007**

124. SACN (2011). *The influence of maternal, fetal and child nutrition on the development of chronic disease in later life.* Available at: **https://assets.publishing.service.gov.uk/media/5a7e0601ed915d74e33ef8d3/SACN_Early_Life_Nutrition_Report.pdf**

125. Sinn N, Bryan J (2007) Effect of supplementation with polyunsaturated fatty acids and micronutrients on learning and behaviour problems associated with child ADHD. *Journal of Developmental & Behavioural Behavioural Pediatrics,* 28 82-91

126. McCann D, Barrett A, Cooper A et al. (2007). Food additives and hyperactive behaviour in 3-year-old and 8/9-year-old children in the community: a randomised, double-blinded, placebo-controlled trial. *The Lancet,* 370(9598), pp.1560–1567. **https://doi.org/10.1016/s0140-6736(07)61306-3**

127. Whiteley P, Haracopos D, Knivsberg AM et al. (2010). The ScanBrit randomised, controlled, single-blind study of a gluten- and casein-free dietary intervention for children with autism spectrum disorders. *Nutritional Neuroscience,* 13(2), pp.87–100. **https://doi.org/10.1179/147683010x12611460763922.**

128. Elder J, Kreider C, Schaefer N et al. (2015). A review of gluten- and casein-free diets for treatment of autism: 2005–2015. *Nutrition and Dietary Supplements,* 1(7) p.87-101. **https://doi.org/10.2147/nds.s74718**

129. NICE (2021). *Autism spectrum disorder in adults: diagnosis and management.* Available at: **https://www.nice.org.uk/Guidance/CG142**

130. Public Health England (2019). *Psychotropic drugs and people with learning disabilities or autism: results.* Available at: **https://www.gov.uk/government/publications/psychotropic-drugs-and-people-with-learning-disabilities-or-autism/psychotropic-drugs-and-people-with-learning-disabilities-or-autism-results#adults-with-learning-disabilities**

CHAPTER 3

Principles of Good Nutrition

Principles of Good Nutrition

This chapter explores the importance of good nutrition and physical activity for children, young people and adults.

The nutrient-based standards for groups of people discussed in Chapter 10 of this report are expressed as the amounts of energy (calories) and nutrients that are needed for good health. The term 'nutrients' refers to the substances in food and drink which humans need to function, grow and repair (for example, after illness or injury). The term nutrients includes:

- fat
- carbohydrates
- protein
- vitamins
- minerals
- water

Most foods contain a variety of nutrients, so it is the balance of different foods within a person's eating pattern that determines whether the recommendations for 'healthy eating' are met. It is important for everyone to have a diet that contains a variety of foods if they are to obtain all the nutrients their bodies need.

There are no magic foods or food supplements that can compensate for a poor diet. Eating well does not mean that people have to eat unusual or expensive foods.

The Eatwell Guide is a visual representation of how different foods and drinks can contribute towards a healthy, balanced diet. The image is not meant to represent the balance required in any one meal, or over a particular timescale; rather, it represents the overall balance of a healthy diet. The sizes of the segments for each of the food groups are consistent with government recommendations for a diet that would provide all the nutrients required for a healthy adult or child (over the age of 5).

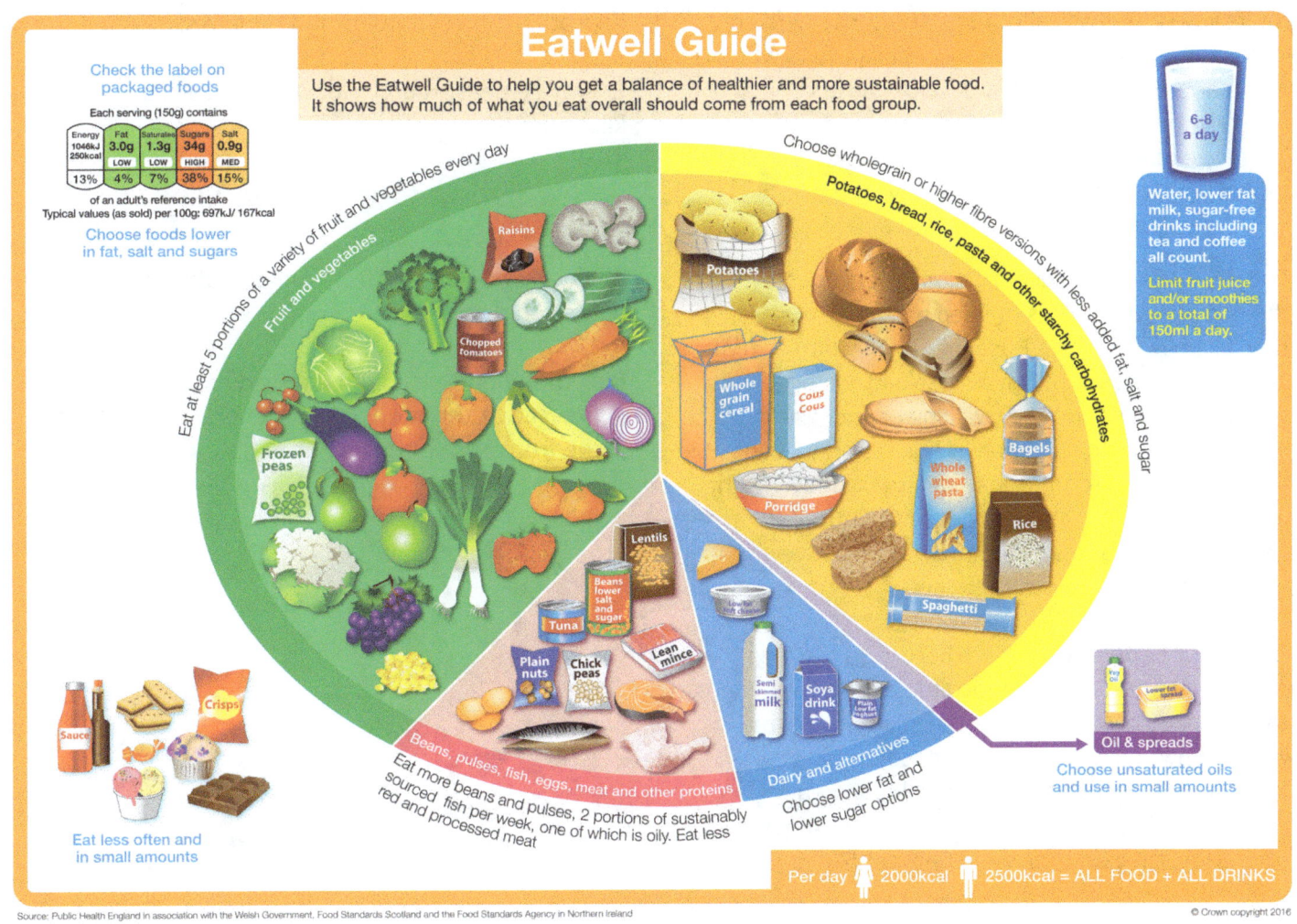

The Eatwell Guide is based on the five food groups and shows how much of these we need:

- Eat at least 5 portions of a variety of fruit and vegetables every day.
- Base meals on potatoes, bread, rice, pasta and other starchy carbohydrates, choosing wholegrain versions where possible.
- Eat some beans, pulses, fish, eggs, meat and other proteins (including 2 portions of fish every week, 1 of which should be oily).
- Have some dairy or dairy alternatives (such as soya milk); choosing lower fat and sugar options.
- Choose unsaturated oils and spreads and eat in small amounts.
- Drink a minimum of 6 to 8 cups/glasses of fluid a day.
- If consuming foods and drinks high in fat, salt or sugar have these less often and in small amounts.

For more suggestions on how to incorporate each of these food groups into the diet, see Chapter 9.

Energy (Calories)

We all need energy for our bodies to function and be active. Children and young people also need energy for growth and development.

People require a different amount of energy (calories) depending on their level of activity as well as their gender, age and basic bodily needs (basal metabolic rate, or BMR).

Adults who are physically small, and those who are inactive, will have lower energy needs. Adults who are larger, and those who walk, pace or shake constantly are likely to have greater energy needs.

The range of energy needs for people with learning disabilities will therefore vary widely, and it is important that everyone is aware of the types and amounts of food needed by individuals who have greater or lesser needs.

Even when energy intakes are lower, the amounts of most micronutrients (vitamins and minerals) required remain the same, so it is essential that low-energy diets are nutrient-dense – that is, they need to be rich in protein, fibre, vitamins and minerals.

Energy is measured in kilocalories (kcals) or kiloJoules (kJ).

Where does energy (calories) come from?

The body gets energy from fat, carbohydrate, protein and alcohol.

Recommendations for a healthy diet are often expressed as the proportion of energy that should come from each of those nutrients.

The energy we need every day is determined by both the basic requirements to keep our bodies functioning (called the Basal Metabolic Rate or BMR), and by the amount of physical activity we do (for example, moving around, walking or exercising). People who are inactive have lower energy needs and require less food to maintain their body weight. It becomes much harder to get all the nutrients needed for good health if people are inactive and eat only small amounts.

Overweight and obesity have become a growing problem in the UK. Doing too little activity and eating too much both contribute to weight gain. People who are overweight should be encouraged to increase their activity levels (as able) and eat healthily. Information about strategies to prevent excess weight gain is given in Chapter 5.

Fat

Fat provides the most concentrated form of energy in the diet. It provides 9kcal per gram, compared with 4kcal per gram for protein and carbohydrate.

Some fat in the diet is essential, and fat in foods also helps with the uptake of fat-soluble vitamins – vitamins A, D, E and K.

There are two types of fat found in foods:
- **Saturated fat**
- **Unsaturated fat**

Both types of fat can be found in varying amounts in oils and other fat-containing products.

Diets high in total fat and saturated fat are associated with high blood cholesterol levels. This is a major risk factor for coronary heart disease. People are encouraged to use oils lower in saturated fats for cooking and spreading, and most people would benefit from eating less fat in their diet, particularly saturated fat.

Omega-3s are a family of unsaturated fat. They are essential for the health of the heart, blood vessels, lungs and the immune and hormone systems. Some claims have been made about the ability of omega-3 fats to improve behaviour and learning. This is discussed on page 39. The richest dietary sources of long-chain omega-3 fats are fish oils. It is recommended to aim for one portion of oily fish per week. If the diet is plant-based or vegetarian, there are non-animal sources of short-chain omega-3s.

If you are considering taking a fish oil or omega-3 supplement, talk to a qualified health professional.

> Stocks of some fish species are declining. To ensure the sustainability of our fish stocks, you can try to choose fish from sustainable sources. Look for products certified by the Marine Stewardship Council. The Good Fish Guide from the Marine Conservation Society provides details of sustainable fish sources.

Trans fats are a particular type of fat found in some manufactured foods that use hydrogenated oils. The trans fats found in these foods are harmful and have no known nutritional benefits.

Foods that have 'hydrogenated oils' or 'hydrogenated fat' in the list of ingredients are likely to contain trans fats.

Foods it is found in

UNSATURATED FATS

Monounsaturated fats	Polyunsaturated fats	Omega-3 fats
■ Olive oil and rapeseed oil	■ Corn oil, sunflower oil and soya oil	■ Long-chain omega-3s: Oily fish such as herring, mackerel, pilchards, sardines, salmon, fresh crab, whitebait, trout
■ Avocado		
■ Nuts and seeds (almonds, cashews, hazelnuts, peanuts and pistachios)	■ Nuts and seeds (walnuts, pine nuts, sunflower seeds and sesame seeds)	■ Short chain omega-3s: vegetable oils such as rapeseed oil, walnuts, pumpkin seeds, linseeds, chia seeds, soya and soya products.
■ Some margarines and spreads are made from monounsaturated fats.	■ Some margarines and spreads are made from polyunsaturated fats.	■ Some foods have long-chain omega-3s added, including certain brands of eggs, milk, yoghurt, bread, and spreads. Check the labels.

SATURATED FATS

- ■ Butter
- ■ Fat in meat and poultry
- ■ Biscuits and Cakes
- ■ Cream
- ■ Meat products (such as sausages, processed meats, and meat pies)
- ■ Hard cheese
- ■ Suet
- ■ Coconut oil and palm oil
- ■ Lard
- ■ Ghee
- ■ Dripping

Carbohydrates

Carbohydrate is the term used to describe both starch and sugars in foods. Carbohydrates provide energy. The term sugars is often assumed to describe something white and granular found in sugar bowls, but in fact, the sugars found in foods can be quite variable. In order to clarify the roles of different sugars in health, the sugars in foods have been distinguished as intrinsic sugars, milk sugars and free sugars.

CARBOHYDRATES

STARCH
Starch is the main component of cereals, pulses, grains and root vegetables.

SUGARS

Intrinsic Sugars and Milk Sugars
These sugars are found naturally in foods such as milk, vegetables and fruits.

Free Sugars
This includes table sugar, sugar added to food and drinks, plus sugars naturally present in honey, syrups and fruit juices.

In its report on Carbohydrates and Health, the Scientific Advisory Committee on Nutrition (SACN) recommended that free sugars should not exceed 5% of total dietary energy intake for adults and children from the age of 2 years. Reducing the intake of free sugars in the diet lowers the risk of tooth decay, and may offer additional health benefits such as lowering the risk of type 2 diabetes, hypertension, coronary artery disease and hyperlipidaemia as well as some types of cancer and other diseases through the reduction of overall energy (kcal) intake and risk of obesity.

	WHAT ARE THEY?	FOODS THEY ARE FOUND IN
STARCH	Starch is the major component of cereals, pulses, grains and root vegetables (for example, yams) and tubers (such as, potatoes).	- All types of bread and rolls, chapattis and other flat breads - Rice and other grains - All types of pasta and spaghetti - Noodles - Breakfast cereals - Potatoes, yams, plantains
SUGARS **Intrinsic sugars and milk sugars**	Intrinsic sugars are those naturally incorporated into the cellular structure of foods such as milk, vegetables and fruits. Intrinsic sugars can be found in fresh, frozen, dried, canned, stewed and pressed fruit and vegetables	- Fruits - Vegetables - Milk and dairy products (lactose)
Free sugars	Free sugars are those which are no longer incorporated into the cellular structure of food. They include sugars such as sucrose, fructose, glucose and starch hydrolysates (glucose syrup, high-fructose syrup) which are added to foods and beverages by manufacturers, cooks or consumers. Free sugars are also present in honey and syrups, as well as fruit juices and fruit juice concentrates. Free Sugar intake should be kept to a minimum by both children and adults.	- Table sugar - Honey - Sweets - Chocolate - Cakes - Biscuits - Most soft drinks and squashes fruit/vegetable juices, smoothies, purees and pastes

Glycaemic index refers to the speed with which carbohydrate foods increase the level of sugar in the blood after they are eaten. It is suggested that foods with a low glycaemic index keep you fuller for longer and may be beneficial for people with diabetes and those who are overweight. Many foods with a low glycaemic index are also high in fibre and low in free sugars, such as higher-fibre cereals, oats, whole grains, fruits and vegetables (not juices).

Fibre

Fibre is a part of cereal and vegetable foods which is not broken down in the small intestine and reaches the large intestine intact. Fibre is particularly important to prevent constipation and maintain healthy bowels. Some types of fibre are important for lowering blood cholesterol levels.

FOODS IT IS FOUND IN

Wholemeal bread and pasta
Brown rice
Wholegrain breakfast cereals
Pulses (peas, lentils and beans – including baked beans, kidney beans and chickpeas)
Dried and fresh fruit and vegetables
Nuts and seeds
These foods provide good sources of other nutrients too.

Protein

Protein is needed for growth and the maintenance and repair of body tissues such as muscles and bones. Most people in the UK have plenty of protein in their diets (including vegetarians and vegans).

FOODS IT IS FOUND IN

Tofu and soya products (e.g. soya milk, soya yoghurt)
Quorn
Pulses such as peas, lentils and beans (including baked beans, kidney beans, chickpeas and butter beans)
Nuts and seeds
Dairy Milk
Meat, poultry and fish
Eggs
Cheese
Cereal foods such as bread and rice

Vitamins

Vitamins and minerals are also known as 'micronutrients' because they are needed by the body in much smaller amounts [milligrams (mg) or micrograms (µg) per day] than carbohydrates, protein and fat (called macronutrients).

VITAMINS

Fat-soluble vitamins	Water-soluble vitamins
Vitamin A	Some of the most important water-soluble vitamins are: B vitamins: thiamin, riboflavin, niacin, vitamin B6, vitamin B12, folate and vitamin C
Vitamin D	
Vitamin E	
Vitamin K	
These are stored in the body.	These are not stored in the body.
They are less easily destroyed by heat, sunlight or oxidation.	They are more likely to be destroyed by overcooking, or by being left exposed to sunlight or the air.

Vitamins are divided into two groups: those that are fat-soluble and those that are water-soluble. Some vitamins are found predominantly in animal foods – for example, vitamin B12 and vitamin D. Others are found predominantly in foods of vegetable origin – for example vitamin C.

Fresh produce starts degrading as soon as it is picked, so it is important to eat and prepare foods as fresh as possible. This is also why it is important to prepare vegetables close to the cooking time and not to overcook them.

Frozen fruits and vegetables have been found to have comparable, and sometimes higher, vitamin and mineral content than fresh produce. Canned varieties can also be a good source of vitamins to help meet requirements.

	WHY WE NEED IT	FOODS IT IS FOUND IN
Vitamin A	Vitamin A plays an important role in maintaining the immune system. It is also associated with good vision in dim light, as retinol is essential for the substance in the eye which allows night vision. Vitamin A comes in two forms: ■ retinol, which is only found in animal foods. ■ carotene, which is the yellow or orange pigment found in fruit and vegetables.	*(See also Appendix 1.)* ■ Liver* ■ Liver pâté* ■ Carrots and other orange foods, such as sweet potatoes ■ Mango, melon and apricots (dried or fresh) ■ Green leafy vegetables such as kale, spinach, watercress and broccoli ■ Tomatoes ■ Red peppers.
Vitamin D	Vitamin D is needed for healthy bones and teeth. It helps the body to absorb dietary calcium. Prolonged deficiency of vitamin D in children results in rickets, the main signs of which are skeletal malformations (such as bowed legs) with bone pain or tenderness and muscle weakness. Vitamin D also has important roles in the immune system and muscle function. Most people in the UK will benefit from taking Vitamin D supplement, see page 61 for more information.	■ Oily fish such as salmon, sardines, and mackerel ■ Egg yolk ■ Liver*, liver pâté * ■ Some fortified foods – such as some margarines and breakfast cereals
Vitamin E	Vitamin E is involved in a number of body processes and protects cell walls as it acts as an antioxidant.	■ Plant oils such as soya, corn and olive oil ■ Nuts and seeds ■ Wheatgerm in bread and cereals
Vitamin K	Vitamin K is important for normal bone health, wound healing and blood clotting.	We can make vitamin K in the body, but it is also found in green leafy vegetables such as broccoli and spinach, and in vegetable oils and cereals. Small amounts can also be found in meat (such as pork) and dairy foods (such as cheese).

* *As these foods can contain high levels of vitamin A, it is suggested that they are not eaten more than once a week. Anyone who is pregnant should avoid eating liver and liver pâté (and avoid dietary supplements which contain vitamin A), as very high intakes may damage the foetus.*

	WHY WE NEED IT	FOODS IT IS FOUND IN
B vitamins – thiamin, riboflavin and niacin	These vitamins are particularly important for the heart and nervous system. The body also needs these vitamins to be able to use the energy in food, reducing tiredness and maintaining normal psychological function.	**Thiamin and niacin** (See also Appendix 1.) - Bread - Fortified breakfast cereals - Pork (including bacon and ham) - Liver* and kidney - Oily fish - Yeast extract (such as Marmite) - Nuts - Potatoes **Riboflavin** - Milk and milk products such as yoghurt and cheese - Meat, offal* and poultry - Fortified breakfast cereals - Almonds - Eggs
Folate	Folates or folic acid are a group of compounds found in foods. Folate is a B vitamin that is essential for many body processes, including forming red blood cells, making new cells, and using protein in the body. Deficiency can lead to a particular type of anaemia known as megaloblastic anaemia. Low folic acid intakes at conception and in early pregnancy are associated with an increased risk of neural tube defect births (such as spina bifida).	- Green vegetables (including cabbage and spinach) - Oranges - Liver* - Yeast extract - Potatoes - Fortified breakfast cereals
Vitamin B^6	Vitamin B6 is the name given to a whole group of substances that are commonly found in both animal and vegetable foods and which are involved in a number of body processes, including healthy immune responses, hormone regulation and reduction in tiredness.	- Fortified breakfast cereal - Meat and poultry - Fish - Potatoes - Bananas - Nuts - Avocado
Vitamin B^{12}	Vitamin B12 interacts with folate and vitamin B6. Together, these vitamins help the body to build up its own protein, especially for nervous tissue and red blood cells. If someone avoids all animal products, it is important to make sure that they include a source of vitamin B12 in their diet.	- All foods of animal origin, for example: meat, white fish, eggs and milk. - Some other foods are fortified with vitamin B12, such as fortified breakfast cereals and fortified milk alternatives (e.g. some soya or oat milks) - Some yeast extracts also contain this vitamin. * See footnote on page 55.

	WHY WE NEED IT	**FOODS IT IS FOUND IN**
Vitamin C	The body needs vitamin C to produce and maintain collagen, the foundation material for bones, teeth, skin and tendons. It is important in wound healing and immunity. It is an antioxidant vitamin which has a role in protecting cells and tissues in the body. Consuming vitamin C in the same meal as iron helps the body to absorb iron.	(See also Appendix 1.) - Most fruit, vegetables and fresh juices. **Good sources include:** - Citrus fruits such as oranges - Red peppers and tomatoes - Potatoes - Blackcurrants and strawberries.

Minerals

	WHY WE NEED IT	**FOODS IT IS FOUND IN**
Iron	Iron is an essential part of the pigment in red blood cells called haemoglobin, which carries oxygen. A deficiency in iron will cause anaemia. In a person with anaemia, the blood transports less oxygen, which limits the person's ability to be physically active. People with anaemia may become pale and tired, and their general health, resistance to infection, and vitality will be impaired. Sometimes there are no apparent symptoms, and anaemia may be undetected. Iron deficiency during childhood can impair brain function, and children with iron deficiency have been found to perform less well in motor and mental development tests. Sufficient iron during pregnancy is important for the health of both the mother and baby.	(See also Appendix 1.) There are two forms of iron in foods: - Haem iron, and - Non-haem iron. Haem iron is found in foods of animal origin such as beef, lamb, chicken and turkey, liver and kidney, and in fish such as sardines and tuna. Haem iron is absorbed by the body more easily than non-haem iron. Non-haem iron is found in foods of plant origin, including cereal foods, such as bread, pulses (such as peas, beans and lentils), dried fruits and green vegetables. It is also found in fortified breakfast cereals.
	Lower intakes and lower iron status are more frequently reported among younger women. For those women who have higher iron needs – either because they have heavy menstrual losses or because they have been found to have low haemoglobin or serum ferritin levels – good sources of iron should be included in the diet regularly and, if iron status is found to be low, iron supplementation should be considered after consultation with a medical practitioner.	

	WHY WE NEED IT	FOODS IT IS FOUND IN
Calcium	Calcium is needed for building bones and teeth, keeping them strong, for transmitting nerve impulses and muscle actions and for many other body functions. Adequate calcium intakes (and vitamin D levels) are essential for long-term bone health. Breastfeeding mothers and people with coeliac disease, bowel disease or osteoporosis will have higher requirements.	■ Milk and fortified plant-based alternatives ■ Yoghurt ■ Cheese and cheese spread ■ Bread ■ Tinned fish (eaten with the bones) ■ Tofu ■ Egg yolk ■ Pulses such as beans, lentils and chick peas ■ Green leafy vegetables ■ Nuts ■ Sesame products
Zinc	Zinc is important for a wide range of enzymes involved in body processes, including the normal metabolism of protein, fat and carbohydrate, and is particularly important for the normal functioning of the immune and reproductive systems. In babies and children, it supports the growth and development of the brain and nervous system and also plays a role in healthy bone development. Studies suggest that people with a learning disability (specifically children and adolescents with Down's Syndrome) have lower zinc levels than those without a learning disability, suggesting that this population group may be at higher risk of zinc deficiency.	■ Meat, fish, shellfish ■ Eggs ■ Milk, cheese ■ Wholegrain cereals ■ Pulses ■ Tofu ■ Nuts
Sodium	Salt (sodium chloride) is the main source of dietary sodium. Sodium is essential for fluid balance, but too much sodium is associated with raised blood pressure in later life, and this is a risk factor for heart disease and stroke. There is also evidence that people with obesity may be particularly sensitive to the effect that salt has in raising blood pressure. *(See page 135 for more information on salt in the diet)*	Foods to which salt is added in processing or preparation – for example, sauces, soups, processed meat and fish products, some canned foods (including those canned in brine, beans and spaghetti in sauce), bacon, ham, sausages, smoked cheese or smoked fish, crisps and other snacks, some breakfast cereals, breads, biscuits and other bakery products. Take-away and fast foods such as pizzas, burgers and coated chicken products are also likely to be high in salt.

	WHY WE NEED IT	FOODS IT IS FOUND IN
Copper	Copper is an essential component of many substances which control body functions. It can be found in a wide variety of foods, particularly in vegetables, fish and liver.	■ Vegetables ■ Fish ■ Liver
Iodine	Iodine helps to make the thyroid hormones necessary for maintaining metabolic rate. It also promotes normal cognitive function and normal growth in children	■ Milk ■ Fish
Magnesium	Magnesium is important for the development of the skeleton and for maintaining normal nerve and muscle function.	■ Cereals, including bread ■ Green vegetables ■ Nuts
Phosphorus	About 80% of the phosphorus in the body is present in the bones, and phosphorus, with calcium, provides rigidity to the skeleton.	Phosphorus is found in all plant and animal cells, so people will get enough phosphorus as long as they eat a varied diet.
Potassium	Potassium helps regulate body fluids and blood pressure, and also has a role in nerve and muscle function.	A large range of foods contain potassium, and it is particularly abundant in: ■ Vegetables ■ Potatoes ■ Fruit and fruit juices.
Selenium	Selenium is involved in protecting body cells from damage due to oxidation and promotes normal immune function.	■ Cereals ■ Meat ■ Fish ■ Brazil nuts

Water

Water is the main constituent of the body and accounts for 50%- 60% of body weight. Water is vital to many functions in the body including, the maintenance of cell structure, the transport of nutrients and oxygen through the body via the bloodstream, the transport of white blood cells to fight infection, enabling normal cognitive function, and getting rid of the body's waste products via the excretory systems, such as through the formation of urine. Water is lost from the body as urine, in faeces and by evaporation from the skin and lungs. The amount of water required by the body varies depending on dietary factors, physical activity level, environmental conditions, metabolism and health status. There is evidence that dehydration among people with learning disabilities in residential settings is common, which is why monitoring people's fluid intake is so important.

To ensure people are adequately hydrated, it is recommended that adult women and men should have at least 1.6 and 2.0 litres of fluid a day, respectively, equating to around 7-10 glasses. If someone breathes through their mouth, dribbles or sweats a lot, or has a high temperature, they will have increased requirements for fluid and should seek advice on the amount appropriate to their needs. *(See also Drinks on page 143.)*

Signs that someone you are caring for might be dehydrated include headaches, confusion, irritability, tiredness and lack of concentration, as well as constipation and urinary tract infections. #ButFirstADrink is an initiative championed by the National Hydration Association to help prevent dehydration for those in care settings.

Alcohol

Alcohol provides energy, and alcoholic drinks can make a substantial contribution to daily calorie intake among regular consumers. Alcohol affects multiple parts of the body: the stomach, gut, brain and especially the liver. In the brain, the first thing to be switched off are our inhibitions, which can make people behave in a way they would not normally, and this can lead to risk-taking behaviours.

Men and women are advised to drink no more than 14 units of alcohol a week, spread across 3 days or more. Women who are planning a pregnancy or who are pregnant are advised to avoid having alcohol.

1 unit of alcohol is equivalent to half a pint of ordinary-strength beer or lager, half a glass of wine, or a single pub measure of spirits.

Improving health outcomes: heart disease, bone disorders, cancer and infections

Coronary heart disease and stroke

Diseases of the circulatory system were the leading cause of death for people with a learning disability who had a LeDeR review following their death (LeDeR 2022).

High-fat diets and increasing lifespan of people with learning disabilities, combined with obesity and low activity levels, have been linked to the reported increases in coronary heart disease seen in people with learning disabilities.

The current high levels of salt habitually consumed by the UK population increase the risk of high blood pressure, which increases the risk of stroke and premature death from cardiovascular disease (coronary heart disease and stroke).

What can help prevent coronary heart disease and stroke?
Eating patterns shown to be cardioprotective include:
- Five or more portions of a variety of fruit and vegetables every day.
- A maximum of 6g of salt per day.
- Monounsaturated fats in place of saturated fats *(see page 52)*
- Eating plenty of fibre. Soluble fibre such as that found in oats, oat bran, and pulses such as baked beans, kidney beans, soya beans, peas, lentils and chickpeas is proven to help lower harmful LDL cholesterol.

> High levels of LDL cholesterol in the blood are associated with an increased risk of heart disease. Some foods are fortified with plant sterols and stanols (natural plant substances which reduce the absorption of cholesterol in the gut). There is evidence to show that plant sterols and stanols can help to reduce LDL cholesterol levels by up to 10-15 per cent when 2g per day is regularly consumed as part of a healthy balanced diet. These include spreads, yoghurt drinks and yoghurts, produced by companies such as Benecol and Flora Proactiv, with supermarket own-brands also available.

- Oily fish (such as salmon, trout, herring, mackerel or sardines) at least once a week.

Useful information about how to eat well to protect your heart can be found on the British Heart Foundation website **www.bhf.org.uk.**

Bone disorders

Low bone mineral density – osteoporosis, osteopenia and fractures – are found at higher prevalence rates in people with learning disabilities compared to the general population. Evidence suggests that over half of adults with a learning disability aged between 20 and 64 have abnormal bone mineral density, and that most of these individuals and their carers are unaware of it.

People with a learning disability are at higher risk of poor bone health due to a combination of factors, including; polypharmacy (including anti-epileptic and antipsychotic medications), poor diet, sedentary lifestyles and lack of weight-bearing exercise, comorbid health complications (e.g. hypothyroidism), lack of screening at annual health checks and low levels of Vitamin D.

Vitamin D
People with learning disabilities in England have been found to be nearly twice as likely to be either Vitamin D insufficient, or Vitamin D deficient, compared to the general population. Some of the reasons for this are:
- Less exposure to sunlight – particularly for those in secure services.
- Increased use of high-factor sunblock, sun avoidance and smaller exposed skin surface areas, especially in those prescribed medications known to be photosensitive.
- Increased incidence of obesity, which reduces bioavailability of vitamin D.
- Increased incidence of malnutrition, resulting in reduced intake of micronutrients.
- Use of antiepileptic medications, antipsychotic medications, or levothyroxine, which increase 25-hydroxyvitamin D metabolism, thus reducing vitamin D levels.

Cardiovascular conditions and osteoporosis are the two long-term conditions with the strongest association with dying from an avoidable death for people with a learning disability (LeDeR 2022)

What can help prevent bone disorders?

To reduce the possibility of low bone density, people with learning disabilities should be encouraged to be as mobile as possible, to spend time outside in the summer sunshine safely, and to ensure adequate vitamin D, protein, and micronutrients: calcium, magnesium, manganese, phosphorus, vitamin K, vitamin C and zinc. Bone density should be reviewed as part of the annual health check, and advice should be sought from a physiotherapist or GP about how to undertake weight-bearing exercises. Regularly reviewing medications and body weight. with consideration to their impact on bone health, is also advised.

The Department of Health and Social Care recommends that adults and children over 4 take a daily supplement containing 10 micrograms (400 IU) of vitamin D throughout the year if they:

- are not often outdoors – for example, if they are frail or housebound.
- are in an institution like a care home.
- usually wear clothes that cover up most of their skin when outdoors.
- are over 65 years of age.
- are pregnant or breastfeeding.

Those with dark skin, for example, people from an African, African-Caribbean or South Asian background, may also not make enough vitamin D from sunlight and should consider year-round supplementation.

Everyone in the UK should consider taking a daily

What happens if I take too much vitamin D?

- Taking too many vitamin D supplements can cause damage to the bones, kidneys and heart.
- If you choose to take vitamin D supplements, 10 micrograms a day will be enough for most people.
- Adults should not take more than 100 micrograms (4,000 IU) of vitamin D a day as it could be harmful.
- Children aged 1 to 10 years should not have more than 50 micrograms (2,000 IU) a day.
- Infants under 12 months should not have more than 25 micrograms (1,000 IU) a day.
- Some people have medical conditions that mean they may not be able to safely take as much. If in doubt, you should consult your GP.
- You cannot overdose on vitamin D through exposure to sunlight but remember to cover up or protect skin if out in the sun for long periods to reduce the risk of burning and skin cancer.

Cancer

Cancers are the third highest cause of death for people with a learning disability and account for 15.7% of avoidable deaths.

Cancers with the highest mortality rates in people with learning disabilities are those of the digestive organs, such as the bowel, oesophagus and pancreas. There is evidence that cancers of the intestinal tract are linked to lower intakes of fruits, vegetables and fibre, and higher intakes of alcohol and processed meats. People with a learning disability have been found to have higher rates of helicobacter pylori infection, which can cause reflux, gastritis, and peptic and gastric ulcers, and which significantly increases the likelihood of developing stomach cancer.

What can help?

The possibility of helicobacter pylori infection should be considered in health checks, as this can increase a person's risk of developing stomach cancer.

Cancer Research UK estimates that around 13% of bowel cancer cases in the UK are linked to eating too much red and processed meat, and 30% of cases are linked to eating too little fibre. Healthier eating can reduce these risks.

Supporting people to access cancer screening programmes is also essential for identifying cancers earlier and ensuring better outcomes.

Infections, immune function and recovery from illness and surgery

A recent study by the Scottish Learning Disabilities Observatory (SLDO) found that people with learning disabilities of all ages are almost 11 times more likely to die from respiratory illness compared with the rest of the population. The rate of death from pneumonia was almost 27 times higher.

They highlighted the importance of people with a learning disability receiving appropriate vaccinations, for example, the annual flu and Covid-19 vaccines, to help with lowering this risk. The increased risk of recurrent chest infections, which are secondary to dysphagia, was also highlighted, with a high proportion of aspiration pneumonia-related deaths occurring among individuals with severe and profound intellectual disabilities. Dysphagia is discussed in more detail on page 97.

What can help?

It is well established that good nutrition plays an vital role in the immune system and that optimal nutritional status is associated with shorter hospital stays and fewer infections among hospitalised patients. There is significant evidence that adequate nutrient intakes are essential for those recovering from illness and surgery as tissue repair requires increased energy and nutrients. Key nutrients particularly linked to the immune system includes vitamins A, C, D, B12, B6, zinc, iron, folate, copper and selenium. For more on these, see page 55.

CHAPTER 3 – Principles of Good Nutrition

References

1. Public Health England (2016). *Government Dietary Recommendations: Government recommendations for energy and nutrients for males and females aged 1 – 18 years and 19+ years.* [online]. Available at: https://assets.publishing.service.gov.uk/media/5a749fece5274a44083b82d8/government_dietary_recommendations.pdf

2. World Health Organization (2015). *WHO calls on countries to reduce sugars intake among adults and children.* Available at: https://www.who.int/news/item/04-03-2015-who-calls-on-countries-to-reduce-sugars-intake-among-adults-and-children

3. Foresight (2007). *Tackling Obesities: Future Choices - Project Report* [online] Available at: https://assets.publishing.service.gov.uk/media/5a759da7e5274a4368298a4f/07-1184x-tackling-obesities-future-choices-report.pdf

4. NHS (2024). *Alcohol Units.* Available at: https://www.nhs.uk/live-well/alcohol-advice/calculating-alcohol-units/

5. NHS (2023). *Salt in your diet.* Available at: https://www.nhs.uk/live-well/eat-well/food-types/salt-in-your-diet/

6. NHS England (2023). *Health and Care of People with Learning Disabilities, Experimental Statistics 2022 to 2023.* Available at: https://digital.nhs.uk/data-and-information/publications/statistical/health-and-care-of-people-with-learning-disabilities/experimental-statistics-2022-to-2023

7. King's College London (2021). *Learning from Lives and Deaths – People with a Learning Disability and Autistic People (LeDeR).* Available at: https://www.kcl.ac.uk/research/leder

8. Srikanth R, Cassidy G, Joiner C et al. (2010). Osteoporosis in people with intellectual disabilities: a review and a brief study of risk factors for osteoporosis in a community sample of people with intellectual disabilities. *Journal of Intellectual Disability Research,* 55(1), pp.53–62. https://doi.org/10.1111/j.1365-2788.2010.01346.x

9. Chen PH, Chen CY, Lin YC et al. (2015). Low bone mineral density among adults with disabilities in Taiwan: A cross-sectional descriptive study. *Disability and health journal,* 8(4), pp.635–41. https://doi.org/10.1016/j.dhjo.2015.03.010

10. Harper L. (2017). Optimal nutrition for bone health in people with a learning disability. *Learning Disability Practice,* 20(1), pp.31–35. https://doi.org/10.7748/ldp.2017.e1783

11. Frighi V, Morovat A, Stephenson MT et al. (2014). Vitamin D deficiency in patients with intellectual disabilities: prevalence, risk factors and management strategies. *The British Journal of Psychiatry*, 205(6), pp.458–464. doi:https://doi.org/10.1192/bjp.bp.113.143511

12. CIPOLD (2011). *The Confidential Inquiry into the deaths of people with learning disabilities.* 16(5), pp.18–25. https://doi.org/10.1108/13595471111185729

13. Truesdale M, Melville C, Barlow F et al. (2021). Respiratory-associated deaths in people with intellectual disabilities: a systematic review and meta-analysis. *BMJ Open,* 11(7), p.e043658. https://doi.org/10.1136/bmjopen-2020-043658

14. Cancer Research UK (2024). *Risks and causes of Bowel cancer.* Available at: https://www.cancerresearchuk.org/about-cancer/bowel-cancer/risks-causes

15. Barišić A, Ravančić ME, Majstorivić D et al. (2023). Micronutrient status in children and adolescents with Down syndrome: systematic review and meta-analysis. *Journal of intellectual disability research,* 67(8), pp.701–719. https://doi.org/10.1111/jir.13042

CHAPTER 4

Nutrition through the Lifespan for People with Learning Disabilities

Nutrition through the Lifespan for People with Learning Disabilities

This chapter looks at some of the nutritional factors which may impact people with learning disabilities throughout their lifespan – as infants, young children, teenagers, adults, and into older age.

It is important to recognise that our nutritional needs and vulnerabilities will change over time and ensure our eating patterns and food and drink choices reflect this.

Infants

The nutritional needs of infants are very specific, and advice about infant feeding is available from midwives, health visitors and other health professionals. Exclusive breastfeeding is the best way to feed babies, and for the first six months, a baby can receive all his or her nutritional requirements from breast milk alone. Supporting women to breastfeed and finding innovative ways to ensure that all infants receive breast milk, regardless of their mother's disability or any disability in the child, should be seen as a priority. Breast milk is hygienic, easily digestible, nutritionally unique, and contains essential antibodies to help babies fight infections. Breastfeeding can also protect women from some diseases of later life. Women with learning disabilities should be offered specific and tailored support to help them breastfeed their infants if they wish to do this.

Some infants with learning disabilities may have feeding difficulties, and this may lead to 'faltering growth', which means they are not growing as well as other children of their age. Mothers of learning-disabled infants should be aware that they may experience feeding difficulties and should be offered tailored support to help with feeding as well as emotional and practical support if breastfeeding is unsuccessful.

A learning disability may be first observed when children are slow to reach typical developmental milestones – for example, a failure at six months to show interest in their surroundings or to attempt to sit up and grasp objects. Diagnosis of a learning disability is rarely possible, and with a few exceptions, unwise in the first six months of life. The most important exception is infants born with Down's syndrome. Once a learning disability has been confirmed, a multi-disciplinary team of health professionals will be able to support the family, and where there are dietary-related problems, a paediatric dietitian will be consulted. Feeding tubes may be used in some cases where necessary.

It is recommended that solid foods start being offered to babies, where developmentally appropriate, from about six months of age. When complementary foods are introduced, the following points are important.

- No salt should be added.
- No sugar should be added.

The first foods recommended are vegetables that aren't sweet, such as cauliflower, broccoli and green beans.

Unprocessed finger foods, such as fruit and vegetables should be offered to encourage independence.

Mealtimes will be messy as babies learn about food and feeding.

It is crucial that parents are given guidance on appropriate foods, portion sizes and mealtime behaviour and that they are aware of safety issues such as never leaving a baby or toddler alone with food.

Useful information is available at the **NHS 'Start 4 Life'** website www.nhs.uk/start-for-life/

It is important that parents and other carers with a learning disability or those caring for a baby with a learning disability receive careful and individually tailored advice on feeding in the first year of life.

From birth to 12 months, a daily vitamin D supplement of 8.5mcg should be given to all breast-fed babies. This increases to 10 mcg after the first year. From 6 months to 5 years of age, daily vitamin A, C and D supplements are recommended. Babies receiving 500 ml or more of formula per day do not need a separate supplement as these vitamins are added to the formula already.

For further information on vitamin drops for infants, see page 68. For more detailed information on infant feeding, see the **Caroline Walker Trust** publication **Eating well: first year of life.**

Children

Eating well and being active in the early years are essential for proper growth and development. This is true for all children, regardless of whether they have a learning or physical disability or not. It is the responsibility of everyone who cares for and supports young children to ensure that they are exposed to good experiences around food and encouraged to develop positive attitudes to eating and physical activity. It is recommended that all parents and carers of children with learning disabilities, and all parents with learning disabilities themselves, are given appropriate information on eating well for their children, to ensure that they can establish appropriate eating habits and prevent underweight, overweight and other nutritionally-related health problems. Some of the key points to consider when helping children eat well are outlined opposite.

Children with learning disabilities

Various research studies have examined the nutritional status of children with learning disabilities. Children with disabilities and neurological impairment

Key issues for eating well among children

Children should be encouraged to eat a varied diet. They should eat foods from each of the four main food groups every day.

The four main food groups are:
- Fruit and vegetables.
- Starchy carbohydrates such as potatoes, bread, rice and pasta, choosing wholegrain versions where possible.
- protein-rich foods such as beans, pulses, fish, eggs, meat and other proteins (including 2 portions of fish every week, 1 of which should be oily).
- Dairy or dairy alternatives (such as soya milk).

Fruit and vegetables are particularly important for good health. Children should be encouraged to have at least five portions of a variety of fruits and vegetables every day.

Most children consume **too much sugar and too little fibre**. Children do not need sugary foods or drinks, such as sweets, chocolate, soft drinks or honey, for energy, and these foods are a cause of tooth decay. Starchy foods, such as potatoes, bread, rice, pasta and yam, are better sources of energy as these foods contain other important nutrients too.

Choosing wholegrain varieties increases fibre intakes to support regular bowel movements. If children have sugary foods and drinks as an occasional treat, they should be served with meals rather than as snacks between meals.

The **iron and zinc** intake of children is lower than recommended, and there is evidence that low iron and zinc status is common. Children should therefore include a range of iron-rich and zinc-rich foods in their diet, such as wholegrain cereals, pulses (peas, beans and lentils), tofu, nuts, seeds, lean meat and fish.

It is recommended that breastfed infants and children aged 6 months to 5 years should receive **vitamin drops** containing vitamins A, C and D.

Children should be encouraged to be **physically active,** and it is important to fit activity into children's daily routines throughout the year. Physical activity, including active play, builds up muscle strength, bone density and overall fitness. It also helps develop motor skills such as balance and coordination, is good for mental health, and provides a release for children's energy.

(conditions which impact the brain and spinal cord, including cerebral palsy, brain injury and epilepsy) are more likely to experience nutritional problems, and in particular insufficient energy intake, which can impact growth. Children with learning disabilities are also more likely to be underweight or shorter than expected for their age, and children with more severe disabilities are more likely to experience nutritional problems.

Micronutrient deficiencies have been reported in children with developmental disability and may be under-recognised. For example, children with feeding difficulties may rely on a milk-based diet, which makes it more likely that they will get insufficient amounts of other nutrients, particularly iron. Children with learning disabilities may experience difficulties with controlling food or fluids in their mouths, sensory sensitivity (e.g. an exaggerated response to touch in the mouth or around the face), or difficulty managing cutlery. Advice on managing eating difficulties can be found in Chapter 8.

Parents of children with disabilities and eating difficulties have reported that meat, fruits and vegetables are often avoided, and this can have an impact on vitamin, fibre, iron and zinc intakes. For information about the role of nutrients for health, see page 55.

It is recommended that all children between 1 and 5 years receive daily vitamin drops (containing vitamins A, C, D).

These are free to anyone eligible for the Healthy Start scheme. Information on vitamin supplements can be obtained from health visitors or the **Healthy Start** website on www.healthystart.nhs.uk.

Children with learning disabilities want to be treated like other children and to be included in ordinary activities. All children with additional needs should be encouraged to eat the same healthy diet and, wherever possible, do this in the same way as other children.

> For more detailed practical guidelines on eating well for children, including example meal plans and portion pictures, see the **Caroline Walker Trust** publications: **Eating well: 1-4 year olds** and **Eating well: 5-11 year olds**.

Teenagers

The teenage years are characterised by a move to greater independence for almost all children as they forge their own identities and make more decisions about their own lifestyles. Adolescence is often seen as a time of rebellion, experimentation and increasing financial independence, which may affect food choices. For example, irregular eating, increased snacking or grazing, missed meals, unconventional meals and an increase in the consumption of fast food, soft or energy drinks and confectionery. Many young people with learning disabilities will face the same pressures as other teenagers to adopt a more risk-taking lifestyle, and it has been suggested that teenagers with low self-esteem and less hope for their own futures are more likely to adopt behaviours which put their health at risk.

An increase in body image awareness and body image concerns also makes this a vulnerable age for thedevelopment of eating disorders such as anorexia nervosa and bulimia nervosa. Helping teens to develop a healthy self-image should be a priority.

As young people move on from child and adolescent healthcare and educational provision, they and those who support them may find it more difficult to access services which support eating well and being active.

Increased access to food, increased exposure to food advertising, and reduced physical activity put teenagers at risk of weight gain, so this can be a crucial time to establish good eating habits and regular physical activity. Both diet and activity will help to prevent other physical health difficulties and boost mental health. It is essential that each person's nutritional needs are considered whenever their health is reviewed. Support may be needed to help young people develop the skills to identify, access and prepare healthy foods that they enjoy. Likewise, support may be required to embed physical activity in daily routines, for example walking, dancing, trampolining, gardening or structured sporting activities.

Pregnancy

A healthy diet during pregnancy is important for the health of the mother and the baby. Women should be offered appropriate advice on eating and drinking well throughout their pregnancy and ideally before they become pregnant. For women with learning disabilities, it is important that the advice is specifically tailored to their particular condition and geared to their level of understanding.

It is very important that women attend all the appointments made with health professionals throughout their pregnancy so that they can be appropriately supported. Those with learning disabilities should be enabled to access that support. Those caring for or supporting women with learning disabilities who are or who may become pregnant should ensure that medical advice is always accessible and accessed.

Women with learning disabilities who are planning a pregnancy, those who have obesity, and those who may become pregnant (that is, if they are sexually active and not using contraception) should take a daily supplement of 400 mcgs of folic acid before pregnancy and during the first 12 weeks of pregnancy. Women who have a history of neural tube defects or diabetes mellitus, or who take anti-convulsant drugs, should talk to a health professional about the amount of folic acid they need, as they have greater needs than other women. Folic acid is essential for the early development of the foetus and for preventing the development of neural tube defects such as spina bifida.

Vitamin D is essential for ensuring healthy bones for both the mother and the infant, and a 10 mcg daily supplement is recommended.

Some women may be entitled to free vitamins, which contain folic acid, vitamin C and vitamin D, as part of the Healthy Start programme. More information about who is eligible for free vitamins and about food vouchers in pregnancy can be found at **www.healthystart.nhs.uk**.

> When considering an over-the-counter vitamin supplement women should not take cod liver oil or any supplements containing vitamin A (retinol) when pregnant as too much vitamin A could harm the baby. It is best to choose a supplement that is specifically designed for pregnancy and to take advice from a health professional.

During pregnancy women should avoid eating certain foods. These include some types of cheeses, unpasteurised milks, uncooked fish and seafood, raw and undercooked meats, pate, liver, and certain types of eggs (if undercooked). Consumption of some types of fish (including oily fish and tuna) should also be limited.

Care should be taken with caffeine intake, and alcohol should be avoided completely.

Check the NHS website for more detailed information on which foods to avoid during pregnancy: **www.nhs.uk/pregnancy/keeping-well/foods-to-avoid/**

For women with learning disabilities who are planning a pregnancy, pregnant or breastfeeding, medications should be prescribed cautiously, and regular medication reviews carried out, to minimise the risk of harm to the foetus.

Women who are overweight or obese before they conceive have an increased risk of complications during pregnancy and birth, which pose health risks to both the mother and baby.

Women who are overweight at the start of pregnancy should be given accessible advice, tailored to their needs and circumstances, on how to eat healthily during pregnancy and after they have given birth.

All women should be encouraged and supported to breastfeed their infants. Breastfeeding women should be advised that losing weight through a combination of healthy eating and regular physical activity will not affect the quantity or quality of their milk.

Parenthood

Parents with learning disabilities often face additional challenges to parenting, including poor physical or mental health, poverty, discrimination and lack of social support. They are far more likely than other parents to have their children removed from them and permanently placed outside the family home. Appropriate help and support should be provided to ensure they know how to offer an appropriate diet for their child at every stage of development. Support may also be needed to know how to store and prepare healthy food for their children, and how to budget.

The Menopause

Women with learning disabilities have the same menopausal symptoms as other women, but generally experience the menopause earlier, particularly those with Down's syndrome. The symptoms of the menopause can be particularly distressing for women with learning disabilities as they may lack the cognitive ability or education to understand why they are experiencing symptoms such as hot flushes, headaches, weight gain or anxiety.

Hormone replacement therapy (HRT) can be prescribed to relieve the symptoms of the menopause, but some women will be unable to make an informed decision about the treatment. Research has shown that most women with learning disabilities are influenced by the beliefs of those who care for

> *Women who are overweight or obese before they conceive have an increased risk of complications during pregnancy and birth, which pose health risks to both the mother and baby.*

them regarding symptom management. Maintaining a healthy weight, eating a diet rich in fibre, fruits and vegetables, reducing caffeine, alcohol and salt intake, and being as active as possible, may help mitigate some of the symptoms associated with menopause. Including foods containing plant oestrogens (such as soya milk, soya yoghurts, edamame beans and linseeds) several times per day can improve the symptoms of hot flushes in some women. The principles of eating for good bone and heart health also become increasingly important with the onset of the menopause.

Older age

Older people with learning disabilities are at risk of the same age-related physiological changes as the general population. The nutritional needs of older people have been summarised in the The Caroline Walker Trust practical guide 'Eating Well: Supporting older people and older people with dementia.'

Depression is common among older people and this may be a particular problem among those with learning disabilities if they have poor communication or verbal skills. For older adults in the general population, there is usually a good outlook once depression is treated, but there is some evidence that, among older people with learning disabilities, mental ill health can be more persistent. The mental health needs of older people with learning disabilities have been reported to be overlooked and unmet, and this is likely to be an increasing problem as this population ages.

Many older people with learning disabilities have limited social networks and few opportunities to use ordinary leisure provision in the community. This social isolation is in marked contrast to the experiences of many non-learning-disabled people who, as they grow older, take up new hobbies and other leisure pursuits. People with learning disabilities need support to share these opportunities, and it is essential that support systems are well-equipped to meet age-related needs.

Provision for people with learning disabilities who develop dementia is a key area of concern. People with Down's syndrome are at greater risk of developing Alzheimer's disease and will do so at a younger than average age. However, in the case of people with learning disabilities other than Down's syndrome, the prevalence of Alzheimer's disease and other forms of dementia is no greater than for the rest of the population.

End-of-life

End-of-life planning for people with learning disabilities should be given the same care and attention as it is for any other member of society. Caring for people at the end of their lives is an important role for health and social care professionals. End-of-life care requires an active, compassionate approach that treats, comforts and supports individuals who are living with or dying from progressive or chronic life-threatening conditions. Such care is sensitive to personal, cultural and spiritual values, beliefs and practices, and encompasses support for families and friends up to and including the period of bereavement. Conversations about death, dying and preferred end-of-life plans require information that a person can understand. A person with a learning disability may need to have familiar people around them. Appropriately skilled healthcare professionals can provide effective care for people with learning disabilities at the end of their lives and work in partnership with their family and carers.

One of the key elements in supporting people at the end of their lives is to find out what their preferences and wishes are regarding to how they would like to be cared for and documenting these to ensure they are accessible to anyone involved in their care. This might include completing of a Respect (Recommended Summary Plan for Emergency Care and Treatment) form. More information on this, including an Easy-Read version of the form, is available at is available from the Resuscitation Council UK website's Useful information on end-of-life planning has been produced by NICE:
https://www.nice.org.uk/guidance/ng96
An Easy Read version is also available.

There are frequently specific issues around the provision and acceptance of food and drink at end-of-life, and it is essential that any concerns or changes around nutrition and hydration are carefully discussed with all those involved in end-of-life planning for an individual.

References

1. UNICEF (2016). *The benefits of breastfeeding.* Available at: https://www.unicef.org.uk/babyfriendly/about/benefits-of-breastfeeding/
2. NICE (2018). Faltering Growth. Available at: https://cks.nice.org.uk/topics/faltering-growth/
3. NHS (2023). Weaning – Start for Life. Available at: https://www.nhs.uk/start-for-life/baby/weaning/
4. Sullivan PB, Juszczak E, Lambert BR et al. (2002). Impact of feeding problems on nutritional intake and growth: Oxford Feeding Study II. *Developmental Medicine & Child Neurology,* 44(07). https://doi.org/10.1017/s0012162201002365.
5. Batra A, Marino LV, Beattie RM. (2022). Feeding children with neurodisability: challenges and practicalities. *Archives of Disease in Childhood,* 107, pp967-972. https://doi.org/10.1136/archdischild-2021-322102.
6. Public Health England (2015). *SACN Carbohydrates and Health Report.* Available at: https://www.gov.uk/government/publications/sacn-carbohydrates-and-health-report
7. British Nutrition Foundation (2024). *Nutrition for teenagers.* British Nutrition Foundation. Available at: https://www.nutrition.org.uk/nutrition-for/teenagers/
8. NHS (2020). *Keeping well in pregnancy.* Available at: https://www.nhs.uk/pregnancy/keeping-well/
9. NHS (2020). *Overweight and pregnant.* Available at: https://www.nhs.uk/pregnancy/related-conditions/existing-health-conditions/overweight/
10. Anna Freud. *Supporting parents with learning difficulties or disabilities.* Available at: https://www.annafreud.org/resources/under-fives-wellbeing/working-with-families-facing-challenges/parents-and-carers-with-learning-difficulties/
11. Chou YC, Jane Lu ZY, Pu CY. (2013). Menopause experiences and attitudes in women with intellectual disability and in their family carers. *Journal of Intellectual & Developmental Disability,* 38(2), pp.114–123. https://doi.org/10.3109/13668250.2013.768763
12. BDA (2019). *Menopause and diet.* Available at: https://www.bda.uk.com/resource/menopause-diet.html
13. Willis DS, Wishart JG, Muir WJ. (2010). Menopausal Experiences of Women with Intellectual Disabilities. *Journal of Applied Research in Intellectual Disabilities,* 24(1), pp.74–85. https://doi.org/10.1111/j.1468-3148.2010.00566.x
14. NICE (2018). *Care and Support of People Growing Older with Learning Disabilities.* Available at: https://www.nice.org.uk/guidance/ng9615. Cooper SA, Smiley E, Morrison 15. J et al. (2007b). Mental ill-health in adults with intellectual disabilities: prevalence and associated factors. British Journal of Psychiatry, 190(01), pp.27–35. https://doi.org/10.1192/bjp.bp.106.022483

CHAPTER 5

Monitoring nutritional status and supporting people with healthy weight

Monitoring nutritional status and supporting people with healthy weight

This chapter looks at: monitoring nutritional status, identifying when people are underweight and overweight, why people with learning disabilities are vulnerable to unhealthy body weight, and how this can be managed.

Monitoring nutritional status

Knowing whether someone is meeting their nutritional needs requires some measure of their nutritional status. This is most frequently done by monitoring a person's weight change over time and recording any changes in food and drink consumption.

It is not easy to spot malnutrition. Often, prolonged periods of insufficient or inappropriate food intake manifest very late as a sudden illness, such as pneumonia or a fracture. Being alert to changing food patterns is essential if poor eating and drinking are to be recognised before malnutrition impacts health and wellbeing.

Several tools can be used to help screen nutritional status, both in the community and in hospitals. Details of some of these are given on page 174. The best fit for a particular setting will depend on who is undertaking the screening, where it is being undertaken, and what information is available.

If there is concern that someone is not eating well, ask the person's GP for a referral to a registered dietitian, or consult with the community learning disability team.

Simple warning signs of changes in nutritional status

These include:
- unexpected weight loss or gain,
- significant changes in eating habits, or drinking or eating more or less than usual,
- food or drinks routinely left over at meals and snack times,
- loss of independence in eating,
- difficulties with swallowing,
- ongoing signs of fatigue, apathy, or disinterest

Identifying underweight and overweight

Evidence shows many people with learning disabilities have inappropriate body weights – either underweight or overweight. However, it is not always easy to tell if people are too thin, and it can be difficult to know if a person's weight gain is impacting their health and wellbeing. To assess people's weight in relation to their health, we rely on some simple measurements, which are described below.

Growth charts

Growth charts show how a child's height, weight and head circumference compare with other children of the same age and sex. Children come in all shapes and sizes, and will not all track the same, but the chart helps to check whether a child is growing and developing as expected for good health. Certain genetic conditions will change the expected patterns of growth. As such, specific growth charts are available for boys and girls with Down's syndrome, Williams Syndrome, Prader-Willi Syndrome and for those with Cerebral Palsy. There are also specific height charts available for children with Turner syndrome.

Measuring height

Height measurements should be taken using a height stick (stadiometer) where possible. Ensure it is correctly positioned, with the person standing upright, shoes removed, feet flat, and heels against the height stick or wall. This could be requested at the GP surgery during a person's annual health check. Where this measurement is made difficult due to physiological changes such as scoliosis, height can be estimated by measuring the length of the person's ulna from the elbow to the wrist.

More guidance on how to do this is available in the MUST Toolkit at **bapen.org.uk**.

Body mass index

Deviations from 'ideal weight' are most commonly defined in terms of body mass index (BMI). This is calculated by dividing a person's weight (in kilos) by the square of their height (in metres). The classification of weight among adults by the National Institute for Health and Clinical Excellence (NICE) is shown in the table below:

Classification of weight among adults	
Classification	**BMI (kg/m^2)**
Underweight	Less than 18.5
Healthy weight	18.5-24.9
Overweight	25.0-29.9
Obese	30.0 or over
Class I	30.0-34.9
Class II	35.0-39.9
Class III	40.0 or over

Source: NICE, 2025

BMI does not consider the distribution of body fat, or body composition (e.g. the amount of muscle a person has). There are no predetermined correction factors available specifically for use with those with Down's syndrome, who tend to be shorter compared to the general population and have lower muscle tone. BMI may not be appropriate for those who have a physical disability and complex anatomy, or have muscle wasting due to limited mobility.

It is also important to recognise that people with an Asian, Middle Eastern, Black African or African–Caribbean background are at an increased risk of chronic health conditions at a lower BMI than people from a white background. NICE suggest using lower BMI thresholds to classify overweight and obesity for these populations:

Overweight: BMI 23 kg/m^2 to 27.4 kg/m^2,

Obesity: BMI 27.5 kg/m^2 or above.

Calculating appropriate BMI thresholds for children and young people requires adjustments for age and sex, and the use of BMI centile charts. The NHS website has a Healthy Weight Calculator you can use to calculate BMI for children, young people and adults, available at:

https://www.nhs.uk/health-assessment-tools/calculate-your-body-mass-index/

Waist measurements

NICE guidance also advises measuring the waist-to-height ratio to assess central adiposity (fat stored around the waist). An easy way to explain it to people is to suggest that they aim to keep their waist measurement to less than half their height measurement (resulting in a waist-to-height ratio of under 0.5). This is a simple way to understand health risks associated with being overweight.

The correct position for measuring the waist is midway between the top of the hips and the bottom of the ribs, just above the belly button.
To calculate the waist-to-height ratio, measure the waist circumference and height in the same units (either both in cm or both in inches) and divide the waist measurement by height measurement.

Care must be taken with anyone who may have an inappropriate waist measurement for other reasons (e.g. related to the use of medicines, pregnancy or another illness). Also, these measurements have not been validated in a learning-disabled population; therefore, they should be viewed as a general guide only.

The measurement of waist circumference is a measure of risk for conditions such as coronary heart disease, high blood pressure, and type 2 diabetes.

A healthy central adiposity is defined as a waist-to-height ratio of 0.4 to 0.49, indicating no increased health risks

Increased central adiposity is indicated by a waist-to-height ratio of 0.5 to 0.59, indicating increased health risks

High central adiposity is defined as a waist-to-height ratio of 0.6 or more, indicating a further increased risk to health.

These classifications can be used for people with a BMI under 35 kg/m^2 of both sexes and all ethnicities, including adults with high muscle mass, children and young people.

Tools to help monitor weight

It is essential that support staff are able to both easily monitor weight changes and act on changes appropriately. There are several tools available to assist with this, and we recommend using them both to record and monitor weight and to assess nutritional status (see page 176).

A simple tool has been developed for use with people with learning disabilities. It allows support staff to plot a person's weight on a chart and, with input from a health professional, lines can be added that show when attention should be sought for an inappropriate weight.

An example of a completed weight chart is shown, and a blank version is provided in Appendix 3.

The scales used to measure people must be accurate. They should be checked (and ideally calibrated) regularly and should not be moved. Wheelchairs or hoist scales should be available to weigh people where needed. It is useful to have discussions with each person about how frequently weighing should take place, whether weights will always be taken with clothes on or off, and the time of day, to ensure consistency. Shoes should be removed, and only light clothing should be worn. The same set of scales should be used at each weigh-in. Constipation can add 0.5kg to 1.5kg, and this should be considered when instances of short-term weight change are noticed, as should water retention, which may occur as part of a woman's menstrual cycle.

A person is at risk of malnutrition if they have unplanned weight loss of 5%-10% in the past 3 to 6 months. This risk becomes more significant if they have unintentionally lost more than 10% of body weight in the past 3 to 6 months. This would mean, for example:
– If someone weighing 60kg had unintentionally lost 3kg in the past 4 months (equivalent to 5% of weight), they may be at risk of malnutrition and should be monitored carefully.
- If someone weighing 50kg had unintentionally lost 5kg in the past 3 months (equivalent to 10% of weight), they are at high risk of malnutrition, and advice should be sought from a medical practitioner as a matter of urgency.

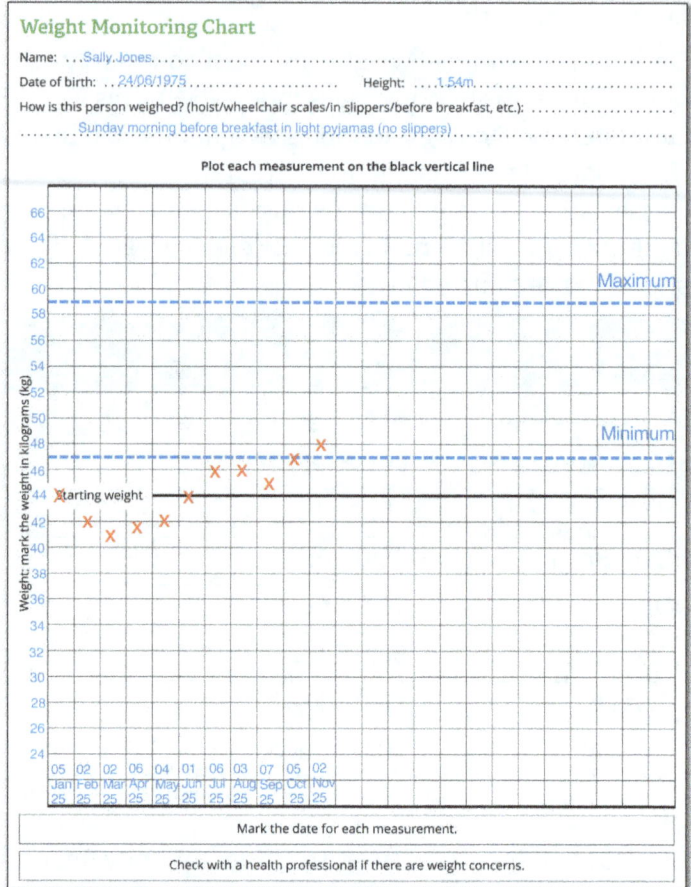

It is important to remember that, even if people appear to be of normal weight or overweight, they can still be at risk of malnutrition if they lose a significant amount of weight unintentionally.

Underweight and malnutrition risks

What do we know about underweight among people with learning disabilities?

Recent data from NHS Digital shows significant inequality in the prevalence of malnutrition risk in those with a learning disability compared to the rest of the population. For example, 3.6% of 25- to 34-year-olds with a learning disability are underweight, compared with 0.8% in the general population. A study of 1,542 adults in supported accommodation found that 14% of those with learning disabilities were low weight (BMI less than 20), and a review of 25 studies concluded that between 35% and 72% of those with severe learning disabilities were significantly underweight (BMI less than 17). This was most common in those who were immobile, unable to feed themselves or tolerate solid foods, or who exhibited regurgitation, rumination or chronic vomiting.

It is not uncommon for severe undernutrition to go unrecognised by support staff and health professionals, particularly when it is longstanding ("they have always been thin"). Thinness can appear to be resistant to obvious practices like offering more food ("no matter what we do, we can't get weight on them. They are just like that and always will be"). It has even been suggested that some support staff accept low weight and resist change, as the person they care for may be easier to manage if they remain underweight. Challenging the perception of what normal body weights are for people with learning disabilities is essential. Health professionals in particular need clear information on the 'normal' growth and development that should be expected among people with learning disabilities, and the importance of intervention if an individual is below a healthy body weight for their health.

Why does underweight matter?

Being significantly underweight increases a person's susceptibility to infection, their risk of bone fracture, and is associated with increased mortality. Sudden death from respiratory illness typifies the end-of-life story for people who have insufficient food intake. Undernutrition also increases the risk of specific nutrient deficiencies, which can lead to various health-related conditions that significantly impact quality of life. Individuals who are underweight often experience weaker muscle tone, which can impair their ability to perform everyday physical tasks and may also affect their appetite. Reduced activity levels can reduce appetite and establish a cycle of poor food intake, illness, reduced appetite and further reduced food intake that can lead to chronic undernutrition.

How to identify malnutrition risks

Malnutrition can be identified using the Malnutrition Universal Screening Tool (MUST), which provides a user-friendly scoring system and can be used by support staff and healthcare teams. An online calculator or a 'toolkit' is used to determine whether a risk is low, medium, or high. For each score, an action is advised:

- A score of 0, low risk, advises to repeat periodically,
- A medium malnutrition risk (MUST score 1), recommends detailed observation and implementation of nutritional intervention,
- A score of 2, high risk, recommends referral to a dietitian.

Page 176 lists other recommended tools for identifying malnutrition. Healthcare teams may use additional measures to assess co-occurring frailty and muscle loss, such as handgrip strength or the Rockwood Frailty Scale.

It is essential that all support staff are alert to undernutrition, malnutrition and use of nutritional screening as a way of recognising and validating concerns. Training may be available locally or can be accessed via focusonundernutrition.co.uk.

What to do if someone is underweight

It is possible to restore weight with considered support for eating and drinking. A medium malnutrition risk, with a score of 1, indicates that steps can be taken to improve nutritional status and prevent further deterioration in weight. Strategies to improve weight in those who are malnourished include:

- keeping weight records and following up if there is unexplained weight loss of over 5%,
- keeping records of food eaten and leftovers,
- providing a fortified diet (see page 78),
- providing prescribable nutritional supplements or over-the-counter nutritional drinks (see page 78),
- investigation of any underlying medical problems which might be related to weight loss,
- ensuring robust bowel management,
- increasing physical activity among those who are able, to increase appetite and interest in food,
- improving techniques to support people who have eating difficulties (see page 117),
- offering small meals regularly (e.g. six small meals a day) – sometimes called 'little and often' eating,
- stimulating the appetite by making food look and taste good and ensuring meals are served at appropriate times, in a calm and pleasant environment,
- nutrition support (see following page),
- enteral feeding (see following page).

Nutrition support

When an individual has significant difficulties with eating and drinking, and malnutrition risks are high (MUST score 2 or more), they should be offered nutrition support. This may be in the form of an oral supplement to be taken alongside the usual intake. These are available in various sizes and flavours, and in different consistencies suitable for those with dysphagia. Alternatively, if oral intake is compromised, supplemental nutrition can be administered through a tube, allowing liquid food to pass straight into the stomach (enteral nutrition). In extreme circumstances, such as disease of the gut or a very serious illness, individuals may be offered parenteral nutrition, where nutrients are administered directly into the bloodstream.

Decisions around how best to manage malnutrition risks in people who have a significant disability can be challenging to make. Many people who experience this will lack the capacity to make informed decisions about managing this risk. The decision will be highly personal, depending on the individual's health, support needs, living situation, tolerance, and a variety of other factors. Exploring the risks and benefits of the surgical procedure and placement of a gastrostomy (feeding tube) is a necessary and legal part of the best interest process if it is evidenced that the individual lacks capacity regarding this decision.

For many people, the addition of nutritional support does not mean an end to eating, and it is essential that it is not viewed as an either/or scenario. Where the provision of food and drink is extremely time-consuming (e.g. more than 45 minutes per meal), this can become very fatiguing for both the person involved and their caregiver. Nutritional support, in conjunction with oral intake, can significantly reduce the time spent at meals. Following advice from a speech and language therapist, there may be no need to deny a person the social aspects of eating or the pleasant tastes of foods and drinks. Gastrostomy tubes can be discreetly hidden under clothing and allow for the accurate administration of medication.

Food fortification

The fortification of commonly eaten foods can be a valuable way of increasing nutrient intake. Adapting common meals and snacks to increase their energy and protein content can be particularly useful when appetites are reduced but people can eat and drink normally. Advice should be sought on suitable fortification tips and ideas where there are special dietary needs.

Examples of how to fortify the diet and foods to increase calorie and nutritional content:

- Add dried milk powder to whole milk and use in drinks ('fortified milk').
- Add dried milk powder or cream to custard.
- Make soups with fortified milk, add cream, coconut cream, crème fraîche or pureed tofu.
- Add cream, coconut cream or condensed milk to puddings.
- Add butter, cream, grated cheese or soft cheese to soups, mashed potato, pasta dishes, curries.
- Use butter, mayonnaise, olive oil or salad cream in sandwiches, on potatoes and salads.
- Add extra butter to vegetables, scrambled eggs and bread.
- Add nut butters, seed butters, tahini, hummus or mashed avocado to toast, crackers or sandwiches.
- Choose thick and creamy yogurts
- Add jam, honey, nuts or nut butters, seeds or seed butters, dried fruits or milk powder to porridge, breakfast cereals or puddings.
- Choose nourishing drinks between meals, such as milkshakes or hot milk drinks.

Oral Nutritional supplements

A wide range of commercially produced high-energy, vitamin- and mineral-enriched food supplements are available. These are prescribed by a doctor, medical practitioner or on the advice of a dietitian. Examples include Fortisip, Ensure, Altraplen & Foodlink. These supplements should not be seen as long-term food substitutes but can be useful for short-term use after illness or operations, or where there has been sudden unexpected weight loss.

Various flavours and bottle sizes are available, and it can be helpful to provide a trial of flavours before prescribing. Supplement fatigue is common if these products are used for a long period. Regularly reviewing the need to offer new flavours or present them in a new way (e.g. stirring into a hot chocolate or coffee) can be helpful.

How to use food supplement products safely
- Check the use-by date on products before you use them.
- Do not use damaged bottles or packets.
- Store in a cool place.
- Follow the prescriber's instructions for use, and the manufacturer's instructions for storage.
- Remember good hygiene practice.
- Ask for a regular review of the prescription to ensure that these supplements are needed.

More information on food supplements and food fortification is available at **malnutritiontaskforce.org.uk**.

NUTRITION SUPPORT TERMINOLOGY	
Enteral Nutrition	Passing liquid food directly into the stomach or small bowel via a feeding tube
Parenteral Nutrition	Passing nutrients directly into the blood for people who cannot digest or absorb food
Gastrostomy tube (often referred to as a PEG)	A tube which passes into the stomach via which liquid food, fluids and medications can be given
Jejunostomy tube	A tube which passes into the jejunum (small bowel) via which liquid food, fluids and medications can be given

Living with artificial nutrition support

People who are enterally fed will often rely on the support of family carers and/or support staff to manage their feed, along with support from a dietitian or nutrition support nurse. Training should always be provided so that family, friends, and support staff know how to support enteral feeding and resolve any practical problems people may encounter.

Some people may find living with a gastrostomy straightforward, while others may find that it impacts various aspects of their daily life. One small study reported that 90% of parents of children with learning disabilities were happy with the tube-feeding regimen for their child, but that some parents would have liked more support when their child first needed a gastrostomy. The most common difficulties dealt with by parents in this study were vomiting, leakage, infection, diarrhoea and nausea.

To make life with a gastrostomy as normal as possible, it is worth considering the following:
- Feeding regimens should consider the individual's lifestyle, and feeding should not dominate each day.
- Individuals may choose to join in with the social aspects of mealtimes, which should be encouraged wherever possible.
- Oral intake of food and drink at meals may still be possible, but should only be given under the guidance of a speech and language therapist and dietitian.
- It is essential that oral hygiene (e.g. regular toothbrushing) continues even if food and drink are not consumed orally.

People may feel self-conscious about their tube and feel tied down by the gastrostomy. Talking to other people can be helpful, and there are several organisations that offer support (see Appendix 2).

Overweight and obesity

What do we know about overweight and obesity among people with learning disabilities?

When the total amount of calories in the food and drink consumed exceeds expenditure, the excess is stored as body fat. Obesity is defined as a condition in which the stores of body fat have increased to a level which impairs health.

Obesity in the general population has risen rapidly (House of Commons, 2023); statistics from NHS Digital Data 2022 estimate that 29% of adults in England have obesity, and a further 35% are overweight. Overweight (BMI 25-29.9) and obesity (BMI 30 or above) are more common among people with a learning disability. People with learning disabilities also experience obesity at a younger age than the general population. People aged 18 – 24 years with a learning disability are six times more likely to experience obesity than those without a learning disability.

Why is obesity higher among some people with learning disabilities?

It has been suggested that the increased rates of obesity among young adults with learning disabilities are linked to:

- living in poorer households,
- increased dependence on others,
- lower levels of activity, and
- use of food to manage boredom, social isolation, or behaviours that challenge.

Obesity may be higher in young people with learning disabilities when they leave school, as many find it challenging to move into employment or continuing education, or to access purposeful activities. This results in less daily structure, and hence less structure to eating patterns in general.

A propensity to weight gain can be compounded by using food as a reward or comfort, or by engaging in disordered eating. For example, recent evidence suggests that about 13% of service users with a learning disability in South London had a diagnosable binge eating disorder associated with obesity. Children and adolescents with learning disabilities are four times more likely to have an emotional disorder, and this is more common among girls and those who live in poverty.

Certain specific conditions can also increase the predisposition to weight gain. Hypotonia (low muscle tone) is a feature of Prader-Willi Syndrome and Down's Syndrome, resulting in a person having lower energy needs. Additionally, these conditions are linked to an increased incidence of hypothyroidism, which in turn can increase the likelihood of weight gain.

In the general population, increasing rates of obesity and poor nutrition have been linked to:

- a lack of understanding of what constitutes a balanced diet,
- limited access to fresh fruit and vegetables,
- a sedentary lifestyle,
- diets high in fat and sugar, particularly sugary drinks,
- environments (e.g. home, school, high streets, etc.) where less healthy foods are widely available and/or promoted, and
- overly large portion sizes.

Studies have reported that people with learning disabilities living in supported living or residential care, who rely on their support staff for advice and help with their diets and lifestyle, are also subject to these issues.

Support staff are paramount to facilitating nutritional changes. However, they may find it challenging to balance individual choice with the promotion of healthy foods. Often, individual choice is limited to that available within the care setting, which itself may be an obesogenic environment. Additionally, food options available are determined by service providers who may have limited nutritional knowledge and skill.

Capacity

The Learning from Lives and Deaths - people with a learning disability and autistic people (LeDeR) reports identify the application of the Mental Capacity Act as a strong influencing factor in effective delivery of care and health outcomes. In the case of dietary risks, such as malnutrition, obesity, or diabetes, it is essential to assess whether someone has the capacity to manage their health risk. Understanding whether someone has the capacity to manage their diet-related health risks allows interventions to be more effectively personalised to meet their needs. To have capacity, someone will be able to understand, communicate, retain, and weigh up information pertinent to a specific decision. In this case, it might include information about the health risk, its consequences, how this is likely to impact the individual themselves, and the pros and cons of any dietary changes. More information on capacity is included in Chapter 7. The British Dietetic Association offers training on this topic, which is available to all healthcare professionals.

The health consequences of overweight and obesity

It is known that overweight and obesity in the general population are linked to an increased risk of developing coronary heart disease, type 2 diabetes,

Type 2 diabetes

People with a learning disability in England have higher rates of diabetes than the general population and are likely to be diagnosed at a younger age. Research suggests that rates of diabetes are 16 times higher for those aged 25 – 54 with a learning disability than those without a learning disability.

Nine out of every ten people with type 2 diabetes are overweight or obese, with a BMI score over 25 considered a significant risk factor for developing the disease. Maintaining a healthy weight, combined with regular physical activity, is strongly linked to a reduced risk of developing type 2 diabetes.

Having diabetes is particularly problematic for some people with learning disabilities. They might experience difficulty adjusting to or understanding the importance of making diet and lifestyle changes. However, many are able to learn to manage their diabetes with support. It is important to ensure that diabetes is taken seriously, as failure to manage the disease properly can result in serious medical problems, such as blindness, nerve damage (resulting in amputations), and an increased risk of atherosclerosis, which can cause kidney failure, heart disease, and stroke. In some people with learning disabilities, the responsibility for managing diabetes is likely to rest with their family, friends and support staff. A diagnosis of diabetes can, in some cases, encourage supporters to find out more about eating and drinking well and pay closer attention to the foods and drinks available. For most people with diabetes, the diet of choice is the one recommended for the general population – namely, a diet rich in fruits, vegetables, and whole-grain carbohydrates, and lower in fat, saturated fat, sugar, and salt, as outlined in the Eatwell Guide. Special diabetic products and strict dietary regimens are generally not recommended. For support on how to manage your diet with diabetes, contact Diabetes UK (see *Organisations* in Appendix 2).

certain cancers, stroke and osteoarthritis. It is estimated that a BMI of 30-35 kg/m2 reduces life expectancy by around 2-4 years, increasing to 8-10 years for those with a BMI of 40 - 50 kg/m^2, when compared to those living without obesity.

In 2023, diseases of the circulatory system were the leading cause of death in the learning disability and autistic communities (LeDeR, 2023). Obesity is a risk factor for circulatory disease; hence, effective interventions to prevent and treat obesity have the potential to significantly improve health outcomes for people with a learning disability.

Having obesity can affect everyday activities, such as walking up steps or keeping all areas of the body clean during washing. It can contribute to skin infections, which may develop into abscesses if left untreated. There is also social stigma associated with being overweight, which means that those with a larger body size can be viewed negatively, which can impact mental health.

Managing overweight

In simple terms, weight management involves balancing the amount of energy (calories) consumed with the amount of energy used for the body's normal metabolic processes and physical activities. Weight reduction requires either a decrease in energy intake or an increase in energy expenditure, or a combination of both. Maintaining weight requires a consistent balance between energy intake and expenditure.

Focus on health not weight

Being overly focused on body weight can be negative and unhelpful. Positive messages, focused on health rather than weight, are more likely to engage people.

Promoting healthy body weight and body image is particularly important for people who might be vulnerable to feelings of shame, anxiety or low self-esteem. Healthy people come in all shapes and sizes. Family, friends and support staff need to be sensitive to body shape dissatisfaction and ensure they do not make derogatory comments about their own or other people's body shape and do not aim for unrealistic media images of body shape and weight.

NICE Clinical Guidance NG246 and Public Health England guidance 'Obesity and weight management for people with learning disabilities' offer approaches and considerations for supporting weight reduction.

There is, however, no simple solution to weight gain as the large number of the population who are currently overweight would testify.

Weight loss interventions

A review of weight loss interventions for people with learning disabilities concluded that moderate weight loss can be achieved. The factors that were related to weight reduction included:

- the teaching of behavioural techniques (e.g. how to manage meals, portion sizes and eating patterns),
- the involvement of support staff,
- increased physical activity, and
- the sharing of nutritional and health information.

Adults with learning disabilities often collaborate in their decision-making with support staff; hence, the motivation and awareness of support staff are key in helping individuals manage their weight.

There is evidence that the health knowledge and skills of adults with learning disabilities can be enhanced, and various resources (see Appendix 2) are available to support caregivers, families, and individuals with learning disabilities in learning more about healthy eating and understanding some of the risks associated with being overweight.

However, it is not easy to lose weight, and it may be particularly difficult for people with learning disabilities if they have mobility difficulties. It is therefore useful to consider the following questions before starting attempts at weight loss, and to be realistic about what can be achieved:

Is it really necessary for the person to lose weight?

If a person's health and mobility are not affected by their weight and it is stable, and especially if someone is over the age of 65, caution should be taken in encouraging weight loss unless there is a clear rationale for doing so.

Is weight increasing rapidly?
If someone is gaining weight rapidly and consistently – for example, if they have gained 3kg (half a stone) or more in a year - it can be more successful to encourage weight maintenance than weight loss to start with, and this can seem more achievable. The St Andrews Nutrition Screening Instrument (SANSI) is a useful tool to measure nutritional risks associated with both weight loss and weight gain, as is the combined use of waist circumference (discussed earlier in the chapter).

Have there been any lifestyle changes that can be compensated for?
Simple changes in lifestyle can often trigger weight gain. If someone changes their place of accommodation, education, work, or transport route, this can result in a decline in small amounts of regular activity. If someone walks 15 minutes to a bus stop twice a day, this adds up to 150 minutes of exercise over five days. Losing this regular activity can tip the balance from weight maintenance to weight gain. Encouraging small, regular amounts of exercise every day is often preferable to and more realistic than a weekly visit to a gym. Three 10-minute walks a day may be more achievable than a more vigorous exercise plan. For more information on physical activity, please refer to page 85.

Medication can also be associated with weight changes, and monitoring should be a priority at times when medication doses are being altered. The 'Safe and Wellbeing Reviews: thematic review and lessons learned' from 2023 identified weight gain following admission to long-stay hospitals, which increased the risk of diabetes. The most common reasons for this were a lack of opportunities for physical activity, limited access to fresh air, an over-reliance on treats, and a lack of means to prepare food. Boredom was also a problem, as well as a lack of ongoing advice to promote healthier lifestyle choices, and side effects of medication, particularly psychotropic medications.

Have there been any changes in eating patterns?
Weight gain may be related to a change in eating habits. This might be triggered by a change in lifestyle or a change in the individuals providing care and support. Be alert to simple changes or additions to the diet (e.g. extra puddings, larger portions) that might be related to changing circumstances, as it is often small changes to daily patterns that can trigger weight gain.

What weight is ideal?
It may be more constructive to aim for an achievable and comfortable weight than to aim at an 'ideal' weight, which might require considerable discomfort and sacrifice to achieve. To keep the need for weight loss in perspective, it is essential to balance a healthy body weight with a person's need for quality of life and the circumstances in which they live. Where there is disagreement or uncertainty about an appropriate target weight, carers may wish to seek guidance from a healthcare professional.

Practical tips to help people reduce their calorie intake

- Aim to have five portions of fruit and vegetables every day and make this a priority when menu planning.
- Offer water as a drink. Place personalised and fun bottles of tap water in the fridge each day and encourage people to drink from these.
- If people are frequently hungry and impatient while waiting for meals to be served or prepared, offer slices of raw fruit or vegetables, such as carrots and peppers, to eat while waiting, rather than biscuits or crisps.
- Follow the guidance in this report for good snack and drink choices and look at the example meal ideas in Chapter 10 to see how much food people typically need to provide all the nutrients they require.
- Look at portion sizes carefully; people may be accustomed to overly large food portions and may eat them because they are given, rather than because they are needed. Using smaller plates can help reduce portion sizes. Be aware that people may not need the same portion sizes as their caregivers would have themselves. Useful information on portion sizes is available at the British Heart Foundation at https://www.bhf.org.uk/informationsupport/support/healthy-living/healthy-eating/healthy-eating-toolkit/food-portions.
- Consider individually portioning items such as breakfast cereals, biscuits, uncooked pasta, uncooked rice, etc., into Tupperware containers after purchase. This then enables the person to independently select and prepare food themselves whilst sticking to appropriate portions. This is particularly helpful for people who need to 'finish' in order to move on to the next part of their day and may therefore finish everything on the table or a whole packet of biscuits to feel that the eating occasion is complete and they can move on. It is also helpful for those who are less able to recognise internal cues of fullness (differences in interoception) and are prone to overeating if given access to larger portions of foods. Providing an alternative cue for the end of a meal, e.g. bringing out a pot of mint tea, can be helpful for signalling a meal is finished.
- Home-made vegetable soup is filling yet low in calories and contributes to vegetable intake.
- After the main course, offer fruit rather than high-calorie desserts.
- Simple changes in the kitchen can be helpful. For example, switching to skim milk and reduced-fat spreads, using less oil in cooking, grilling rather than frying certain foods (or using an air fryer), buying leaner meats and using smaller quantities of them, purchasing fewer ready-prepared foods, and avoiding pies and pastries. Refer to the food-based guidance in Chapter 9 for additional tips.
- If food is eaten for comfort, be sensitive to the relationship the person may have with food. If possible, encourage them to discuss their feelings and explore the connection between their food intake and mood. It may be possible to find non-food ways of stimulating a feeling of wellbeing, such as encouraging people to take up hobbies and pastimes that are creative, taking walks with family, friends and support staff, having a haircut or massage, or spending time in the garden. If food appears to be a way of dealing with difficult emotions, support from a psychologist may be useful.
- If food is eaten for sensory feedback in the mouth, then try offering foods which are highly flavoured or provide plenty of sensory feedback, e.g. celery sticks or sugar-free ice lollies. Chewelry can also be used to provide feedback between meals to prevent unhelpful snacking.

Physical activity

Why is physical activity important?

Inactivity can be disabling. Physical activity builds muscle strength and overall fitness, encourages better mobility and balance, and burns calories, supporting maintenance of a healthy body weight. Exercise is also crucial for preventing constipation and osteoporosis, which affects people with learning disabilities more than the rest of the population (LeDeR, 2020; OHID, 2024). There is also significant evidence to show that activity can be beneficial in treating depression, and this might be particularly important for many people with learning disabilities. Activity is essential for underweight people, too, as it helps to increase appetite.

What do we know about physical activity levels among people with learning disabilities?

Physical activity levels in adults with learning disabilities are extremely low, with international studies showing that less than 10% of people achieve the minimum recommended activity guidelines. In England, a large-scale survey revealed that nearly 60% of all participants had not taken part in any form of sport in the previous month, despite over a third stating that they would like to.

Why are people with learning disabilities often inactive?

Physical disabilities and illnesses can create extra obstacles to exercising at all ages. Among younger people with learning disabilities, there is an increased incidence of epilepsy, sensory conditions, underweight and overweight, congenital heart disorders, and neurological problems, all of which can be barriers to exercise. Among older people with learning disabilities, impaired mobility, respiratory problems, arthritis, deafness and heart disease are common health problems that can negatively impact engagement in physical activity. One study showed that low levels of physical activity in adults with a learning disability were more common in those of older age, those with more severe learning disabilities, females, those with epilepsy, immobility, faecal incontinence, and those living in supported or residential care.

Additionally, adults with learning disabilities are often prevented from being physically active due to financial difficulties, transport barriers, or a shortage of support staff.

People with learning disabilities in residential care may have even more limited opportunities for community leisure, or to be active as part of tasks of daily life or employment. Secondary attitudinal barriers may also impact the activity patterns of people with learning disabilities. Individuals may be less motivated themselves, they may be less encouraged to be active, may have an overprotective family, friends and support staff, and staff in leisure facilities may not be aware of the age-appropriateness or safety of different forms of activity.

Perceived barriers to being active reported by people with learning disabilities include:

- Insufficient support staff and resources to enable physical activity.
- Location, availability and accessibility of leisure services.
- Personal finance and budgeting.
- Lack of choice and autonomy.
- Lack of time.
- Poor weather conditions preventing outdoor activities.
- Perceived safety of local environment.
- Concern over injury or health problems made worse by activity.
- Overprotection and negative attitudes to activity by support staff.

Work and activity

Data from 2019 and 2020, respectively, shows only 4.1% and 5.1% of adults with a registered learning disability known to their local authority in Scotland and England were in paid work (SCLD 2019, NHS Digital, 2021). Increased work activity may help to increase activity levels, as may involvement in community activities or volunteering, where people spend time outdoors being active. It has been suggested that, when lack of exercise is combined with unemployment, there is likely to be apathy and boredom, which can contribute to mental ill health and behavioural disorders.

What can help?

The recommendation for the general adult population is to engage in at least 150 minutes of moderate-intensity activity per week. Examples of moderate-intensity activity include brisk walking, riding a bike, dancing, and water aerobics. If the exercise is more vigorous, such as rope skipping, running, or aerobic workout videos, the aim should be at least 75 minutes a week.

Additionally, we should aim to include strengthening activities that work all the major muscle groups (legs, hips, back, abdomen, chest, shoulders and arms) on at least 2 days a week. Examples of muscle-strengthening activities include Pilates, yoga, tai chi, weight training, working with resistance bands, wheeling a wheelchair, or exercises such as push-ups and sit-ups.

For children and young people (ages 5-18 years) the recommendation is at least one hour of activity a day. This should include a variety of types and intensities of physical activity throughout the week.
All age groups should aim to reduce the time spent sitting or lying down.

While these are the ideal recommendations, any activity is beneficial. If people have been inactive, they should be encouraged to start at a level of activity they feel comfortable with and gradually increase the duration and intensity of their activity. Where people with learning disabilities also have physical disabilities, which make movement difficult, it is vital that they are given as much help as possible to be as active as they can be, even if this involves only very limited chair-based movement.

The key to achieving and maintaining a more active lifestyle for people with learning disabilities is to find activities that they personally enjoy, which can be easily incorporated into their routine and fit in with other activities of daily living.

Consider the benefits of structured exercise programmes, as these have been found to improve the health of adults with learning disabilities. Research has shown that a 12-week aerobic exercise programme resulted in significant improvements in a range of health indicators, including body mass index (BMI) and blood pressure. Participation in an eight-week aquatic exercise programme improved balance and endurance.

Simple ways to increase activity levels include playing active games, walking, swimming, social dancing, climbing stairs, cycling, gardening, doing household chores, DIY projects, and exercises such as chair, bed, and wheelchair exercises. Some activities might include specific mobility, stretching and strengthening exercises. Postural awareness, balance, and coordination are important considerations.
Where practical, children and young people with learning disabilities should be encouraged to engage in moderate-intensity activities, such as playing with friends in a playground, swimming, or playing football, for at least an hour a day. Home-based programmes are an important option and can supplement other activities.

Activities must:

- consider safety issues associated with a particular disability or health condition,
- take place in a safe, supportive environment to minimise the risk of injury and to promote confidence and avoid unnecessary feelings of embarrassment, and
- take account of an individual's needs.

> NHS England has produced training for paid carers of adults with a learning disability entitled 'Supporting Healthy Weight for Carers of Adults with a Learning Disability'. The E-learning package consists of three online modules featuring trusted information and practical ideas for change. It is available at the e-learning for health website and is free to all those working in health and social care. https://www.e-lfh.org.uk/

Appropriate medical advice should always be sought before a person with learning disabilities begins an exercise programme.

People may find activities more enjoyable when participating with others, and support staff should consider taking part in activities with service users whenever possible.

A parent's view...

"It takes imagination and research to explore what there is to do locally. Also, for staff to take the time and trouble to find out what an individual is really interested in participating in. The activity may change on a regular basis for some individuals, whilst others may take a long time to be happy participating in an activity and then settle down."

The Clem Burke drumming project has been investigating the benefits of drumming on varioius aspects of wellbeing, including as an enjoyable form of exercise. Learn more at: https://clemburkedrummingproject.org/scientific-publications/

Eating after activity

It is common for people to overeat after exercising, as they believe that physical activity burns a significant number of calories. While being active is essential for those who want to maintain their weight or lose weight, it is crucial to keep the amount of calories burned in perspective.

It will take around 40 minutes of walking to burn off the calories in a standard bar of chocolate, or 40 minutes of running to burn off the calories in one iced cinnamon roll.

Encourage those who have exercised to drink water rather than sweetened drinks or sports drinks and keep post-exercise snack choices healthy (e.g., fresh fruit, yoghurt, or a portion of nuts), unless there is concern about underweight or excessive weight loss.

References

1. Royal College of Paediatrics and Child Health (2011). *UK-WHO growth charts – Down Syndrome, 0-18 years.* RCPCH. Available at: https://www.rcpch.ac.uk/resources/uk-who-growth-charts-down-syndrome-0-18-years
2. Martin NDT, Smith WR, Cole TJ et al. (2007). New height, weight and head circumference charts for British children with Williams syndrome. *Archives of Disease in Childhood,* 92(7), **pp.598–601.** https://doi.org/10.1136/adc.2006.107946
3. International Prader-Willi Syndrome Organisation. *PWS Growth Charts.* Available at: https://ipwso.org/information-for-medical-professionals/pws-growth-charts/
4. Brooks J, Day S, Shavelle R et al (2011). Low Weight, Morbidity, and Mortality in Children with Cerebral Palsy: New Clinical Growth Charts. *Pediatrics,* 128(2), pp.e299–e307. https://doi.org/10.1542/peds.2010-2801.
5. Isojima T, Yokoya S (2023). Growth in girls with Turner syndrome. *Front Endocrinol,* 13. https://doi.org/10.3389/fendo.2022.1068128
6. NICE (2025). Update information: *Overweight and obesity management: Guidance.* Available at: https://www.nice.org.uk/guidance/ng246/chapter/Update-information.
7. Rose C, Parker A, Jefferson B et al. (2015). The Characterization of Feces and Urine: A Review of the Literature to Inform Advanced Treatment Technology. *Critical Reviews in Environmental Science and Technology,* 45(17), pp.1827–1879. https://doi.org/10.1080/10643389.2014.1000761
8. BAPEN (2025). *'MUST' Calculator.* Available at: https://www.bapen.org.uk/must-and-self-screening/must-calculator/
9. NHS Digital (2022). *Health and Care of People with Learning Disabilities, Experimental Statistics 2021 to 2022.* Available at: https://digital.nhs.uk/data-and-information/publications/statistical/health-and-care-of-people-with-learning-disabilities/experimental-statistics-2021-to-2022
10. Glover G, Emerson E, Eccles R. (2012) *Using local data to monitor the Health Needs of People with Learning Disabilities.* Available at: https://www.researchgate.net/publication/265748530_Using_local_data_to_monitor_the_Health_Needs_of_People_with_Learning_Disabilities
11. Hove O. (2004). Weight survey on adult persons with mental retardation living in the community. *Research in Developmental Disabilities,* 25(1), pp.9–17. https://doi.org/10.1016/j.ridd.2003.04.004.
12. Gravestock S. (2000). Eating disorders in adults with intellectual disability. *Journal of Intellectual Disability Research,* 44(6), pp.625–637. https://doi.org/10.1046/j.1365-2788.2000.00308.x.
13. Stewart L. (2003) Development of the nutrition and swallowing checklist: a screening tool for nutrition risk and swallowing risk in people with intellectual disability. *Journal of Intellectual and Developmental Disability;* 28(2), pp.171-187. http://doi:10.1080/1366825031000106945
14. Ptomey L et al. (2023) Weight management recommendations for youth with Down syndrome: Expert recommendations. *Frontiers in Pediatrics,* 10. http://doi:10.3389/fped.2022.1064108
15. The British Medical Association (2024). *Clinically-assisted nutrition and hydration toolkit.* Available at: https://www.bma.org.uk/advice-and-support/ethics/adults-who-lack-capacity/clinically-assisted-nutrition-and-hydration.
18. Learning Disability Practice (2006) News: PEG feeding can lead to children being shunned. *Learning Disability Practice.* 9(3), pp.4-4. http://doi:10.7748/ldp.9.3.4.s3
19. Ng M, Gakidou E, Lo L. et al. (2025) Global, regional, and national prevalence of adult overweight and obesity, 1990–2021, with forecasts to 2050: a forecasting study for the Global Burden of Disease Study 2021. *The Lancet,* 405. https://doi.org/10.1016/S0140-6736(25)00355-120.
20. NHS Digital (2020). *Health Survey for England 2019.* Available at: https://digital.nhs.uk/data-and-information/publications/statistical/health-survey-for-england/2019
21. NHS Digital (2024). *Health and Care of People with Learning Disabilities, Experimental statistics 2023 to 2024.* Available at: https://digital.nhs.uk/data-and-information/publications/statistical/health-and-care-of-people-with-learning-disabilities
22. Stiebahl S. (2025). Obesity Statistics. *House of Commons Library.* Available at: https://commonslibrary.parliament.uk/research-briefings/sn03336/
23. NHS England (2022). *Health Survey for England, 2021: Data Tables.* Available at: https://digital.nhs.uk/data-and-information/publications/statistical/health-survey-for-england/2021/health-survey-for-england-2021-data-tables

24. NHS Digital (2022). Health and Care of People with Learning Disabilities, Experimental Statistics, 2017 2018 to 2021 2022. Page 3. Available at: https://app.powerbi.com/view?r=eyJrIjoiNTYyNDM4MGYtZDRmYi00NTAxLTkzY2QtMjcwZTY2YTQ0MzNkIiwidCI6IjUwZjYwNzFmLWJiZmUtNDAxYS04ODAzLTY3Mzc0OGU2MjIlMiIsImMiOjh9

25. NHS England (2024) Health Survey for England, 2022, Part 2: Data tables. [online] *NHS Digital.* Available at: https://digital.nhs.uk/data-and-information/publications/statistical/health-survey-for-england/2022-part-2/health-survey-for-england-hse-2022-part-2-data-tables

26. LeDeR (2023). *Learning from Lives and Deaths People with a Learning Disability and Autistic People* (LeDeR) - Report 2022. Available at: https://www.kcl.ac.uk/research/leder

27. Aslam AA, Baksh RA, Pape SE et al. (2022). Diabetes and Obesity in Down Syndrome Across the Lifespan: A Retrospective Cohort Study Using U.K. *Electronic Health Records. Diabetes Care,* 45(12). https://doi.org/10.2337/dc22-0482

28. Vancampfort D, Schuch F, Van Damme T et al. (2022). Prevalence of diabetes in people with intellectual disabilities and age- and gender-matched controls: A meta-analysis. *Journal of Applied Research in Intellectual Disabilities,* 35(2), 301– 311. https://doi.org/10.1111/jar.12949

29. Clegg J, Sheard C, Cahill J et al. (2001). Severe intellectual disability and transition to adulthood. *The British journal of medical psychology,* 74(2), pp.151–66. Available at: https://pubmed.ncbi.nlm.nih.gov/11453168/

30. Emerson E, Hatton C. (2007), The Mental Health of Children and Adolescents with Learning Disabilities in Britain, *Advances in Mental Health and Learning Disabilities,* 1(3), pp. 62-63. https://doi.org/10.1108/17530180200700033.

31. Ello-Martin JA, Ledikwe JH, Rolls BJ (2005). The influence of food portion size and energy density on energy intake: implications for weight management. *The American Journal of Clinical Nutrition,* 82(1), pp.236S241S. https://doi.org/10.1093/ajcn/82.1.236s

32. Melville CA, Cooper SA, McGrother CW et al. (2005). Obesity in adults with Down syndrome: a case-control study. *Journal of Intellectual Disability Research,* 49(2), pp.125–133. https://doi.org/10.1111/j.1365-2788.2004.00616.x

33. Baksh R A, Gulliford M, Chauhan U et al. (2023) Onset and Care of Type 2 Diabetes Mellitus in People with a Learning Disability – A 2022 Deep Dive report. *Autism and Learning Disability Partnership.* Available at https://www.kcl.ac.uk/ioppn/assets/fans-dept/diabetes-deep-dive-2022.pdf

34. Diabetes UK (2025). *Complications of diabetes.* Available at: https://www.diabetes.org.uk/about-diabetes/looking-after-diabetes/complications

35. Public Health England (2018). *The Eatwell Guide.* Available at: https://assets.publishing.service.gov.uk/government/uploads/system/uploads/attachment_data/file/742750/Eatwell_Guide_booklet_2018v4.pdf

36. Public Health England (2020). *Obesity and weight management for people with learning disabilities: guidance.* Available at: https://www.gov.uk/government/publications/obesity-weight-management-and-people-with-learning-disabilities/obesity-and-weight-management-for-people-with-learning-disabilities-guidance

37. Hamilton S, Hankey CR, Miller S et al. (2007). A review of weight loss interventions for adults with intellectual disabilities. *Obesity Reviews,* 8(4), pp.339–345. https://doi.org/10.1111/j.1467-789x.2006.00307.x.

38. Lunsky Y, Stiko A, Armstrong S. (2003) Women be healthy: evaluation of a women's health curriculum for women with intellectual disabilities. *Journal of Applied Research in Intellectual Disabilities,* 16 pp.247-254. https://doi.org/10.1046/j.1468-3148.2003.00160.x

39. St Andrew's Healthcare (2022) St Andrew's Healthcare Nutritional Screening Instrument (SANSI). Available at: https://www.stah.org/assets/SANSI-Paper-version-2022.pdf

40. NHS England (2023). *Safe and wellbeing reviews: thematic review and lessons learned.* Available at: https://www.england.nhs.uk/long-read/safe-and-wellbeing-reviews-thematic-review-and-lessons-learned/

41. LeDeR (2022). *Learning from lives and deaths – People with a learning disability and autistic people Annual Report.* Available at: https://www.kcl.ac.uk/ioppn/assets/fans-dept/leder-main-report-hyperlinked.pdf

42. Office of Public Guardian (2007). *Mental Capacity Act 2005: Code of Practice.* Available at: https://assets.publishing.service.gov.uk/media/5f6cc6138fa8f541f6763295/Mental-capacity-act-code-of-practice.pdf

43. British Dietetic Association (2025). *Completing capacity assessments for diet related health risks.* Available at: https://www.bda.uk.com/practice-and-education/education/cpd/bda-classroom-courses/completing-capacity-assessments-for-health-risks.html

44. Croot L, Rimmer M, Salway S et al. (2018). Adjusting a mainstream weight management intervention for people with intellectual disabilities: a user centred approach. *International Journal for Equity in Health,* 17(1). https://doi.org/10.1186/s12939-018-0871-4

45. Dunn MC, Clare ICH, Holland AJ (2010). Living 'a life like ours': support workers' accounts of substitute decision-making in residential care homes for adults with intellectual disabilities. *Journal of Intellectual Disability Research,* 54(2), pp.144–160. https://doi.org/10.1111/j.1365-2788.2009.01228.x

46. Melville CA, Hamilton S, Miller S et al. (2009). Carer Knowledge and Perceptions of Healthy Lifestyles for Adults with Intellectual Disabilities. *Journal of Applied Research in Intellectual Disabilities,* 22(3), pp.298–306. https://doi.org/10.1111/j.1468-3148.2008.00462.x

47. Smyth CM, Bell D. (2006). From biscuits to boyfriends: the ramifications of choice for people with learning disabilities. *British Journal of Learning Disabilities,* 34(4), pp.227–236. https://doi.org/10.1111/j.1468-3156.2006.00402.x

48. Spanos D, Hankey CR, Boyle S et al. (2013). Carers' perspectives of a weight loss intervention for adults with intellectual disabilities and obesity: a qualitative study. *Journal of Intellectual Disability Research,* 57(1), pp.90–102. https://doi.org/10.1111/ j.1365-2788.2011.01530.x

49. Public Health England (n.d.) *Health Inequalities: Osteoporosis.* Available at: https://fingertips.phe.org.uk/documents/Health_inequalities_osteoporosis.pdf

50. Public Health England (2015). *Public Health Profiles.* Available at: https://fingertips.phe.org.uk/profile/learning-disabilities

51. NHS (2021). *Measures from the Adult Social Care Outcomes Framework – NHS Digital.* Available at: https://digital.nhs.uk/data-and-information/publications/statistical/adult-social-care-outcomes-framework-ascof

52. Scottish Commission for People with Learning Disabilities (2019). *Scotland Learning Disability Statistics Scotland.* Available at: https://www.scld.org.uk/wp-content/uploads/2019/12/Learning-Disability-Statistics-Scotland-2019.pdf

53. Finlayson J, Jackson A, Cooper SA et al. (2009). Understanding Predictors of Low Physical Activity in Adults with Intellectual Disabilities. *Journal of Applied Research in Intellectual Disabilities,* 22(3), pp.236–247. https://doi.org/10.1111/j.1468-3148.2008.00433.x

54. NHS (n.d.) *Exercise.* Available at: https://www.nhs.uk/live-well/exercise/

55. Kastanias VT, Douda HT, Batsiou AS et al. (2015). Effects of aerobic exercise on health-related indicators in individuals with intellectual disability with or without the Down syndrome. Available at: https://www.researchgate.net/publication/312372696_Effects_of_aerobic_exercise_on_health-related_indicators_in_individuals_with_intellectual_disability_with_or_without_the_Down_syndrome

56. Hakim RM, Ross MD, Runco W et al. (2017) A community-based aquatic exercise program to improve endurance and mobility in adults with mild to moderate intellectual disability. Journal of Exercise Rehabilitation; 13(1), pp.89-94. http://doi: 10.12965/jer.1732838.419

57. McKenzie K et al. (2018) Encouraging physical activity in people with learning disabilities. *Nursing Times,* 114: 8, 18-21. Available at: https://www.nursingtimes.net/learning-disabilities/encouraging-physical-activity-in-people-with-learning-disabilities-16-07-2018/

CHAPTER 6

Gastrointestinal disorders, swallowing difficulties and oral health

Gastrointestinal disorders, swallowing difficulties and oral health

This chapter looks at gastrointestinal disorders and swallowing difficulties, which can affect many people with learning disabilities throughout the lifespan. It also looks at the importance of maintaining good oral health.

Gastrointestinal disorders

'Gastrointestinal disorders' include conditions such as constipation, diarrhoea and coeliac disease. There are also some structural problems associated with specific conditions such as Down's syndrome whereby small bowel obstruction, abnormalities of the anus, and Hirschsprung's disease are more likely. Gastrointestinal disorders are also more commonly seen in those with cerebral palsy, and can include malrotation, dysmotility and reflux.

Constipation

Constipation is a common complaint in people with learning disabilities and is mainly caused by a lack of fibre, inadequate fluid intake and inactivity. One study found that constipation was registered as a health problem for nearly 60% of people with profound learning and multiple disabilities, of whom 65% had been prescribed laxatives in the previous year. LeDeR (2019) found that approximately 55% of the learning disabilities population were constipated at the time of death, and 12 deaths were reported between 2015 and 2018 due to constipation.

Major tranquillisers, opioid analgesics (painkillers), anti-seizure medications, and any drugs with anti-cholinergic effects (drugs given for tremor and shaking) can produce constipation as a side effect. Other factors contributing to constipation include thyroid disorders, weak bowel muscles (hypotonia), anxiety, overuse of laxatives, food refusal, and inactivity. Failure to report a lack of bowel movements or inability to communicate pain or discomfort might result in constipation going unnoticed in some people with learning disabilities. This could lead to rectal and womb prolapse, ulcers, hernias, and changes in behaviour. Fear of unfamiliar environments or lack of privacy can also stop a person with a learning disability from going to the toilet, e.g. while in a hospital.

Support staff should be aware that some people may be at particular risk of constipation because of the drugs they take or the health conditions they have. Support staff should be alert to signs which may indicate constipation, such as a reluctance to go to the toilet, obvious discomfort, long periods spent in the toilet, a change in eating habits, a swollen or hard abdomen, rectal probing or manual evacuation, unexplained diarrhoea, or unexplained changes in behaviour, including smearing faeces. Constipation is a significant driver for reduced appetite and weight loss; it should always be considered when food is refused. Routinely documenting bowel habits is good practice. This may be assessed via self-report for individuals who toilet independently. Taking opportunities to check for blood in stools is also essential, as it may be an indicator of bowel cancer or inflammatory bowel disease.

What can help?
To avoid constipation, it is vital that people remain as active as possible and maintain a diet with sufficient fluid and fibre.

Fluid and hydration. How much fluid?
There is debate about the amount of fluid needed, and it is challenging to estimate a general requirement due to the wide variability in fluid intake within and between individuals. If someone is of a larger body size, they will need more fluids. If someone is of a small body size, they will need less. To ensure people are adequately hydrated, it is recommended that adults consume about 6 to 8 glasses of water per day. More accurate estimates of fluid requirements can be calculated by multiplying 35 ml per kg of body weight. For example, if someone weighs 60 kg, they will need 60 x 35 ml = 2100 ml (note that this calculation is less reliable for those with very high or low body weights). If someone breathes through their mouth, sweats or drools excessively, has diarrhoea, or has a high temperature,

they will have increased requirements, and advice should be sought on the amount appropriate for their needs.

> **Establishing helpful toileting routines**
>
> - Allow for a regular, unhurried toilet routine, giving time to ensure that defecation is complete.
> - Respond immediately to the sensation of needing to defecate.
> - Ensure that people with limited mobility have appropriate help to access the toilet and adequate privacy.
> - Ensure access to supported seating if people are unsteady on the toilet.
> - Ensure that people know the best position for effective bowel movements and have access to a foot stool if helpful.
> - Consider any sensory adjustments to the bathroom which may make it a more comfortable environment. For instance, strong air fresheners may be pleasant for some and unpleasant for others.
> - Encourage people to talk openly about their bowel habits so that any changes are picked up early by supporters.

Fluid intake comes from drinks, and from foods such as fruit, soups, milk puddings, yoghurt, gravy, and sauces. Foods such as mousses, jellies, ice cream, sorbets, and ice lollies also provide fluid but should be eaten less often as they are high in sugar. Taking small amounts of fluids regularly throughout the day may be necessary.

Those who experience swallowing difficulties may need to consume thickened fluids, and it may be more challenging to obtain enough fluids each day. Ensure that a variety of hot and cold drinks are available, as people may become bored with the same options. Some people may find it easier to drink through a straw, while others find cold drinks easier to tolerate than hot drinks. For more information about drinks, please refer to page 143.

The National Hydration Association offers ideas and resources for enhancing hydration in care settings (see page 147).

Fibre

High-fibre foods include whole-grain bread and cereals, fruits, vegetables, and pulses. SACN (2015) recommends that adults eat 30g of fibre daily to support good bowel health and transit time. For children and young people, recommended intakes are outlined below:

- Children aged 2 to 5 years – 15g/day.
- Children aged 5 to 11 years – 20g/day.
- Children aged 11 to 16 years – 25g/day.
- Adolescents aged 16 to 18 years – 30g/day.

Most people eat less fibre than is recommended. Increasing the amount of fibre eaten can help to alleviate constipation, but it must be done carefully. Fibrous foods are bulky and can reduce the energy density of the diet; some people may find that sudden increases in fibre intake cause bloating and wind. It is recommended that fibre intake be increased gradually, starting with an increase in fruit and vegetable consumption, followed by the addition of peas, beans, and lentils, and then higher-fibre cereal foods such as wholemeal breads or higher-fibre cereals. When increasing the amount of fibre in the diet, it is vital to ensure adequate fluid intake. Some people with advanced disease (such as cancer)

> A focused review of bowel health should be an essential part of Annual Health checks. Family and carers can support this by providing as much background information as possible on the toileting habits of the person they support.

> **The Rome IV criteria define constipation as any two of the following symptoms**
>
> - Straining (during more than ¼ of defecations).
> - Hard stool (for more than ¼ of defecations).
> - Feeling of incomplete evacuation (for more than ¼ defecations).
> - Sensation of blockage (for more than ¼ defecations).
> - Manual evacuation required (for more than ¼ defecations).
> - Fewer than 3 bowel movements per week.
> - Loose stools are rarely present without the use of laxatives.

or functional (dysmotility) dyspepsia will struggle with high-fibre diets. Additionally, in individuals with poor appetites, care should be taken to ensure the diet does not become too bulky or unpalatable.

Here are some suggestions for simple ways to increase fibre intake for those who are safe to do so:

- Serve vegetables, salad or baked beans with meals.
- Add canned beans, e.g. haricot, cannelloni, butter beans, kidney beans, chickpeas, and lentils to chilli, curries or stews.
- Use canned beans or lentils puréed into soups.
- Add sweetcorn and peas to stews and casseroles.
- Use wholemeal pasta in pasta dishes.
- Use brown rice in rice dishes.
- Switch to higher-fibre white bread (e.g. Best of Both varieties) if wholemeal bread is not liked.
- Switch to wholegrain breakfast cereals.
- Sprinkle flaxseeds on cereal or plain yoghurt.
- Leave the skins on potatoes.
- Add nuts and seeds to salads, stir-fries, etc.
- Add puréed tinned peaches, apricots, prunes or mango to porridge, custard, yoghurt or ice cream.
- Use hummus as a sandwich filling or on toast.
- Mix some brown flour into white when baking.
- Use oats and dried fruits when baking.
- Use rhubarb, blackberries, plums, prunes, kiwis and other fruits as desserts.

> Children and young people with complex needs who are constipated should seek advice from a dietitian or medical practitioner on the amount of fluid and fibre appropriate to their needs.

> Serious case reviews into deaths of people with a learning disability have highlighted that people at risk from constipation should have a bowel management and escalation plan, which should not be stopped without good reason.

Activity

The importance of being as active as possible is discussed on page 85. Even for those who are chair-bound or bed-bound, simple exercises, abdominal massage, or time spent stretched out (as opposed to sitting upright in a chair) can help reduce constipation. Everyone should be encouraged to be as active as possible. Support staff should always be aware that a sudden loss of mobility due to an accident or worsening of a longstanding condition is likely to be associated with constipation. They should ensure that, if a person's level of activity changes, they receive a review of their bowel management plan as a priority.

What does 30g fibre look like?

For more information on fibre, see page 53.

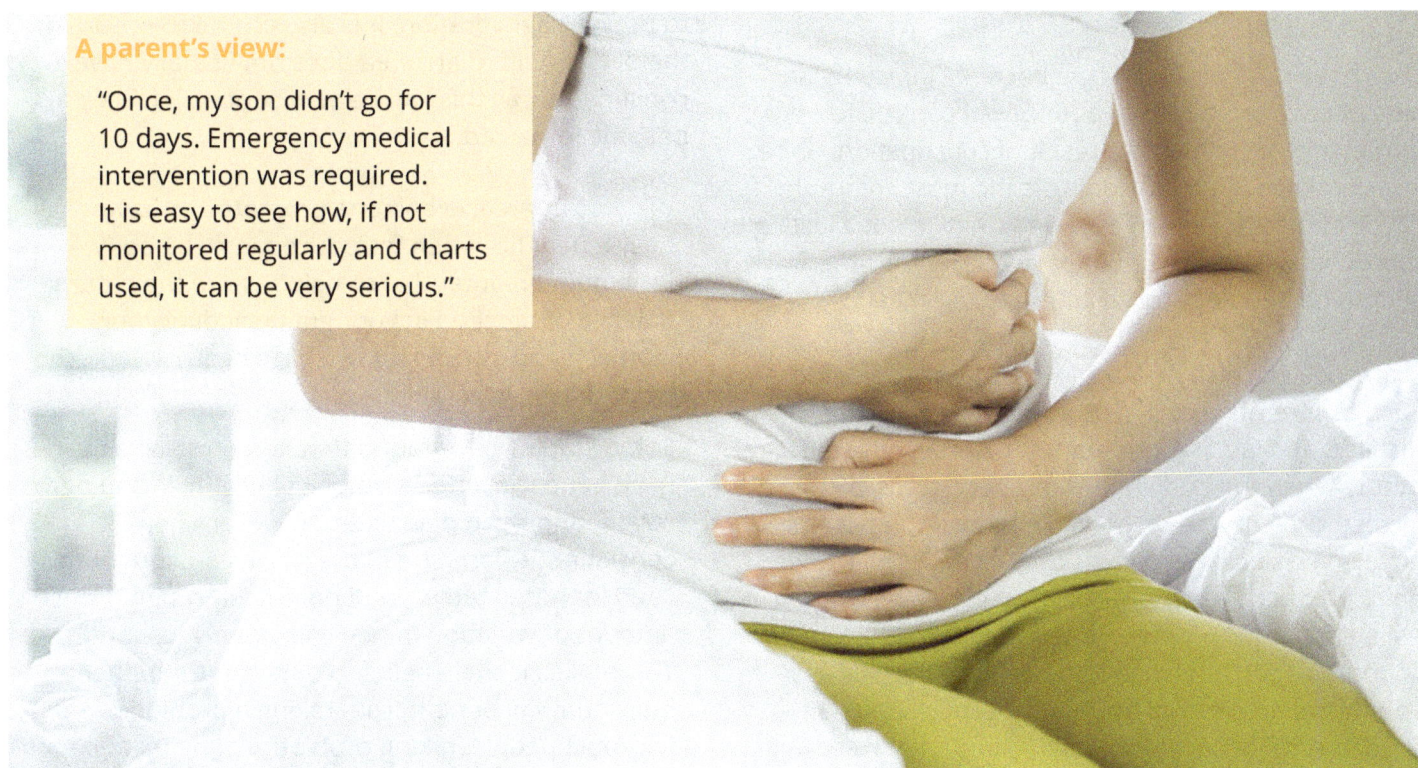

> **A parent's view:**
>
> "Once, my son didn't go for 10 days. Emergency medical intervention was required. It is easy to see how, if not monitored regularly and charts used, it can be very serious."

Medicines

If a diagnosis of constipation is confirmed and any underlying conditions have been investigated, constipation should be managed in the first instance by increasing mobility and increasing fluid and fibre intake. Where these simple measures are ineffective or impractical (for example, because people are immobile or take medications that contribute to constipation), a short course of laxatives may relieve symptoms and restore normal bowel function. The most commonly used laxatives are:

- bulk-forming (for example, ispaghula husk or methylcellulose),
- softeners or lubricants (for example, docusate sodium),
- osmotic laxatives (for example, lactulose or macrogols), and
- stimulant laxatives that directly stimulate colonic nerves to cause movement of the faecal mass (for example, senna or bisacodyl).

Laxatives should be chosen on a case-by-case basis according to symptoms and side effects.
Particular care should be taken when using macrogol laxatives (e.g. Movicol, Laxido, CosmoCol), which must be mixed with exactly the recommended volume of water to be effective.

The recognition and management of constipation is the responsibility of everyone who cares for a person with learning disabilities, as it is a condition that benefits from a holistic approach with multidisciplinary input.

Resources

Derbyshire Healthcare produces 'Poobusters' Constipation Awareness video. It is an accessible video for people with a Learning Disability, to facilitate conversation around constipation and what to do about it, available at:
https://www.youtube.com/watch?v=R16WY6MLBBU

NHS England developed tools and resources illustrating the risk that constipation can pose to people with a learning disability, and how it can be prevented, recognised and treated. These are available on the NHS England and NHS Improvement website at https://www.england.nhs.uk/publication/constipation-learning-disability-resources/

NHS England also supported the development of a Books Beyond Words picture story book, 'The Trouble with Poo,' which is available at
https://booksbeyondwords.co.uk/. It aims to increase awareness and understanding of the risks associated with constipation and the importance of seeking help when needed.

Diarrhoea

Diarrhoea can be caused by a bacterial infection, a side effect of medication, poor bowel control, food intolerance, overflow as a result of constipation, or be stress-related. Food poisoning is the most common cause of diarrhoea, and anyone with diarrhoea lasting more than 48 hours should have a stool specimen sent to bacteriology for testing.

Diarrhoea can also be a symptom of bowel disorders such as ulcerative colitis, Crohn's disease, coeliac disease, and lactose intolerance. Lactose intolerance occurs when the body fails to produce sufficient lactase, the enzyme responsible for breaking down lactose. This enzyme digests the lactose in milk and dairy products. It is more common in people from Asia, Africa, South America, and Mediterranean countries. Diarrhoea has also been reported as a common side effect of antibiotics, especially when used in conjunction with tube feeding.

What can help?

Determining the underlying cause of diarrhoea will aid in its management. If difficulties are associated with tube feeding, seek advice from the home enteral feeding team.

If problems are caused by infection, ensure that everyone is aware of the importance of food hygiene and hand washing.

If someone is lactose intolerant, they may be able to tolerate a small amount of milk products in the diet. If milk and milk products are excluded or reduced, care must be taken to ensure that the diet still contains enough calcium. (For good sources of calcium. If someone appears to have a food intolerance or condition that requires a special diet, this should be undertaken with the advice of a registered dietitian. People who have diarrhoea should be encouraged to follow a diet which has sufficient fibre. For some people, simply restricting the amount of foods and drinks which contain polyalcohol sweeteners (e.g. sorbitol) consumed each day may help reduce the severity of diarrhoea, especially if someone is consuming a lot of 'sugar-free' drinks, sweets, or chewing gum.

People who experience diarrhoea will need extra fluids. If the diarrhoea is severe and prolonged, or if it occurs in a child, it is essential to seek medical advice to prevent dehydration. It is also crucial to ensure that the person with diarrhoea does not actually have constipation, as this can be very serious if faeces become impacted.

Probiotics are live bacteria promoted as having health benefits when introduced into the body. Probiotics are intended to help restore the natural balance of bacteria in your gut (including your stomach and intestines) when it's been disrupted by an illness or treatment.

Some studies have found that certain strains may have beneficial effects on bowel health, including constipation and diarrhoea. However, there is considerable variation in the strains and quantities used in these studies, and potentially a significant amount of variation in how individuals respond. This makes it challenging to determine whether an individual will benefit from taking a probiotic. For most people, taking probiotics appears to be a safe practice. It is suggested that if you are trialling a particular brand, you continue for a minimum of 4 weeks to see if it improves symptoms.

Care should be taken if the person considering using probiotics has a weakened immune system. In this instance, speak to a doctor first.

Coeliac disease

People with Down's syndrome or Turner syndrome are more likely than the rest of the population to have coeliac disease. Coeliac disease means that gluten* (a protein found in wheat, rye and barley) cannot be tolerated, and this may cause diarrhoea and malabsorption of nutrients, which can lead to weight loss, osteoporosis and iron deficiency. It can also present with more vague symptoms such as tiredness, mouth ulcers, constipation or abdominal pain. Those at high risk should be considered for regular screening (via a simple blood test).

Once diagnosed, people require a strict gluten-free diet for life, and advice on how to manage this should be given by a registered dietitian.

Coeliac UK (coeliac.org.uk) provides a valuable resource for further information.

note that care will be needed with oats in the diet due to the high risk of cross-contamination.

Swallowing difficulties (dysphagia)

There is a high incidence of dysphagia (eating, drinking and swallowing difficulties) among people with learning disabilities. Dysphagia is more common in people with more severe learning disabilities and in those with cerebral palsy. Specific syndromes can also increase the risk, including Down's syndrome, Rubinstein Taybi syndrome, and Rett syndrome. People with learning disabilities have also been shown to be at a higher risk of choking.

Health risks associated with dysphagia include poor nutritional status, dehydration, asphyxiation and aspiration (breathing in of food, fluid or other materials to the lungs), which can lead to respiratory tract infections – a common cause of death for people with learning disabilities.

Dysphagia not only results in a reduced ability to swallow food and drink safely but also leads to inadequate food intake, which may result in either general undernutrition or insufficient intake of specific nutrients. Problems resulting from eating and drinking difficulties are not always obvious, and the gradual changes that accompany eating difficulties may go undetected or be accepted as part of the person's normal condition.

What can help?

Intervention to manage dysphagia is a multi-disciplinary approach usually coordinated by a specially trained speech and language therapist who both assesses swallowing difficulties and advises support staff and family carers in management techniques. Family carers can be very expert in positioning to aid swallowing and avoid choking, and it is important that support staff work in partnership with family and friends where appropriate, so that their valuable experience is not lost. The need for training of all support staff who support people with learning disabilities in recognising, understanding and managing dysphagia is essential.

Management of swallowing difficulties can involve:

- Modifying the texture of food and drink
- Altering the position of the person while he or she is eating (see page 118).
- Use of specialised equipment and eating aids (see page 117).

> ### Signs of a swallowing problem
>
> Coughing and/or choking before, during or after swallowing.
>
> Recurrent chest infections.
>
> Difficulty in controlling food and drink in the mouth.
>
> Regurgitating food into the nose or mouth.
>
> Change in breathing patterns.
>
> Unexplained weight loss or chronic low body weight.
>
> 'Wet voice' – gurgly sounds when speaking.
>
> Hoarse voice.
>
> Drooling.
>
> The person reports difficulty and/or painful chewing and/or swallowing or feelings of obstruction in the throat.
>
> Heartburn.
>
> Frequent throat-clearing.
>
> Change in eating pattern – for example, eating more slowly or avoiding foods or meals.
>
> Eating with mouth open.
>
> Unexplained temperature spikes.

- Training for people with learning disabilities themselves on how to manage their dietary requirements, and eat and drink safely.
- Training for support staff on how to support people to eat and drink safely, e.g. with particular prompts when eating.

Evidence suggests a need for ongoing support for people with learning disabilities themselves, to help them understand the reasoning behind the management strategies suggested. There can be conflicts between foods that people with dysphagia want to have and safety issues. Support staff need to handle these conflicts sensitively. Altered textured foods should look and taste appealing and should always be discussed in a positive manner.

The following factors can all contribute to safely supporting people with dysphagia to eat and drink:

- Sufficient numbers of skilled staff.
- Sufficient time to offer relaxed mealtime support.
- Consistency in approach between supporters.

- Maintaining a good posture when eating and drinking.
- Ensuring consistent and correct food and fluid textures in all settings.
- Appropriate spacing of meals and drinks throughout the day.
- Ensuring food is kept warm if mealtimes are lengthy.
- Ensuring good communication and rapport between the individual and their supporter to allow for prompting at mealtimes without people resenting interference in how they manage their eating.
- Ensuring any management/care plans are communicated effectively amongst all those who support eating and drinking or prepare food and fluids.

A person with dysphagia will often be unable to swallow tablets or other medication or supplements, and medication reviews must consider swallowing difficulties.

For more information on the texture modification of food and drink, see page 162. Strategies to help manage difficulties related to eating and drinking can be found on page 119. The importance of staff training is considered on page 110.

Oral health

Good dental health is linked to overall happiness and improved health outcomes. Poor teeth may limit the range of foods that can be eaten, and can impact a person's self-esteem, confidence, and enjoyment of food.

Research consistently shows that people with learning disabilities have higher levels of gum (periodontal) disease, higher plaque levels, and greater gingival inflammation. Consequently, there are higher rates of missing teeth and toothlessness in people with learning disabilities, and these rates increase with age.

For those with poor oral health, infections and soreness of the mouth lining and tongue can occur easily, causing considerable distress and difficulties with eating and drinking (e.g., thrush in the mouth, canker sores, and mouth ulcers).

Poor oral hygiene and gum disease also increase the risk of bacteria being transferred into the bloodstream during certain surgical or dental procedures. If the bacteria transfer to damaged or abnormal heart valves, a life-threatening infection of the heart can result. Having healthy teeth and gums is therefore essential.

Difficulties accessing dental services can be a reason for poor oral health, as can cognitive, physical and behavioural difficulties that impact someone's ability to undertake effective daily oral care. These include:

- not understanding the importance of tooth brushing or forgetting to do this,
- limited mobility, making it physically difficult to brush teeth effectively,
- sensory problems, meaning someone doesn't like being touched inside or around the mouth area,
- behaviour that makes it hard for others to support oral care, and
- limited communication between the patient and dentist, which is a major barrier to successful dental treatment.

Research has also demonstrated a lack of knowledge, support and training about oral health available to family, friends and support staff of people with learning disabilities. Oral healthcare is often given a low priority by support staff, and there is a shortage of training, particularly in community-based and residential accommodations. Family and friends may be able to provide valuable insights on how to approach oral care effectively.

A person with learning disabilities suffering dental pain may be unable to express discomfort and may exhibit a change in behaviour such as loss of appetite, unwillingness to participate in activities, sleeplessness, irritability or self-harm. It is vital for family carers, friends, and support staff to be alert to such changes and to determine if mouth or tooth pain is a possible cause of behavioural change.

Oral health and diet

Poor oral health can adversely affect the intake of a balanced diet, especially of foods that require chewing (such as vegetables and meat), and can result in a preference for soft foods that are easily swallowed. This can increase the risk of nutritional deficiencies and obesity.

Diets which are high in sugar lead to the development of dental caries (tooth decay). This is because the sugars provide food for bacteria living in dental plaque.

Tooth erosion is an irreversible loss of dental enamel, usually caused by acids other than those produced by plaque bacteria. One of the leading causes of tooth erosion is the frequent consumption of fizzy drinks. Acidic foods, such as citrus fruits and pickles, can also contribute to acid reflux if eaten between meals. Gastro-oesophageal reflux, vomiting and rumination can also cause tooth erosion.

Frequent food and drink consumption allows little time for remineralisation of the teeth between snacks or meals, and therefore, those who may need to eat or drink 'little and often' should pay particular attention to their oral health. People who require high-energy food supplements between meals and those who take sugar-based medication will also have an increased risk of dental decay.

In children with a learning disability, who may be slow to clear food or who may 'pouch' food in their mouth, there is a need for good oral hygiene both at home and at school.

People who take medication which causes dry mouth are also at greater risk of tooth decay. There may be conflict between health professionals, family, friends, and support staff when conflicting messages about oral health are given, for example, when high-sugar snacks are recommended between meals to increase energy intake. Health professionals must consider the consequences of their recommendations on other health issues and seek advice on how to manage these effectively.

What can help?
Research suggests that between 40% and 60% of people with learning disabilities will struggle to cope with dental treatment when it is needed. Accessible videos and factsheets to support understanding of the process are available at NHS Team Smile (nhsteamsmile.co.uk) (also see page 175).

Additionally, people with learning disabilities have fewer dentures provided for them than people in the general UK population. Those who wear dentures often experience problems related to poor dental hygiene.

Some suggested barriers to people with a learning disability accessing dental services include not having a regular dentist, the cost of treatments, and reliance on carers to make and support appointments. All those who support and care for people with learning disabilities should be offered training on the importance of oral health and how to assist individuals in cleaning their teeth.

The recommendations outlined in this report pertain specifically to basic oral hygiene and the impact of food and drink on oral health. However, PHE guidance recommends that staff in all community dental services have disability awareness and

Non-nutritive sweeteners (also referred to as artificial sweeteners)

Examples of non-nutritive sweeteners (NNS) include aspartame, saccharin, sucralose and stevia. They are used to replace sugar in many foods and drinks because they give a sweet taste with fewer or no calories. Replacing sugar with NNS may help prevent dental caries and also aid in weight reduction or weight management. However, it is preferable to have food and drinks that are not sweetened with sugar or NNS, as it is unclear how artificial sweeteners might impact health in the long term.

There are some concerns about the metabolism of sweeteners, particularly aspartame, in children with syndromes which may compromise the phenylalanine-tyrosine-dopamine-serotonin metabolic pathway. Aspartame causes significant increases in plasma phenylalanine (and probably brain phenylalanine) and therefore has the potential to interfere with neurotransmitter production.

There is also concern that, if people become accustomed to sweet tastes from artificially sweetened foods, this may hinder their ability to make long-term, permanent, and beneficial changes to their diet to reduce high sugar intakes. Moderation in the amount of artificially sweetened foods and drinks included in the diet would therefore be recommended.

communication skills training. Additionally, there is a legal obligation for dental services to make reasonable adjustments to ensure that their patients with learning disabilities can use their service in the same way as other people.

If dental services are to respond to the needs of all community members, it is essential that community dentistry teams are trained and confident in treating individuals with learning disabilities. Guidance and resources on how to achieve this are available through the British Dental Association.

Further information around the barriers to good oral care and accessing dental services for people with learning disabilities can be found in the PHE Guidance 'Oral Care and People with Learning Disabilities.'

For details on resources related to oral health for people with learning disabilities and general information on good dental health, see Appendix 2.

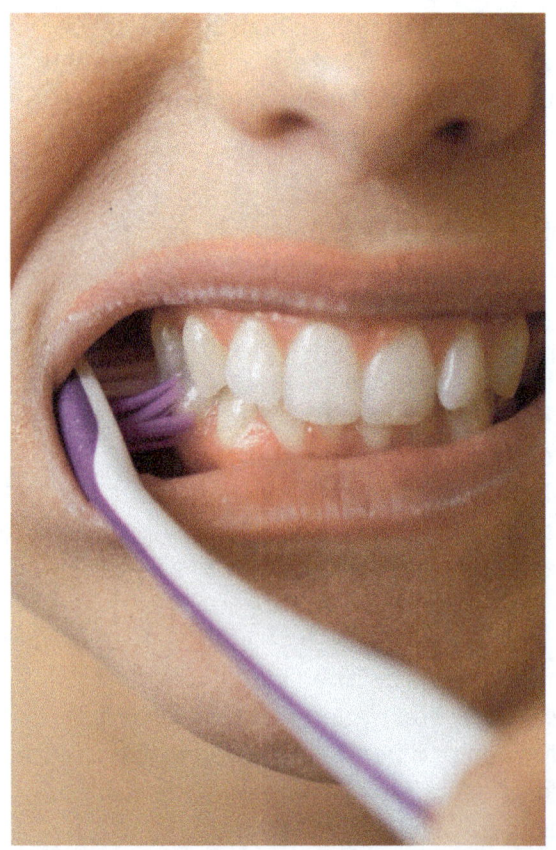

Tips on oral health

- All children, young people and adults with learning disabilities should visit the dentist twice a year.
- Brush teeth for about 2 minutes before bed and on one other occasion every day.
- Parents, guardians or support staff should help with teeth brushing for children under the age of 8 years, and anyone who may have difficulty in brushing their teeth independently.
- If helping someone to brush their teeth, use the procedure suggested in the box on the next page.
- Three-sided toothbrushes can support oral hygiene.
- Medicines, where possible, should be sugar-free unless they are consumed with meals.

Toothpastes

- Adults should use a toothpaste that contains at least 1,350 parts per million (ppm) fluoride.
- Children from the age of 7 can use toothpaste with 1,350 to 1,500 ppm fluoride. Children aged 6 and under who don't have tooth decay can use a children's toothpaste, but ensure it contains at least 1,000 ppm fluoride.
- Children under the age of 3 should use just a smear of toothpaste. Children aged 3 and over should use a pea-sized blob of toothpaste. Ensure children don't lick or eat toothpaste directly from the tube.

Food and drink

Limiting the intake and frequency of consumption of sugary foods and drinks is the most important way of preventing tooth decay:

- The only drinks that should be given in a bottle are milk or water.
- Sugar should never be added to milk or other drinks for infants or children.
- It is particularly important to ensure that drinks other than milk or water are not given at bedtime. This is because the mouth produces less saliva during sleep, which means that teeth are at greater risk of damage.
- As far as possible, keep food and drink with sugar in them for mealtimes only.
- Avoid feeding infants, older children and adults with fruit purees or other foods directly from a pouch.
- Milk, water, and tea or coffee (without sugar) are the only drinks which will not damage teeth between meals. For information about good choices of snack foods between meals, see page 140.

How to help someone clean their teeth

- Always explain what you are going to do first. Brushing someone else's teeth is an invasive procedure and can be frightening.
- Make sure the person is relaxed, comfortable and well supported.
- Encourage the person you are assisting to do as much as they are capable of themselves. Prompt, encourage, or assist as necessary.
- Support staff should wear latex-free gloves when helping with toothbrushing and stand behind the person, slightly to one side.
- Gloves should be changed for each individual.
- Partial dentures should be removed before cleaning natural teeth.
- Gently draw back the lips with the thumb and forefinger on one side of the mouth to gain access to the upper teeth.
- Using a small, soft brush with the appropriate toothpaste, brush the teeth and gums using short, scrub motions and try to brush the outer, inner, and biting surfaces of all teeth to ensure all plaque and food debris have been removed.
- Carefully brush all the teeth in the mouth, trying to reach all areas. If cooperation is limited, it may be necessary to brush different areas of the mouth at different times.
- If possible, gently hold and brush the tongue.
- Prompt the person to spit any excess toothpaste out after brushing. Avoid rinsing with water as it dilutes the protective effect of the fluoride from the toothpaste.
- If someone has no natural teeth, it is still important to clean the gums and the inside of the mouth daily with a soft toothbrush or gauze to maintain good oral health.
- Consider the use of disclosing tablets on the teeth to check the effectiveness of toothbrushing and removal of plaque.
- Record the toothbrushing session on an appropriate oral healthcare plan.
- If any changes to the mouth are noticed, contact the person's dentist.
- Avoid using mouthwash straight after toothbrushing. Instead, use this at a different time of day, e.g. after lunch. This prevents the removal of fluoride left on the teeth from the toothpaste.

References

1. Freeman S, Torfs C, Romitti P et al. (2009). Congenital gastrointestinal defects in Down syndrome: a report from the Atlanta and National Down Syndrome Projects. *Clinical Genetics,* 75(2), pp.180–184. https://doi.org/10.1111/j.1399-0004.2008.01110.x

2. Del Giudice E, Staiano A, Capano G et al. (1999). Gastrointestinal manifestations in children with cerebral palsy. Brain & Development, 21(5), pp.307–311. https://doi.org/10.1016/s0387-7604(99)00025-x

3. Romano C, van Wynckel M, Hulst J, Broekaert I et al. (2017). Evaluation and Treatment of Gastrointestinal and Nutritional Complications in Children with Neurological Impairment. *Journal of Pediatric Gastroenterology & Nutrition,* 65(2), pp.242–264. https://doi.org/10.1097/mpg.0000000000001646

4. Robertson J, Baines S, Emerson E et al. (2017). Constipation management in people with intellectual disability: A systematic review. *Journal of Applied Research in Intellectual Disabilities,* 31(5), pp.709–724. https://doi.org/10.1111/jar.12426

5. NHS England (2019). Learning Disability Mortality Review (LeDeR) Programme: Action from Learning NHS England and NHS Improvement. Available at: https://www.england.nhs.uk/wp-content/uploads/2019/05/action-from-learning.pdf

6. Del Giudice E. (1997). Cerebral Palsy and Gut Functions. Journal of Pediatric Gastroenterology & Nutrition, 25, p.22. https://doi.org/10.1097/00005176-199700002-00011

7. Jahromi SR, Togha M, Fesharaki SH et al (2011). Gastrointestinal adverse effects of antiepileptic drugs in intractable epileptic patients. *Seizure,* 20(4), pp.343–346. doi:https://doi.org/10.1016/j.seizure.2010.12.011

8. Flynn M, Eley R. (2015c). A Serious Case Review James. Suffolk Safeguarding Partnership. Available at: https://www.suffolksp.org.uk/adults-reviews

9. NICE (2024) Constipation in adults - *Clinical knowledge summary.* Available at: https://cks.nice.org.uk/topics/constipation/management/adults/

10. Public Health England (2016). *The Eatwell Guide.* Available at: https://www.gov.uk/government/publications/the-eatwell-guide

11. Maslen C, Hodge R, Tie, K et al. (2022) Constipation in autistic people and people with learning disabilities. *British Journal of General Practice,* 72(720), pp.348-351. https://doi.org/10.3399/bjgp22X720077

12. Scientific Advisory Committee on Nutrition (2015). *Carbohydrates and Health Report.* Available at: https://www.gov.uk/government/publications/sacn-carbohydrates-and-health-report

13. Bowling TE (2010). Diarrhoea in the enterally fed patient. *Frontline Gastroenterology,* 1(3), pp.140–143. https://doi.org/10.1136/fg.2009.000547.

14. Ravikumara M, Tuthill DP, Jenkins HR. (2006). The changing clinical presentation of coeliac disease. *Archives of Disease in Childhood,* 91(12), pp.969–971. https://doi.org/10.1136/adc.2006.094045

15. Robertson J, Chadwick D, Baines S et al. (2017). Prevalence of Dysphagia in People with Intellectual Disability: A Systematic Review. *Intellectual and Developmental Disabilities,* 55(6), pp.377–391. https://doi.org/10.1352/1934-9556-55.6.377.

16. O'Neill AC, Richter G.T. (2013). Pharyngeal Dysphagia in Children with Down Syndrome. *Otolaryngology–Head and Neck Surgery,* 149(1), pp.146–150. https://doi.org/10.1177/0194599813483445

17. Heslop P, Blair PS, Fleming P, et al (2014). The Confidential Inquiry into premature deaths of people with intellectual disabilities in the UK: a population-based study. The Lancet, 383(9920), pp.889–895. https://doi.org/10.1016/s0140-6736(13)62026-7

18. Griffiths C, Fleming S, Horan P et al. (2018b). Supporting safe eating and drinking for people with severe and profound intellectual and multiple disabilities. *Learning Disability Practice,* 21(1), pp.26–31. https://doi.org/10.7748/ldp.2018.e1817

19. Glover G, Ayub M. (2010b). *How People with Learning Disabilities Die.* Available at: https://www.researchgate.net/publication/257984926_How_People_With_Learning_Disabilities_Die

20. Thacker A, Abdelnoor A, Anderson C et al. (2008). Indicators of choking risk in adults with learning disabilities: A questionnaire survey and interview study. *Disability and Rehabilitation,* 30(15), pp.1131–1138. https://doi.org/10.1080/09638280701461625.

21. LeDeR (2021). *Learning from Lives and Deaths People with a Learning Disability and Autistic People (LeDeR).* Available at: https://www.kcl.ac.uk/research/leder

22. NICE (2017). *Nutrition Support for adults: Oral Nutrition support, Enteral Tube Feeding and Parenteral Nutrition. Clinical Guidance* [CG32]. Available at: https://www.nice.org.uk/Guidance/CG32

23. Chadwick DD, Jolliffe J, Goldbart J et al. (2006). Barriers to Caregiver Compliance with Eating and Drinking Recommendations for Adults with Intellectual Disabilities and Dysphagia. *Journal of Applied Research in Intellectual Disabilities,* 19(2), pp.153–162. **https://doi.org/10.1111/j.1468-3148.2005.00250.x.**

24. Wilson NJ, Lin Z, Villarosa A et al. (2018). Oral health status and reported oral health problems in people with intellectual disability: A literature review. *Journal of Intellectual & Developmental Disability,* 44(3), pp.292–304. **https://doi.org/10.3109/13668250.2017.1409596**

25. Chadwick D, Chapman M, Davies G. (2018). Factors affecting access to daily oral and dental care among adults with intellectual disabilities. *Journal of Applied Research in Intellectual Disabilities,* 31(3), pp.379–394. **https://doi.org/10.1111/jar.12415**

26. Davies G, Chadwick D, Cunningham D et al. (2008). The dental health of adults with learning disabilities - results of a pilot study. *Journal of Disability and Oral Health.* 9. pp.121-131. Available at: **https://www.researchgate.net/publication/256494709_The_dental_health_of_adults_with_learning_disabilities_-_results_of_a_pilot_study**

27. Mac Giolla Phadraig C, Griffiths C, McCallion P et al. (2018). Pharmacological behaviour support for adults with intellectual disabilities: Frequency and predictors in a national cross-sectional survey. *Community Dentistry and Oral Epidemiology,* 46(3), pp.231–237. **https://doi.org/10.1111/cdoe.12365**

28. Public Health England (2019). *Oral care and people with learning disabilities.* Available at: **https://www.gov.uk/government/publications/oral-care-and-people-with-learning-disabilities/oral-care-and-people-with-learning-disabilities**

29. NHS (2022). *How to keep your teeth clean.* Available at: **https://www.nhs.uk/live-well/healthy-teeth-and-gums/how-to-keep-your-teeth-clean/**

30. Health Education England (2020) *Mouth Care Matters Improving Oral Health.* Available at: **http://www.mouthcarematters.hee.nhs.uk/**

31. Scientific Advisory Committee on Nutrition (2025). *Statement on the WHO guideline on non-sugar sweeteners.* GOV.UK. Available at: **https://www.gov.uk/government/publications/sacn-statement-on-the-who-guideline-on-non-sugar-sweeteners/sacn-statement-on-the-who-guideline-on-non-sugar-sweeteners-summary**

CHAPTER 7

Encouraging eating well

Encouraging eating well

This chapter provides information on practical strategies that can help encourage healthy eating among people with learning disabilities.

Some of the information in this section pertains to residential care environments and the role of support staff; however, much of it is also relevant to other living arrangements and household types. Just as for all members of society, there is no single right way to support people with learning disabilities to eat and drink well. This section aims to stimulate debate on some of the issues and suggest strategies that may help.

Philosophy of care: rights and responsibilities

It is a fundamental human right that everyone should have access to food and drink that is both nutritionally adequate and culturally acceptable. It is essential to work together to ensure that people with learning disabilities are supported in making informed choices and understanding the importance of eating well. The Health and Social Care Act 2008 (Regulated Activities) Regulations 2014, Regulation 14, outlines the responsibilities of care providers in meeting the nutritional and hydration needs of people using their services, and the Care Certificate dedicates Standard 8 to fluids and nutrition. Regulation 14 is one of CQC's fundamental standards. The CQC can prosecute for a breach of this regulation and must refuse registration if providers fail to comply. See Appendix 5 for more information and guidance on what these standards look like in practice.

Person-centred care aims to ensure that the individual remains the most important person in determining how they are supported, promoting the rights of everyone to maximum independence and choice.

Standard 8 of the Care Certificate states:

'As a healthcare support worker or adult social care worker, you are required to promote good nutrition and hydration, encouraging and supporting individuals to have the correct balance of food and fluids according to their care plan.'

Regulation 14 of the Health and Care Social Act states that the nutritional and hydration needs of a service user must be met. This includes:

- provision of food and hydration, which is adequate to sustain life and good health,
- provision of parenteral nutrition and dietary supplements when prescribed by a health care professional,
- the meeting of any reasonable requirements arising from the service user's preferences or their religious or cultural background, and
- where necessary, providing support for a person to eat or drink.

Mental Capacity Act 2005

The Mental Capacity Act 2005, which came into force in 2007, is an essential piece of legislation which outlines how decision-making should be handled for some people with more severe learning disabilities. The terms of the Act are likely to affect everyone involved in caring for someone with a learning disability, whether formally or informally, if at some time the person with a learning disability lacks the capacity to make a particular decision or take a particular action for themselves at the time the decision or action needs to be taken. The Act sets out a single, clear test for assessing whether a person lacks the capacity to make a particular decision at a specific time. It is a 'decision-specific' and 'time-specific' test. No one can be labelled 'incapable' simply because of a particular medical condition or diagnosis. Section 2 of the Act makes it clear that a lack of capacity cannot be established merely by reference to a person's age, appearance, or any condition or aspect of a person's behaviour.

> **The MCA says a person is unable to make a decision if they cannot:**
> - understand the information relevant to the decision,
> - communicate their decision,
> - retain the information,
> - use or weigh up that information as part of the process of making the decision.

The Act is supported by a Code of Practice which provides guidance to anyone working with and/or caring for people over the age of 16 who may lack the capacity to make particular decisions. The Act is underpinned by five key principles:

- **A presumption of capacity.** Every adult has the right to make his or her own decisions and must be assumed to have the capacity to do so unless it is proved otherwise.

  Where someone's eating behaviour is creating a health risk, this raises the question of whether the person understands the risks they are taking, e.g., they have a BMI > 30 and their food and drink intake is very high in fat or sugar.

- **Individuals are being supported to make their own decisions.** A person must be given all practicable help before anyone treats them as not being able to make their own decisions.

  Nutrition messaging is not always clear or accessible for people. It can be confusing, and the consequences of poor nutrition can be long-term rather than immediately apparent.

- **Unwise decisions.** Just because an individual makes what might be seen as an unwise decision, they should not be treated as lacking the capacity to make that decision.

  Many people without a learning disability make unwise decisions around their food and drink choices every day and are free to do so.

- **Best interests.** An act done or decision made under the Act for or on behalf of a person who lacks capacity must be done in their best interests.

  It is vital to consider the viewpoint of the person themselves, alongside that of carers, family, friends, and anyone else who may have insight into the person's past or present wishes, beliefs, and values.

- **Least restrictive option.** Anything done for or on behalf of a person who lacks capacity should be the least restrictive to their basic rights and freedoms.

  Where there is more than one option, it is essential to explore ways that would be less restrictive or allow the most freedom for a person who lacks capacity (e.g., can we find healthier ways of providing a favourite food or reduce intake rather than eliminating it altogether?).

The final decision must always allow the original purpose of the decision or act to be achieved. Sometimes, when the risks of various approaches are weighed, it may be necessary to choose an option that is not the least restrictive alternative if that option is in the person's best interests (e.g., where the risk of choking is very high in relation to particular food items).

An Independent Mental Capacity Advocate, or IMCA, is an individual appointed to support a person who lacks capacity but has no one to speak on their behalf, such as family or friends. The IMCA makes representations about the person's wishes, feelings, beliefs, and values, while also bringing to the attention of the decision-maker all relevant factors that are pertinent to the decision.

Bournemouth University, alongside the Burdett Trust for Nursing, have developed 'The Mental Capacity Toolkit', a free resource for health and social care professionals and for friends or family who may have to make decisions on behalf of another person. Available at mentalcapacitytookit.co.uk.
An example of how a mental capacity assessment for diet and health might be completed is shown in Appendix 6.

Taking responsibility for health

People taking responsibility for their health is part of most government public health strategies, and people with learning disabilities should be encouraged to take the same responsibility for their health as other people in society (if they have the capacity to do so). Access to health facilitators is essential for people with learning disabilities, so that people who may be less able to act as 'expert patients' in a system which increasingly expects well-informed, articulate consumers, do not become further disempowered. It is also important to remember that many people with learning disabilities may live in poorer households and may experience inequalities in their environment and their health. It is vital that access to services is made equally available to all and that all support staff are trained to help those they support in navigating a complex healthcare environment and the challenges of socioeconomic deprivation.

The eating environment

Creating a calm eating environment where individual needs at mealtimes are met is crucial for encouraging people with learning disabilities to eat well. Inadequate or inappropriate nutrition in individuals with learning disabilities can be partly attributed to environmental factors, which are commonly reported in residential care settings. Mealtimes are often hurried, and staff are frequently untrained in nutrition, constrained by limited finances and cooking abilities. This can result in residents not getting a nutritionally balanced diet. It is essential to ensure that people arrive at mealtimes ready for the eating occasion, for example, having had the opportunity to use the toilet and wash their hands, or collect their hearing aid, glasses or dentures, and having been informed of the eating occasion ahead.

Ensuring everyone has the correct cutlery and crockery for their needs, and that the appropriate seating is also provided, is essential.
In residential and day care settings, support staff should also consider the choice of tables and the layout of the room impacting people's mealtime experience. Wherever possible:

- People should choose where they sit and whom they sit with.
- The range of foods available should make it easy for people to select appetizing, healthy foods, including vegetables and fruit.
- People should have the opportunity to serve themselves the food that they would like, from serving dishes brought to the table.
- Tablecloths, colourful table mats, matching crockery and table napkins can all help to make mealtimes more enjoyable and give them a sense of importance and occasion.

- Mealtimes should be protected, and other routine tasks and visits should be avoided during planned meals.

For individuals with learning disabilities who may also have sensory disabilities, using cues to stimulate appetite can be particularly important. The smell of food being prepared, the sound of food preparation and service, and the sight of laid tables may help to orient people to the mealtime ahead.

Food should be appetising and attractively served, to ensure that people enjoy their food. This is particularly important if the food has been altered in form or texture for people with swallowing difficulties. To make mealtimes a time of pleasant social sharing, and as good practice, staff should sit with the people they support during meals and snacks, and where appropriate, share the same foods and drinks. Mealtimes offer an opportunity for support staff to model healthy food choices and eating skills while also encouraging social interaction and conversation. To encourage this, distractions such as television are best avoided during mealtimes.

Helping people make good choices

For some, allowing an individual to drink six cans of cola a day if they choose to do so is seen as an expression of 'individual choice and a person's right'. Others, however, argue that guidance on choice is needed where the choices made can have a negative impact on health. To restrict food and drink choices among people with learning disabilities when these are not restricted to other members of society would seem unfair. To allow someone to become overweight and ill, and in some cases to put their lives at risk, when they may be unable to consider the consequences of their actions, might, however, seem even more unfair. There is a changing mood regarding the 'free choice' of food and drink in the UK. Healthy choices should be the easiest choices, but foods that are highly processed and less healthy are often cheaper and more widely available than healthier foods, which can sway people's choices. For example, the Government has acted to restrict food choices in schools and put regulations around advertising of certain foods in place, as it has had to conclude that many children and young people fail to make good choices on their own in an environment of unlimited choice and that their vulnerability to food-related ill health requires legislation.

The main factors influencing choice and decision-making around food for people with learning disabilities are:
- past experiences,
- an awareness of the range of choices, and
- the role of carers in supporting and encouraging choice.

Directing choice-making around food, without encouraging unhealthy eating, is an essential component of a duty of care for vulnerable adults. To support people with learning disabilities in making good choices about food and drink, family, friends, and support staff themselves must also be confident about what eating well means. We hope that the information in this report will be useful in helping people learn more about eating well, and that employers will support the training and support of their staff.

Most people are likely to have strong opinions about the foods and drinks they like and dislike, and follow routines and eating patterns that they prefer. It is not the role of support staff to dictate what better choices might be. Still, people with learning disabilities have the same right as anyone else to be given relevant information about their health and the impacts of their choices on their health.

A variety of appetising, healthy foods and drinks should be made available to everyone. Support staff should be trained in the basics of good nutrition and the application of the MCA around this topic to help people with learning disabilities make capacitous decisions when they are able. Where there are communication difficulties around food and drink choices and eating, support staff should be encouraged to develop skills in interpreting people's wishes. Each person will have different requirements regarding food and drink; therefore, it is essential to be sensitive to any restrictions that may be necessary (for example, in food texture) when discussing dietary changes and to avoid blanket approaches to food service provision within settings with multiple service users.

Family, friends and support staff will have a significant influence on food choice and availability and may find the following suggestions helpful when considering how to encourage people to consider the choices they make:

- Modelling is an effective approach to encouraging healthy food choices. Sharing snack times and mealtimes with others provides an opportunity for discussion, and people may be more tempted to try healthy foods and drinks if other people around them are enjoying them.
- Keep a record with the service user of their typical eating and drinking patterns over a few days and use this to talk about the foods and drinks they like, the quantities they consume, and their preferred routines, to see if they are actually enjoying their current choices.
- Use pictures or photographs of different types of foods and drinks, in different portion sizes, to encourage people to think about new foods and drinks, or the amounts or balance of foods and drinks they have.
- Games are available, some of which might be suitable for some people with learning disabilities. These can be a helpful springboard for discussion. (see page 174).
- Small changes over time are likely to be more effective. If people consume large amounts of a particular food or drink (for example, if they are heavy consumers of fizzy drinks throughout the day), suggest that one drink be swapped for an alternative to start with. Gently distracting someone from a food or drink habit which may be harming their health by spending time with the person and sharing an alternative can be effective.
- Ensure that the food being offered as an alternative is attractively presented. Using colourful plates with good contrast to the food can be helpful.
- If people need to lose weight, consider some of the strategies outlined on page 84.
- Look at food labels together and explain how to make choices between similar products.

There are several behavioural learning routes which may help encourage people to make positive changes to their dietary habits.

Fading involves gradually replacing some foods or drinks with others. This could take the form of gradually reducing the amount of sugar in tea and coffee, diluting squash over time until water becomes the drink of choice, or replacing some biscuits on a plate with fruit and gradually changing the proportions offered.

Replacement can be used as a method to help individuals with very limited food choices expand their food choices. For example, if someone only likes to eat chips, then other root vegetables can be cut into the same shape and cooked in the same way, and they can be introduced alongside the chips. If accepted, the proportion can be gradually increased. Association can also be used to encourage change. Sometimes people associate pleasant experiences with particular foods. For example, someone may associate eating crisps with enjoying television-viewing as a child. It may be possible to reverse this by introducing other foods in similar situations to create new positive associations.

Role modelling is a powerful social learning tool, and family, friends, and support staff should be encouraged to eat in social situations with people with learning disabilities as much as possible, even when someone may need help with eating. Eating together is a crucial aspect of social inclusion in most cultures and can also be an essential part of the day for sharing information and news.

Organisational culture

In residential care, other supported living arrangements and day care, it is essential that there is a commitment to good nutrition and an awareness of the broader role of food and drink in contributing to wellbeing and quality of life. Managers and staff at all levels need to demonstrate their commitment to good nutrition so that it becomes part of the organisational culture.

A commitment to eating well may necessitate a reassessment of staff shifts, training, and support in light of the need to support service users' eating and drinking needs. For an organisation to work effectively as a team to support eating well, all staff must understand why it matters and know how to assess whether people are eating and drinking adequately. For more information on staff training, please refer to the details below.

The overall ethos of care should be person-centred. Therefore, information from each person, as well as their relatives and friends, should be shared with all staff to ensure continuity of care. This should include their food and drink preferences, desired meal patterns, and choices around where and when to eat. This information should be recorded, shared with all support staff, and regularly updated to ensure accuracy. For those offering respite care, it is essential that family, friends and support staff, as well as the person himself or herself, are given the opportunity to discuss how a change in living arrangements may impact on their usual eating and drinking routines so that everyone can work together to ensure that there is continuity of care.

> Developing a food policy within a supported living, residential, or day care setting can be a useful way to outline the food-related values and actions that all staff are committed to. An example food policy is shown in Appendix 7.

Staff training and support

It is essential that all staff are valued and that their significant contributions to supporting people with learning disabilities are acknowledged. The importance of staff training cannot be overemphasised. To support people with learning disabilities in eating and drinking well, it is essential that everyone who supports them, whether paid or unpaid, has a clear understanding of what eating well means in practice. It is also essential to provide ongoing training for all staff, regardless of whether they are permanent, temporary, employed through an agency, or are voluntary.

It is vital that anyone supporting individuals who need assistance with eating must be trained to help in a sensitive and effective manner. Helping someone with eating difficulties to eat and drink well can be complex and stressful, and staff must be given sufficient support from colleagues when this is challenging.

Currently, there is a lack of training on nutrition and hydration within the health and social care sector as a whole. Qualifications at all levels should include an appropriate section on nutrition and eating well, with oversight of a registered dietitian or registered nutritionist (public health) to ensure the validity of the content.

Additional training in nutrition should be organised by employers for all those who support people with learning disabilities in their care, to supplement the training they receive elsewhere. When training in eating well is provided in a group setting, it should be led or supported by a registered dietitian or a registered nutritionist.

Free training in relation to food allergens is available from the Food Standards Agency via their website at - https://allergytraining.food.gov.uk/

Guidance on Food Hygiene and Food Safety is also available via the Food Standards Agency. All staff involved in the purchase, storage, preparation, or serving of food, or in supporting individuals with a learning disability to undertake these tasks, should have formal training and relevant certification. Your local authority can advise on the courses available in your area.

Involving and listening to family and friends

Food and drink can be an emotive issue, and sometimes it can be challenging to reconcile the wishes of family members and friends with changes in choices or routines that support staff may wish to implement to encourage eating well. Some family members and friends may have strong beliefs about the need for particular foods and feel strongly about whether access to certain foods and drinks is limited or if changes are made to the types of ingredients or foods available. This can be difficult for support staff who are trying to make positive changes, which can be upsetting for families and friends who believe they have the individual's best interests at heart. Below are some suggestions which may be a helpful starting point for staff discussing food and drink issues with family and friends:

- Think about making small changes over time. It may be easier to phase in changes to the menus or daily food and drink routines gradually, discussing and reviewing them as you go along, and ensuring that the views of the person with learning disabilities, as well as those of their families and friends, are taken into consideration.
- Make change familiar. Discussing the changes you want to make and focusing on the positive aspects – perhaps by offering tasting sessions, providing leaflets, or other information to service users and their family and friends – will help the novel become more familiar and less threatening.
- Listen and allow people to discuss ideas. No one likes to change that is forced on them, yet most people respond favourably to change they create themselves. Provide enough background information and a forum for people to reflect on and discuss any changes you suggest, and encourage family and friends to make their suggestions.
- Ensure everyone in the organisation is on board with the changes, so the messages given are united and everyone shares a clear vision of what you are trying to achieve. This is best achieved by completing a capacity assessment on diet, weight and health. Where someone is found not to have the capacity to make decisions regarding this aspect of their care, a best interest nutrition plan can be devised with the support of the GP, social care, family, and carers.
- Avoid confrontation and keep things in perspective. Eating and drinking well means having a variety of food and drink over a period of time, so think in terms of the bigger picture rather than demonising any particular foods or drinks that may be a source of conflict.

Food as a treat or reward

Food plays a significant role in many people's lives, and the use of food as a treat, reward or consolation, or the withholding of food as punishment, are measures most people will be familiar with from their own lives and the lives of others. It is, of course, never acceptable to withhold food or drink from anyone; however, support staff may not be aware of how often food and drink are used as treats and rewards, or that this can lead to unhealthy eating habits. Some support staff offer food and drink that they consider 'treats' to compensate a person with learning disabilities for what they may consider difficult circumstances or conditions. For example, offering sweets and soft drinks more frequently to people with learning disabilities than they would to other people they care for. Likewise, relatives and friends visiting people with learning disabilities might be more likely to bring fizzy drinks, sweets, biscuits and cakes as treats to comfort the person. It is vital that anyone who supports a person with learning disabilities considers the needs of the individual in a holistic way and thinks about how best to support them to good health.

A person with learning disabilities who is overweight or who has dental health problems may not be best supported with sweet treats, but might enjoy non-food gifts from friends and relatives. It may be helpful for the individual to work with a supporter to create a list of alternative treats which are health-promoting or non-food, and which they could ask people to donate instead of sweet treats. For example, this could be a trip or outing, a piece of music or a film, or household or garden equipment. For people on low incomes, some types of fresh and dried fruit can be expensive. Supporters could find out the varieties that would be particularly enjoyed and offer them as treats and gifts.

Rewards are often given to encourage good behaviour or to reward people for performing well in a particular task. Rather than giving sweets, chocolates and sweet snacks such as biscuits to reward good behaviour, rewards can be given in the form of smiles and praise ('soft rewards') or as small, inexpensive items such as stickers or badges ('hard rewards'). Most people enjoy both soft and hard rewards, and it is essential to ensure people feel proud of their achievements, however small.

> **If dessert is offered as a reward for eating vegetables, then vegetables become less desirable and the dessert becomes even more desirable, creating an unhelpful food hierarchy.**

Engaging with health and other professionals

Many health professionals are likely to be involved in supporting people with learning disabilities. Children with learning disabilities usually have their care coordinated by a paediatrician. For adults, most health authorities across the UK have a team providing specialist health and social care to people with learning disabilities living in the community. These are commonly referred to as Community Learning Disability Teams (CLDT), but the names may vary in some areas. The teams are multidisciplinary and may include members from social care, the health service and mental health trusts. CLDTs employ a wide range of specialists, including community learning disability nurses, occupational therapists, physiotherapists, psychiatrists, psychologists, social workers, speech and language therapists, dietitians, hearing and visual therapists, pharmacists, challenging behaviour workers and psychiatric nurses. However, the access of individuals and families to all these specialist services is likely to vary across the country, and it is important that people with learning disabilities remain in contact with their GP throughout their lifespan.

The key personnel supporting eating and drinking are outlined below:

Speech and language therapists (SLTs) provide assessment and intervention for those with swallowing and communication difficulties. Communication strategies from an SLT enable a person to be more actively involved in communicating their needs and preferences, and ensure the support team delivers information (e.g., weekly meal planning) in the most accessible way. SLTs provide guidance to enable safer eating and drinking (including advice on texture modification) developed in partnership with the person with a learning disability, family, friends, support staff and other members of the multi-disciplinary team.

Occupational therapists (OTs) offer support and guidance to help individuals maintain independence and play several key roles in supporting eating well habits. OTs can advise on the immediate eating environment at mealtimes and the use of appropriate equipment to aid eating and drinking. They can advise on positioning to promote function, comfort, and safety, suggest strategies for managing mealtimes, and work with individuals to promote independence. Additionally, OTs can support meaningful engagement where someone may be eating through boredom and a lack of activity in their life.

Dietitians can assess nutritional status and intake, and provide advice on dietary changes to tailor energy and nutrient intake, as well as offer specialised dietary advice for specific medical conditions. Dietitians can also advise on menu planning, recipe development and cooking practices and offer training to support staff and others in eating well. Dietitians work with other health professionals to advise on artificial nutrition and texture modification for individuals with swallowing difficulties.

Physiotherapists help and treat people of all ages with physical problems caused by illness, accident or ageing. Physiotherapy sees human movement as

> **Who can give nutrition advice?**
> The term nutritionist is not a protected title. Therefore, many people offer nutrition advice when they are not qualified to do so. Advice on nutrition should be sought from a registered dietitian (RD) or a registered nutritionist (RNutr). For details of where to access these professionals, see Appendix 2.

central to the health and wellbeing of individuals. Physiotherapists identify and maximise movement potential through health promotion, preventive healthcare, treatment, and rehabilitation and can offer advice on positioning, activity and improving mobility for people with learning disabilities.

Community learning disability nurses are involved in planning programmes of care for individuals, supporting skills development, and ensuring health and social needs are met. They provide nursing care in a variety of settings and offer support and advice to families, friends and support staff. The amount of training on nutrition that nurses receive varies, and nurses may welcome additional, up-to-date, and ongoing training on eating well.

Psychologists within learning disability services can support staff and service users in understanding and managing eating and mealtime behaviour, issues around body image and self-esteem, identity, anxiety and other factors which might contribute to disordered eating.

Social Workers have a key role in organising and monitoring services and support. **Primary Care Liaison Nurses** support GP surgeries in making reasonable adjustments to meet the health needs of people with learning disabilities effectively.

Pharmacists play an increasingly important role in managing medication and providing advice on interactions between certain drugs and foods.

> Making Every Contact Count (MECC) is a vital tool for delivering first-line nutrition advice to people in any setting where they access support from a healthcare worker. It is essential that MECC materials are fully accessible and appropriate for use by people with a learning disability.

Health action plans and annual health checks

Health action plans

A health action plan tailored to each individual should be compiled to explain their health needs. These plans should be drawn up by the individual, supported by a health facilitator, who may be someone from their community learning disability team, a relative, partner, carer or friend. The aim of the health action plan is to provide an accessible, living document. It can be considered as the health section of their person-centred plan and should include information about nutrition and health. The health action plan should be made as accessible for the individual as possible.

Drawings, photos, workbooks, social stories, drama, and group work can all be used to increase the health literacy of people with learning disabilities, enabling them to participate more fully in planning for their health. People may also have more conventional patient-held medical records that they can share with health professionals and take to appointments.

Annual health checks

GPs should proactively offer people with learning disabilities an annual health check. This should look at a range of indicators related to nutritional health such as body weight, weight change, bowel health, oral health, specific medical conditions such as diabetes and coeliac disease, difficulties around eating and drinking, and any other issues that may be related to any of the conditions discussed in this report. Reviewing medication is also important, particularly where medication impacts nutritional status (see page 37). Annual health checks provide a vital opportunity to raise any concerns regarding a person's nutritional health. Good liaison between medical practitioners, specialist learning disability teams and other health professionals should be fostered to ensure that the annual health check is part of a holistic approach to health planning for each individual.

Children, young people and adults with learning disabilities should also visit their dentist twice a year.

> **Introducing material on eating well as part of assessment and care pathways**
>
> It is important that social care professionals and those involved in assessing, planning for and otherwise helping people with learning disabilities, recognise that there are stages in the assessment and care pathway where they can introduce material about nutritional and dietary needs. There may well be opportunities to talk about eating well during:
>
> - person-centred planning,
> - carer and user assessments,
> - case reviews,
> - day service curriculum.
>
> Resources which might be used to discuss issues around food and nutrition can be found on page 174.

Food knowledge and skills of people with learning disabilities

Many people with learning disabilities wish to acquire new skills or enhance existing skills. This may be to enhance employment prospects, to allow them to lead more independent lives or because they enjoy learning purely for its own sake. Opportunities to learn also provide people with new experiences and the chance to meet new people and form new friendships. The provision of learning opportunities for people with learning disabilities is likely to vary across the UK, as different colleges, voluntary sector organisations, and local councils offer varying opportunities to begin, continue, and extend learning. Some areas will provide high-quality provision for people with learning disabilities, while others may provide very little. It is recommended that all learning and skills councils accredit courses in nutrition and health, as well as basic cookery, for people with learning disabilities, and make training accessible to family, carers, and other supporters. Special courses should be considered for people with learning disabilities from ethnic minorities, who are likely to be under-represented in post-school education. Courses should also be made available to individuals with learning disabilities who are parents (or who wish to or are likely to become parents), to help them understand the importance of good nutrition in their children's development and to provide healthy food choices for them.

There are several activities that may enhance the food experience for people with learning disabilities. Details of games and other activities are given on page 174.

Growing clubs and therapeutic horticulture

Gardening is an activity that many people enjoy, and it can encourage them to spend more time outdoors being active.

Social and therapeutic horticulture has been defined as the process by which individuals may develop wellbeing through actively being involved in growing plants. This has been used as therapy and for rehabilitation among people with a range of disabilities. There is evidence that this can be a valuable and effective form of health and social care provision for people with learning disabilities and that individuals benefit from a break in their usual

routines and from being outside. Benefits are reported in social networks, education and training, relaxation and restoration, as well as improvement in self-confidence and self-esteem. Many service users also enjoy consuming the food grown, and this can contribute to better health. For more information about therapeutic horticulture, contact Thrive (see page 172).

References

1. UK Government (2014). *The Health and Social Care Act 2008 (Regulated Activities)* Regulations 2014. Available at: **https://www.legislation.gov.uk/ukdsi/2014/9780111117613/regulation/14**

2. Care Quality Commission (2025) *Regulations for service providers and managers: relevant guidance.* Available at: **https://www.cqc.org.uk/guidance-providers/regulations-enforcement/regulations-service-providers-managers-relevant-guidance**

2. NHS England (2017). *Involving people in their own health and care.* Available at: **https://www.england.nhs.uk/wp-content/uploads/2017/04/ppp-involving-people-health-care-guidance.pdf**

3. Public Health England (2010). *Healthy Lives, Healthy People: Our strategy for public health in England.* Available at: **https://assets.publishing.service.gov.uk/media/5a74fd1640f0b6360e472767/dh_127424.pdf**

4. Robertson J, Emerson E, Gregory N et al. (2000). Lifestyle-related risk factors for poor health in residential settings for people with intellectual disabilities. *Research in Developmental Disabilities,* 21(6), pp.469–486. **https://doi.org/10.1016/s0891-4222(00)00053-6**

5. Rodgers J (1998). 'Whatever's on her Plate': Food in the Lives of People with Learning Disabilities. British *Journal of Learning Disabilities,* 26(1), pp.13–16. **https://doi.org/10.1111/j.1468-3156.1998.tb00040.x**

6. Hoey E, Staines A, Walsh D et al. (2017). An examination of the nutritional intake and anthropometric status of individuals with intellectual disabilities: Results from the SOPHIE study. *Journal of Intellectual Disabilities,* 21(4), pp.346–365. **https://doi.org/10.1177/1744629516657946**

7. Meijer MM, Carpenter S, Scholte FA (2004). European Manifesto on Basic Standards of Health Care For People with Intellectual Disabilities. *Journal of Policy and Practice in Intellectual Disabilities,* 1(1), pp.10–15. **https://doi.org/10.1111/j.1741-1130.2004.04002.x**

8. Smyth CM, Bell D (2006). From biscuits to boyfriends: the ramifications of choice for people with learning disabilities. *British Journal of Learning Disabilities,* 34(4), pp.227–236. **https://doi.org/10.1111/j.1468-3156.2006.00402.x**

CHAPTER 8

Supporting people with eating difficulties

Supporting people with eating difficulties

This chapter explores strategies for maintaining independence in eating, as well as approaches to addressing common eating difficulties, including extreme faddy or selective eating, food refusal, and challenging eating behaviours.

Maintaining independence in eating

It is generally agreed that help with eating, while sometimes essential, can lead to a loss of self-esteem and a sense of powerlessness and dependency. Those who are able to eat independently, even if this is by hand only, should be encouraged to do so to maximise independence and dignity. The use of finger foods can help people maintain and recover their eating skills, and has the advantage of boosting self-esteem and independence, while also allowing individuals to eat at their own pace. (For more on finger foods, see page 159.)

Practical aids to eating and drinking

There are various helpful aids to eating that some people may find useful for feeding themselves, or which family, friends and support staff can use to help individuals to eat and drink more effectively. Occupational therapists can advise on suitable aids, which might include the following:

- Differently shaped cups, with one or two handles, of different weights, materials, transparencies and designs. Cups should not shatter or break if they are bitten.
- A transparent cup can be useful when helping someone to drink so the carer can see how much liquid is taken.
- Cutlery of differing shapes, sizes, depths and materials. Cutlery should not shatter if it is bitten. Solid plastic cutlery or plastic-coated metal might be better for people who have a bite reflex when cutlery is placed in their mouth. Shorter-handled cutlery is easier to manage, and handgrips or irregularly shaped handles may help individuals use a utensil more easily.
- Plates and bowls which do not slip, have higher sides to prevent spillage, or are angled to make access to food easier.
- Insulated crockery that keeps food hot if mealtimes are lengthy.
- Non-slip mats which support crockery.
- Straws which can help those with a weaker suck or which have different widths.
- Automated eating systems, such as Neater Eater, which allow people to feed themselves even when movement is very limited.

For details of sources of specialist eating and drinking equipment, see page 175.

Helping people to eat

Staff involvement and commitment to successful mealtimes are critical in ensuring that people with learning disabilities eat well.

While it is essential that those who can eat independently, either fully or partially, are encouraged and enabled to do so, those who require assistance with eating must be treated with sensitivity. The perspective of assisting people to eat rather than 'feeding' them is essential. Mealtimes should be viewed as a therapeutic time for an activity that involves physical, sensory, emotional and social stimulation. Verbal prompting during eating to 'Open your mouth,' 'Chew,' or 'Swallow' has been suggested as particularly helpful. If direct verbal prompting fails to work, touching food against the person's lips gives a non-verbal cue to open the lips. If someone cannot initiate voluntary movement, it is better to give indirect encouragement to eat, for example, saying, 'This meal looks tasty.' Guidelines for helping a person to eat are given below.

Support staff should receive training in supporting individuals to eat. This training may include experiencing what it is like to be assisted in eating. Other practical suggestions include ensuring that people have an empty bladder before they start eating, and that their glasses or dentures are accessible and well-fitting. Suggestions for addressing

specific problems and behaviours associated with eating are provided on page 122.

Communication tips for mealtimes:

- Speak clearly and at a relaxed pace. Give people time to process the information or instruction you are giving.
- Allow the person to express their feelings about the food.
- Avoid offering too much choice, which can be overwhelming.
- Explain what you are doing so your actions are not a surprise.
- Be respectful and avoid talking over people's heads when they are eating unless absolutely necessary. Give people your full attention and minimise distractions for you and them.
- Reassurance, by holding the person's hand, may be appropriate. Observe signs of anxiety and try to understand the reasons for this - is the environment, positioning, or food choice working for the person?

Positioning when people need help with eating and drinking

The importance of good positioning for eating and drinking cannot be overemphasised. Family carers may be experienced in achieving the best position. The normal position for eating is in the upright position. No two people are the same, and therefore, the position best suited to each individual will vary. However, it is beneficial for everyone to be aware of some basic principles when preparing to help someone eat well.

It is challenging to balance, eat, and drink at the same time, so the advice of a physiotherapist or occupational therapist can be very helpful in finding the best and safest positions for each individual. The general suggestions provided below are designed to stimulate discussion and encourage all those involved in eating and drinking to reflect on their current practices and share ideas. Eating and drinking can be hazardous, and any changes in position or support must be reviewed in light of how someone can be helped if they cough or choke.

- Aim for symmetry and alignment of the body when someone is sitting or standing ready to eat – with the head upright, the back of the neck elongated, and the chin tucked slightly in.
- Usually, both the person eating and the person helping them should be sitting at the same height so that they can have face-to-face contact to help communication during meals. In some cases, people with visual impairments may prefer someone to sit next to them and maintain contact side by side, but eye contact is generally preferred.
- An extended head, neck and body position makes eating and drinking uncomfortable and potentially dangerous, as the person may be more likely to cough and choke. Avoid sitting so that the person has to look up.
- For some people, eating while standing up may be preferable. Standing with the help of a frame or a prone stander may help with stability. Standing can also ease the descent of fluid and food into the stomach and may help prevent gastro-oesophageal reflux.
- Ensure that people are well supported so that they don't push against tables or hyperextend their limbs to make themselves feel safer.
- Headrests and neck supports may be necessary to maintain the head in an upright position and keep the neck elongated.
- How a person is positioned after the meal can also impact wind or reflux problems. Some people may find it easier to stand up for a short time after the meal. For some, a 30-minute period of sitting after a meal may be recommended.
- Regularly reviewing the position that best suits each person at mealtimes is essential.
- If someone needs assistance with eating, it is also vital that the physical needs of the helper are taken into consideration so that they are comfortable and can focus all their attention on the job in hand. Support staff may also need cushions to ensure they are in a comfortable position and avoid neck or back pain when assisting individuals with eating.

Guidelines for helping a person to eat

- The same carer should stay with the person throughout the meal.
- If the person uses glasses, dentures and/or a hearing aid, ensure these are in place.
- Ensure the person is sitting in an upright position.
- The carer should sit at eye level, and either immediately in front of or slightly to one side of the person who needs help.
- Give small mouthfuls, but enough for the person to feel the food in their mouth.
- Allow sufficient time for the person to swallow each mouthful before continuing.
- Assist but never force.
- Maintain eye contact with the person who needs help. Do not talk to someone else while offering food.
- Use verbal prompts: speak clearly about the food you are offering (especially if it is puréed) and use a gentle yet firm tone.
- Discourage the person from distractions (such as talking or laughing with food in their mouth) because of the risk of choking.

Strategies to deal with eating and drinking difficulties

This section makes some suggestions about how to handle eating and drinking difficulties for people with learning disabilities. However, it is important to remember that everyone is an individual, and all those who support a person with learning disabilities should work together to find strategies that best suit that person.

Extreme faddy or selective eating

Some people with learning disabilities may be selective eaters or have phases of only being willing to choose from a small selection of foods and drinks. This is often associated with autistic spectrum disorders (ASD). Autistic children and adults may display strong preferences for foods of a particular colour, smell, texture, taste or temperature. They may also accept only processed foods with familiar packaging. They may find it challenging to try new foods and may be distressed in some mealtime environments, resulting in food refusal. They may only accept foods presented on a plate in a specific manner or using particular crockery or utensils. They may experience a strong aversion to disliked foods or to being around others who are eating.

Strategies which may help with selective eating:

- Make mealtimes predictable by having a structured eating routine.
- At the start of each week, prepare 'visual timetables' using picture symbols, photos or words as appropriate, detailing when, where and what people will eat.
- Ensure there are no underlying health problems that might make eating specific foods uncomfortable. For example, mouth ulcers may deter people from eating fruit or drinking fruit juices, or swallowing difficulties may instill fear in individuals who have previously found food difficult to chew or swallow.
- Try to identify the specific anxieties for each person and devise a step-by-step programme for overcoming them, including any adjustments to the mealtime environment or manner in which food is presented.
- Use activities and stories to talk about new foods and keep a visual list of foods enjoyed and foods they might try.
- Food preferences may be situation-specific, so new environments may offer a good opportunity to introduce new food.

Food refusal

People may refuse food for various reasons, and managing food refusal can be difficult and distressing for those who support them. There can be several reasons why individuals might refuse food, and it is essential that all avenues are explored to determine the cause and that the person is given every opportunity to express their feelings and preferences regarding food and drink.

- There may be physical problems, such as a sore mouth, painful teeth or gums, or thrush, which may require investigation and treatment.
- Food may be refused because there is an underlying swallowing difficulty.
- Medication may make a person feel nauseous. See the next page for strategies to manage nausea.

- Medication may have other side effects which impact eating and drinking. A medication review may therefore be useful.
- Constipation may make a person feel nauseous.
- Food may be refused because it isn't liked. Ensure that people's food preferences are recorded and considered, and that, where possible, a wide variety of foods with different tastes, textures, and temperatures are offered.
- People who refuse food may take it from a specific family member, friend or member of the support staff they know well.
- The mealtime environment may be off-putting.
- Paranoia can mean people are fearful of food and may think, for example, that it has been poisoned. Paranoia can be treated with talking therapy if communication allows, or with medication.
- Depression can cause loss of appetite. Depression can be treated with medication or with talking therapies if communication allows.
- A person at the end stage of life may refuse to open their mouth and accept any food or drink. It is still important to offer food and drink regularly, regardless of the outcome of previous eating occasions. Decisions on how to manage food and drink at the end stage of life should involve doctors, family, friends, support staff and any advocates, including Independent Mental Capacity Advocates.

Individuals who are losing weight and refusing food may benefit from nutritional support while the reasons for food refusal are examined and treated (see page 78).

> **A parent's view...**
>
> "A routine is good, doing the same preparations for each mealtime is a non-verbal cue, and this can be comforting. It can prepare the person and get them ready in their mind for a change about to take place."

Nausea and vomiting

If someone is feeling nauseous or vomiting, the cause must be investigated. In some cases, nausea may be a side effect of essential medication, and simple strategies can help alleviate this. Support staff may find some of the suggestions below helpful but should ensure that the needs of each individual are carefully considered.

- Fresh air before a meal and a well-ventilated room may help.
- Make sure people sit upright for meals and rest after eating.
- Aim for five or more smaller meals a day so that people are not 'overwhelmed' with large portions. Small portions of attractive food may be more tempting.
- Avoid foods with a strong odour and keep cooking smells to a minimum.
- Dry, savoury foods – such as toast, crackers, rice cakes, breadsticks or plain popcorn – may be tolerated. Some people find dry biscuits or toast helpful in relieving nausea upon waking.
- Cold foods may be easier to tolerate than hot ones, for example, thick and creamy yoghurt, jelly, ice cream or egg custard.
- Cold drinks drunk through a straw may cause less nausea.
- Ginger is well known to alleviate nausea: ginger cordials, ginger ale or ginger beer, ginger biscuits or stem/ crystallised ginger might be helpful. Peppermint tea may also alleviate symptoms.

Mouth sensitivity

'Hypersensitive oral reactions' are exaggerated responses to touch in the mouth or around the face. An individual may be hypersensitive for several reasons. Neurological impairment may cause an individual to over-respond to sensory information. Limited motor capabilities, which inhibit someone from touching their face, may mean the area remains sensitive to touch. Additionally, being fed via a gastrostomy tube may limit someone's exposure to oral stimulation.

There is also some evidence that a lack of feeding experiences during critical periods of weaning in the first year of life can lead to oral hypersensitivity. Children or adults with hypersensitive oral reactions may be reluctant to let you into their mouth for feeding or toothbrushing. They may have difficulty transitioning from one food texture to another, spitting out or gagging on any food except pureed food. They may gag when a spoon touches the tip of their tongue, and may gag on a tiny lump of food instead of swallowing it.

Some people become so sensitive and emotional that their reactions become aversive reactions. They may cry, fuss, pull away, push food away, or refuse even to let you near their mouths. Gagging may escalate into vomiting in an aversive reaction. Fears can develop around feeding or any touch around the mouth, and individuals may try to control all aspects of a meal to protect themselves from uncomfortable situations. For example, they may want only certain food textures, specific spoons, plates or cups. An excessive reaction to stimulation may trigger a bite reflex, causing the individual to clench in a biting position.

What can help?

It is crucial to work with a speech and language therapist and an occupational therapist to manage oral hypersensitivity.

- Ensure the person is sitting in a stable, upright position.
- Ensure mealtimes are calm and relaxed. Play calming music and reduce other sensory stimulation.
- Eating involves many different types of touch: the spoon, fork, and cup touch the lips as they bring food to the mouth. Try gradually keeping the spoon or cup at the lips for a longer period each time you help someone to eat, using favourite foods for this activity.

- Providing cues that the spoon is coming may help. Ringing a bell attached to the spoon, stating verbally "Here comes the food", or placing the food on a brightly coloured spoon may provide a cue that the mouth is about to be touched and reduce unwanted reflexes.
- Food temperature can often cause overreactions. Remember that room-temperature foods tend to be easier to handle. Make the temperature change very slowly and with foods that are liked.
- Plastic-coated or silicone spoons may be needed if people bite or are hypersensitive to temperature.
- If people overreact by gagging when you try to switch from strained foods to thicker, more textured or lumpy foods, you probably need to make the transition more slowly.
- Toothbrushing with a regular or electric toothbrush can help, but should only be done with guidance from a speech and language therapist or occupational therapist.
- Wipe the face regularly with warm cloths or soft sponges, using deep pressure. This can be calming.

Drooling or dribbling

The ability to swallow saliva is normally learnt automatically, and most adults swallow the 1 to 1.5 litres of saliva produced a day on 1,000 to 2,000 swallows. Saliva control depends largely on trunk stability and head control, being aware of the need to swallow, as well as factors such as positioning, fatigue and drugs taken. Dribbling can be a common problem among people with learning disabilities. It can lead to a sore mouth, dry mouth, difficulty eating, gum or dental problems, and dehydration, as well as being embarrassing. Drooling or dribbling can also be linked to swallowing difficulties (see page 97). Individuals who drool may need higher fluid intakes.

What can help?

- Good positioning – being well supported and upright with an elongated back of the neck – will help with jaw stability.
- Gently dry the mouth with a small piece of absorbent cloth, explaining what is happening and using small dabs so as not to over-stimulate the mouth.
- Special clothing or the creative use of scarves, which can be frequently replaced, may help with embarrassment.
- Behaviour modification or the development of oral control may be possible among some people.
- Some drugs can be used, but these may have side effects such as drying the eyes as well as the saliva and increasing thirst.
- Travel bands designed to alleviate nausea associated with travel sickness have been anecdotally suggested as useful for some people with mild dribbling.

Bruxism (teeth grinding)

Teeth grinding may be related to oral pain or discomfort, or anxiety, medication or communication difficulties, and dentists should collaborate with family, friends and support staff to explore potential causes of bruxism. Bite guards may be helpful, but should only be used after discussion with a dentist.

Other problem behaviours around food and drink

Individuals with learning disabilities may exhibit other eating behaviours which support staff find challenging to deal with. People may use their behaviour around food to communicate distress – for example, if they have changed carers or places of residence, or if habits and patterns they are used to are disrupted. It is essential that routines around food, drink, and mealtimes are respected, so that as much information as possible is gathered from family carers about the individual's preferences and habits, and that care is taken to interpret signs and signals from the individual about their food choices. Taking the time and trouble to understand the causes of people's behaviour and address any underlying issues may prevent considerable distress.

The observed behaviours on the following three pages, and the suggestions for dealing with them, may be useful in managing problem behaviours around food for people with learning disabilities, including those with dementia. With more extreme eating difficulties, help should be sought from a GP and/or dentist to exclude any underlying physical ill health, or from psychologists, psychiatrists and other team professionals within learning disability services.

Observed Behaviour	Strategies to Support Mealtimes
Style of eating or pattern of intake	
Incorrectly uses a spoon, fork or knife	Try verbal cues, model correct use, or use hand-on-hand techniques
	The person may benefit from adapted cutlery. Consult with an occupational therapist
Incorrectly uses a cup or glass	Try verbal cues and show correct use
	Offer an adapted cup with handles or a straw for easy use. Consult with an occupational therapist
Unable to cut meat	Provide cut meat, soft meat or finger food
Difficulty getting food onto utensils	A plate guard or lipped plate may help
	Try finger foods
Plate moves on the table	Use a no-skid placemat or suction plate
Eats desserts or sweets first	Serve meal components one at a time and keep desserts or sweets out of sight until the main course is finished
	Ultimately, this doesn't matter as long as all courses are eaten during the mealtime
Eats too fast	Offer food in small portions
	Provide verbal cues to slow down, and model slower eating
	Reassure the person that there is plenty of food available and it will not run out
Slow eating and prolonged mealtimes	Serve small portions at a time so the food stays warm, and offer second helpings
	5-6 small meals over the day may work better than 3 larger ones
Eats other people's food	Sit between the client and other people, or keep other people's food out of reach
	Serve small amounts of food at a time
Eats non-food items (pica)	Take non-food items away and replace them with food, drink or another distraction
	Remove commonly eaten non-food items from reach and use simple picture cues to remind people what is not edible
	Make sure the diet includes good sources of iron and zinc every day
	Provide a safe option for oral sensory feedback, such as Chewelry
Mixes food together	Ignore as long as the food is eaten
Drinks excessively	Offer small, regular drinks or ice lollies throughout the day
	Encourage individuals to sit and drink with friends and support staff to help with pacing
	Store drinks in individual-sized bottles, cartons or drink containers
	Agree on a daily limit and set times with a chart for the person and carer to track intake

Observed Behaviour	Strategies to Support Mealtimes
Behaviour which disrupts mealtimes	
Hoards, hides or throws food	Remove specific items
	Keep the number of items on the table to a minimum
	Serve small portions
	Explore if the food provided to the person is acceptable
	Provide a safe store of food for personal use, e.g. breadsticks, to prevent risks of food poisoning associated with hoarding mealtime foods
Interrupts food service or wants to help	Give the person a role in meal service, such as setting the table or pouring water
Plays with food	Explore whether the food provided is acceptable to the person
	Check for any unmet sensory needs (this may be a form of 'messy play')
	Verbal cues to remind of the purpose of the mealtime
	Not a problem as long as food is eaten and hygiene is maintained (ensure thorough hand washing before a meal)
Distracted from eating	Make sure the room is calm and quiet, that the person has everything needed for the meal (e.g. has been to the toilet, has their glasses, dentures or hearing aid if needed), and is sitting comfortably
	Other people modelling eating may help
Stares at food without eating	Use verbal or manual cues to eat: place food or utensils into the person's hands
	Model eating and offer encouragement
Demonstrates impatient behaviour during or before a meal	Make sure that people are not alerted to meals too early, that they are offered something nutritious to eat if they have to wait for a meal to arrive (e.g. a small bowl of vegetable soup or some carrot sticks), or that meals are served in small courses to minimise waiting times
	For individuals who like routine, eating at very specific times may be important. Try to cater to these times where possible to reduce anxiety or discuss in advance if there will be a change in the schedule.
States 'I can't afford to eat' or 'I can't pay for this meal'	Provide visual or verbal reminders of the person's current food budget and how the current meal fits in
	Provide meal tickets or vouchers to reduce anxiety
Wanders during mealtimes and is restless	Make sure that mealtimes are calm and try to encourage people to eat together where possible
	If wandering persists and food intake is compromised, encourage the person to use finger food while wandering
	If there is a time of day when the person will sit for longer periods (for example, first thing in the morning), ensure a good variety of foods is on offer

Observed Behaviour	Strategies to Support Mealtimes
Oral Behaviour (Consult with a speech and language therapist about these problems)	
Difficult chewing	Provide foods that are easier to chew Check dental health
Prolonged chewing without swallowing	Liaise with a speech and language therapist Use verbal cues to chew and swallow
Does not chew food before swallowing	Use verbal cues to chew Consider modifying the texture of the food if choking is a risk
Holds food in the mouth	Use a verbal cue to chew Massage the cheek gently Offer small amounts of different foods with stronger or sharper flavours
Bites on the spoon	Use a plastic-coated or silicone spoon
Spits out food	Check that the food is liked that the temperature is appropriate, and that the food is of an appropriate texture
Doesn't open their mouth	Use a verbal or visual cue to open their mouth Touch the lips with a spoon Use straws for drinks Check dental health

References

1. Ball SL, Panter SG, Redley, M et al. (2012). The extent and nature of need for mealtime support among adults with intellectual disabilities. *Journal of Intellectual Disability Research,* 56(4), pp.382–401. **https://doi.org/10.1111/j.1365-2788.2011.01488.x**

2. Griffiths C, Fleming S, Horan P, et al. (2018). Supporting safe eating and drinking for people with severe and profound intellectual and multiple disabilities. *Learning Disability Practice,* 21(1), pp.26–31. **https://doi.org/10.7748/ldp.2018.e1817**

3. Worsfold J, Kew J (2017). Outcomes from a quality improvement initiative in an eating and drinking difficulties service for people with learning disabilities. *Learning Disability Practice,* 20(6), pp.24–28. **https://doi.org/10.7748/ldp.2017.e1815**

4. Ullian K, Caffrey B (2022). Identifying and managing malnutrition in people with learning disabilities. *Learning Disability Practice.* **https://doi.org/10.7748/ldp.2022.e2181**

5. Murphy JL (2022). Improving nutrition and hydration in older people with dementia in care homes. *Nursing Older People,* 34(5), pp.35–42. **https://doi.org/10.7748/nop.2022.e1389**

6. British Dietetic Association (2021). *Autism and diet.* Available at: **https://www.bda.uk.com/resource/autism-diet.html.**

7. Holmes JH, Murphy J, Scammell JS (2015). *Eating and Drinking Well: Supporting People Living with Dementia Workbook.* Available at: **https://www.ageuk.org.uk/bp-assets/contentassets/2d42698f64294f3993e75b378eb3292a/eating-and-drinking-well-workbook.pdf.**

CHAPTER 9

Food-based guidance

Food-based guidance

This chapter provides information about the five food groups and how to select foods that contribute to a healthy, balanced diet.

Food Labels

It is also useful to look at the nutrition information labels and ingredient lists on food products, and to choose those that are lower in salt, sugar and fat. Some front-of-pack nutrition labels use red, amber and green colour coding. This can make it easier to compare foods in the same category, particularly for those who find interpreting numbers challenging or have visual impairments. Colour-coded nutritional information tells you at a glance if the food has high, medium or low amounts of fat, saturated fat, sugars and salt:

- Red means high
- Amber means medium
- Green means low

Generally, food or drink with all or mostly green on the label is a healthier choice.

The table below provides information on what is 'a lot' of and 'a little' salt, sugar and fat in foods:

Foods **high in fat** have more than 17.5g of fat per 100g of food.	Foods **low in fat** have 3g of fat or less per 100g of food.
Foods **high in saturated fat** have more than 5g of of saturated fat per 100g of food.	Foods low in **saturated** fat have 1.5g of saturated fat or less per 100g of food.
Foods **high in sugar** have more than 22.5g of sugar per 100g of food.	Foods **low in sugar** have 5g of sugar or less per 100g of food.
Foods **high in salt** have more than 1.5g of salt (or 0.6g sodium) per 100 g of food.	Foods **low in salt** have 0.3 g of salt or less (or 0.1g sodium) per 100g of food.

For more information on food labels, see
https://www.nhs.uk/Live-well/eat-well/food-guidelines-and-food-labels/how-to-read-food-labels/

It is essential to interpret the colour coding on nutrition labels with caution. A diet cola drink will have an all-green label, whereas a banana will have an amber (for intrinsic sugars) label. This does not make a diet cola a better choice than a banana. This type of labelling is most helpful when comparing similar items, such as two types of pizzas for dinner or a yoghurt versus a slice of cheesecake for dessert.

Food group: potatoes, bread, rice, pasta and other starchy carbohydrates

ADVICE	WHY?	WHAT'S INCLUDED
Starchy foods should make up around a third of the diet. Choose higher fibre and wholegrain varieties. A variety of starchy carbohydrates should be available throughout the week and served daily with every meal.	Starchy foods are a good source of energy and the main source of a range of nutrients in the diet. As well as starch, these foods supply fibre, calcium, iron, and B vitamins.	All varieties of bread, including wholemeal, granary and seeded breads, chapattis, bagels, roti, tortillas and pitta bread. Potatoes, yams, sweet potato, plantain, cocoyam, dasheen, breadfruit, and cassava. Breakfast cereals. Rice, couscous, bulgar wheat, maize (polenta) and cornmeal. Noodles, spaghetti, and other pastas.

Tips

- When serving rice and pasta, try to use wholemeal, wholegrain, brown or high-fibre versions.
- Some breakfast cereals are nutrient-fortified (that is, with added iron, folic acid and other vitamins and minerals), but check for high sugar content. Choose wholegrain cereals or mix them with other types of cereals.
- Offer a variety of breads, such as seeded, wholegrain and granary.
- If you are making chips or fried potatoes, consider alternative methods of cooking, such as oven-baked or air-fried, to reduce the fat content, and keep the skin on for added fibre.
- Baked potatoes do not need to have butter or margarine added when served with fillings that have a sauce, such as baked beans or chilli.
- For people who avoid gluten in wheat, barley and rye, good alternatives to offer are foods made from maize (e.g. polenta), rice, rice flour, potatoes, potato flour, buckwheat, sago, tapioca, soya and soya flour.
- Cereal foods that are good sources of iron and zinc include fortified cereals, wholegrain cereals, wholemeal bread and flour, couscous and wholemeal pasta.

Food group: fruit and vegetables

ADVICE	WHY?	WHAT'S INCLUDED
Fruits and vegetables should comprise a third of the diet. It is essential to offer a variety. Five portions a day is an achievable target. Aim for 1 or 2 portions with each meal and offer fruits and vegetables as snacks. One portion is about 80g of fresh fruit or vegetables, or 30g of dried fruit.	Fruit and vegetables are good sources of many vitamins and minerals. There is evidence that consuming 400g or more of fruit and vegetables a day reduces the risk of developing chronic diseases such as coronary heart disease and certain cancers. Including fruits and vegetables in the diet will increase the intake of fibre, and can help to reduce the total amount of calories consumed among those who wish to lose weight.	All types of fresh, frozen and tinned vegetables, e.g. broccoli, Brussels sprouts, cabbage, carrots, frozen peas, peppers, swede and sweetcorn. Beans and pulses, including baked beans, chickpeas and kidney beans. All types of salad vegetables, including lettuce, cucumber, tomato, raw carrots, peppers and beetroot. All types of fresh fruit, e.g. apples, bananas, kiwi fruit, oranges, pears, mango and plums. All types of tinned fruit in fruit juice, e.g., pineapple, peaches, mandarins and oranges. Stewed fruit. Dried fruit. A 150 ml glass of 100% fruit juice can count as one portion of fruit each day, but not more than one portion.

> The reason why fruit and vegetables are so beneficial is because of the array of compounds they contain. As well as vitamins and minerals, fruit and vegetables also contain many complex plant components (called phytochemicals), including flavonoids, glucosinolates and phytoestrogens. Some vitamins and phytochemicals also act as antioxidants, helping to destroy free radicals in the body. These free radicals are known to have a role in causing cancer as well as other harmful effects.

Tips

- Steaming or cooking vegetables with minimum amounts of water and serving them as soon as possible will help retain vitamins.
- Use fresh fruit and vegetables as soon as possible, rather than storing them, to avoid vitamin loss.
- Using frozen or tinned vegetables can be cheaper and reduce waste.
- Incorporate fruit and vegetables as snack options.
- Add vegetables and pulses to curries, casseroles or stir-fry dishes and serve at least two types of vegetables with Quorn, soya, fish, chicken or meat.
- Add a handful of dried fruit to cereal or porridge.
- Offer traditional salads as well as raw vegetables, to increase colour, taste and texture at mealtimes.
- Add extra vegetables to savoury dishes.
- Vegetable soups are a useful way of increasing vegetable intake.
- Choose dried fruit without added sugar.
- Buy tinned fruit in juice rather than syrup and drain the juice before serving.
- Pulses count as vegetables. However, if you are serving pulses as a non-dairy protein source for vegetarians, you will also need a separate vegetable serving.
- Aim for a rainbow of colours when putting fruit and vegetables in the basket at the supermarket or planning menus.

Food group: beans, pulses, fish, eggs, meat and other protein foods

GUIDANCE	RATIONALE	WHAT'S INCLUDED
Offer a variety of meat and meat alternatives at main meals.	Beans, pulses, eggs, meat alternatives and nuts all provide good sources of nutrients. Some meat and meat products can have a high fat and saturated fat content.	Beans and pulses such as chick peas, lentils, kidney beans beans, butter beans, textured vegetable protein, nuts, Quorn, and soya products such as tofu.
Fish should be offered at least twice a week. It is strongly recommended that oily fish, such as salmon, trout, mackerel, herring, pilchards or sardines – should be served once a week.	White fish is low in fat. Oil-rich fish provide a good source of omega-3 fats, which may help to protect against heart disease. Oil-rich fish are also a source of vitamin A and D.**	Fish includes fresh, frozen and tinned fish, such as tuna and sardines. Fish products, such as fish cakes, fish fingers, and fish pies, may have a low fish content.
Eggs can be served at breakfast and as part of main meals.	Eggs are a good source of protein, vitamin A, vitamin D and some minerals.	Boiled, poached or scrambled eggs, or omelettes. Meat includes all cuts of beef, pork, lamb, poultry, offal* and meat products such as bacon, sausages, beef burgers, pies and cold meats.

Tips

- Having more meat-free days, including a variety of alternatives, is suggested as being of benefit for health and sustainability.
- Reduce the amount of processed meat products served, such as meat pies and pasties, sausages, burgers and coated chicken products.
- Reduce the amount of processed fish products on offer, particularly those that are fried or coated, such as fish fingers or fish cakes.
- Offer unsalted nuts and seeds as snacks. Sprinkle on salads and yoghurts and add to stir-fries. Choose nut butters and seed pastes that are free from palm oil, added salt, and sugar.
- Use fish from sustainable fish stocks. Look for the Marine Stewardship Council logo.
- Use more vegetables, beans, and pulses to extend dishes further, and add more texture and flavour. Less meat is used, reducing the fat content and the cost of the meal.
- Select the leanest cuts of meat and remove visible fat and poultry skin.
- Roast meat on a rack to let the fat run off.
- Grill, poach or bake meat rather than frying. If you do fry, note that larger pieces of fish and meat absorb less fat.

* Liver and liver pâté are very rich in vitamin A, and it is recommended that these foods be consumed no more than once a week.
** More information on vegetarian/vegan sources of Omega-3 is available on page 52.

Beans, pulses, nuts, fish, eggs, meat and meat alternatives (e.g. Quorn) are a good source of protein and some vitamins and minerals, particularly iron and zinc. The body more easily absorbs the iron in meat than iron from vegetable sources. However, eating processed meat increases the risk of bowel cancer and eating red meat may increase the risk of bowel cancer. Cancer Research UK suggests eating processed and red meat on fewer days of the week, consuming smaller portions, and reducing the number of portions. Ideas for reducing red and processed meat consumption include using chicken, turkey, soya or Quorn mince instead of beef or pork mince, introducing Meatless Mondays, or filling sandwiches with chicken, tuna, or eggs instead of ham.

What is processed meat and red meat?

Processed meat is meat that's been treated to make it last longer or taste better. This could be through smoking, curing, or salting the meat. Processed meat often contains chemical preservatives, such as nitrates and nitrites, added to it.

Examples of processed meat include:
- ham
- bacon
- corned beef
- some sausages, like chorizo and hot dogs
- deli meats, like salami and pepperoni

Red meat is any type of beef, pork, lamb or goat. It can be fresh, minced or frozen.

Food group: milk and dairy foods such as yoghurt and cheese, and fortified alternatives (e.g. soya or oat milks)

GUIDANCE	RATIONALE	WHAT'S INCLUDED
Offer dairy foods and dairy substitutes such as milk, yoghurt and cheese as part of meals and snacks. Offer low-fat options such as semi-skimmed milk, low-fat yoghurt and low-fat cream cheese. Do not regularly rely on cheese as the main protein item for vegetarians. When choosing dairy alternatives, select those fortified with calcium and other essential vitamins and minerals whenever possible.	Milk and dairy are good sources of calcium, protein, vitamin B12, vitamin B2, Iodine and vitamin A. Calcium helps to contribute to good bone health. The fat content of different dairy products vary and much of this is saturated fat.	Skimmed, semi-skimmed, whole milk Oat, rice, coconut, hemp and soya milk, yoghurts and cheeses Dried milk, goat's, and sheep's milk and Kefir. All types of cheeses, e.g. Cheddar cheese, cottage cheese, cheese spreads, quark, Brie, feta, Edam, goat's cheese, paneer, stilton and Parmesan. Yoghurt and fromage frais. Soya, oat, rice, coconut and pea milks and yoghurts.

Tips

- Choose reduced-fat hard cheeses, cottage cheese, quark and skimmed-milk soft cheese.
- Some cheeses can contain high levels of salt, e.g. parmesan. Check labels and look for lower-salt cheeses and use smaller amounts of stronger cheese.
- Use the size of a small matchbox as a guide to the right portion size for cheese.
- For adults and children over 2 years of age, offer semi-skimmed or skimmed milk and low-fat yoghurts and fromage frais.
- Use plain yoghurt, fromage frais or low-fat crème fraiche instead of cream or soured cream in recipes.
- Try serving frozen yoghurts as an alternative to ice cream.
- Avoid sweetened milkshakes and yoghurts, which can be very high in added sugars.

Food group: oils and spreads		
GUIDANCE	**RATIONALE**	**WHAT'S INCLUDED**
Some fat in the diet is essential, but it should be included in small amounts.	All types of fats are high in calories and, therefore, can contribute to excess energy intake and weight gain.	Foods containing fat include: butter, margarine, other spreading fats and low-fat spreads, cooking oils, oil-based salad dressings, mayonnaise, cream, chocolate, crisps, biscuits, pastries, cakes, puddings, ice cream, rich sauces, and gravies.
Ensure that most of the fat in the diet is from unsaturated oils and spreads.	Swapping to unsaturated fats can help lower cholesterol.	

Tips

- Use fat spreads rich in monounsaturated or polyunsaturated fats, e.g. olive spreads, sunflower spreads, and spreads made from rapeseed and vegetable oils.
- Use cooking oils high in monounsaturated fats, such as soya, rapeseed or olive oils.
- Serve pastry dishes infrequently.
- Measure oil for cooking carefully and reduce the amount of oil used when preparing soups, stews and casseroles. Vegetables can often be dry-fried, steamed or stewed to form the basis of sauces and other dishes. Air fryers can be a useful way of reducing the oil used in cooking.
- Use low-fat yoghurt or non-dairy ice cream to complement puddings or pies in place of cream or ice cream.
- Incorporate fresh fruit, tinned fruit in juice or dried fruit into puddings and cakes.

Sugar

Diets which are high in sugar contribute to obesity as well as tooth decay, and very sugary foods may contain few nutrients. Most adults and children in the UK eat too much sugar, and people who drink sugar-sweetened soft drinks regularly or have a 'sweet tooth' are likely to exceed the current recommendations for the maximum amount of sugars in the diet (currently set at no more than 5% of total energy intake from free sugars).

To cut down on sugar:

- Have fewer sugary drinks and snacks. Refer to page 140 for ideas on nutritious snacks. See page 143 for guidance on sugar-free drinks.
- Drink water with and between meals.
- If people take sugar in hot drinks or add sugar to breakfast cereal, gradually encourage them to reduce the amount until they can cut it out altogether.
- Choose tins of fruit in juice rather than syrup, and drain before serving
- Check the labels on items such as breakfast cereals and yoghurts for added sugars.

For information on sources of sugars in the diet, see p.52. For information on non-nutritive sweeteners, see p.99.

Salt

Salt is the main source of dietary sodium. Sodium is essential for fluid balance, but too much sodium is associated with raised blood pressure in later life, which is a risk factor for coronary heart disease and stroke. It is currently recommended that adults consume no more than 6g of salt per day and children proportionally less, depending on their age.

As a nation, salt reduction has been aided by the gradual reduction of the salt added to manufactured foods. Everyone should be encouraged to choose lower-salt foods whenever possible and to adapt recipes to reduce the amount of salt used. While 6g has been set as the maximum (for adults), some flexibility might be required in menu planning, and caterers should look holistically at the foods served and the ingredients used rather than making artificial or unpalatable changes solely to achieve a 'standard'.

How to Reduce Salt in the Diet

Much of the salt we consume is found in processed foods, including soups, sauces, ready meals, meat products such as pies and pasties, bacon and ham, takeaway foods, savoury snacks, and foods like bread and breakfast cereals. Checking the labels and selecting the lower salt option can make a significant difference. There is no need to stop eating foods which are higher in salt, but it may be necessary to eat them less often and in smaller amounts.

Think about the amount of salt you use when cooking and at the table. Try not to add salt automatically – people should always taste food first.

There are lots of ways to add flavour to food without using salt, soya sauce or stock cubes – for example:

- Add fresh or dried herbs to dishes.
- Use tomato purée to add flavour.
- Marinade meat and fish in advance to give them more flavour. Try using citrus juices or yoghurt-based marinades.
- Use garlic, ginger, chilli, lemon or lime to add flavour to meat and fish dishes.
- Use spices such as cumin, coriander and turmeric.
- Use black pepper as a seasoning instead of salt.
- Roast vegetables such as red peppers, courgettes, fennel, parsnips and squash to bring out their flavour.
- Add fruit to meat dishes to give a naturally sweet flavour (e.g., pork and apricots). Make your own sauces and gravies and avoid using stock cubes and instant gravy mixes.
- Use a smaller amount of strong cheese in dishes, rather than a larger amount of mild cheese.

Vitamin, mineral and herbal supplements

Most people can obtain all the vitamins and minerals the body needs by eating a varied diet. Dietary supplements that contain vitamins and minerals may be useful in some cases where nutrient intake is low (for example, if the amount of food eaten is very small for some reason) or where there are increased needs or a deficiency has been identified (for example, for vitamin D or iron). Advice should always be sought from a medical practitioner or dietitian before taking supplements, because high doses of certain vitamins and minerals, as well as some herbal supplements, can cause adverse reactions and may interfere with the absorption of other nutrients. There is no evidence that taking large doses of vitamin and mineral supplements is beneficial to health, and some evidence suggests that they may be harmful.

> High doses of certain vitamins and minerals, as well as some herbal supplements, can cause adverse reactions and may interfere with the absorption of other nutrients.

Herbal supplements are often assumed to be safe because they are 'natural', but this alone does not imply safety, and advice should always be sought before taking any type of supplement. Some herbal supplements can interfere with the effectiveness of certain medicines. For example, St John's Wort should not be taken by people taking medications, including anti-depressants, digoxin, warfarin or the contraceptive pill; ginseng and gingko can interfere with the action of warfarin.

References

1. Public Health England (2016). *Government Dietary Recommendations Government recommendations for energy and nutrients for males and females aged 1 - 18 years and 19+ years.* Available at: https://assets.publishing.service.gov.uk/media/5a749fece5274a44083b82d8/government_dietary_recommendations.pdf

2. Public Health England (2020). *National Diet and Nutrition Survey Rolling programme Years 9 to 11 (2016/2017 to 2018/2019).* Available at: https://assets.publishing.service.gov.uk/media/5fd23324e90e07662b09d91a/NDNS_UK_Y9-11_report.pdf

3. Public Health England (2018). *The Eatwell Guide.* Available at: https://assets.publishing.service.gov.uk/media/5ba8a50540f0b605084c9501/Eatwell_Guide_booklet_2018v4.pdf

4. British Nutrition Foundation (2023). *Vitamins and Minerals – Nutritional Information.* Available at: https://www.nutrition.org.uk/nutritional-information/vitamins-and-minerals/

5. Public Health England (2018). *PHE publishes latest data on nation's diet.* Available at: https://www.gov.uk/government/news/phe-publishes-latest-data-on-nations-diet

6. NHS (2023). *Sugar: the facts.* Available at: https://www.nhs.uk/live-well/eat-well/food-types/how-does-sugar-in-our-diet-affect-our-health/

7. British Nutrition Foundation (2023). *Sugar and Nutrition.* Available at: https://www.nutrition.org.uk/nutritional-information/sugar/

8. NHS (2023). *Facts about Fat.* Available at: https://www.nhs.uk/live-well/eat-well/food-types/different-fats-nutrition/

9. Schulze, M.B., Martínez-González, M.A., Fung, T.T., et al (2018). Food based dietary patterns and chronic disease prevention. *BMJ*, 361, p.k2396. https://doi.org/10.1136/bmj.k2396

10. World Cancer Research Fund. (2024). *What affects your risk of getting cancer?* Available at: https://www.wcrf.org/preventing-cancer/topics/.

11. Public Health England (2015) *Why 5%?* Available at: https://assets.publishing.service.gov.uk/media/5c3381e1ed915d7325fbc294/Why_5__-_The_Science_Behind_SACN.pdf

12. NHS (2022). *5 A Day portion sizes.* Available at: https://www.nhs.uk/live-well/eat-well/5-a-day/portion-sizes/

13. Asher, G.N., Corbett, A.H. and Hawke, R.L. (2017). Common Herbal Dietary Supplement–Drug Interactions. *American Family Physician,* 96(2), pp.101–107. Available at: https://www.aafp.org/pubs/afp/issues/2017/0715/p101.html

CHAPTER 10

Menu Planning

Menu Planning

This chapter looks at some of the practical issues to consider when planning daily meals or weekly menu cycles for people with learning disabilities. We provide some example eating plans and consider the benefits of people being involved in food purchase and preparation.

Eating patterns and timing of meals and snacks

When people with learning disabilities live in their own home, they are more likely to be able to choose when to eat and drink and find patterns of eating and drinking which suit their lifestyle and routines. In residential accommodation, the national minimum standards for care homes for adults provide clear guidance that mealtimes should be flexible and that a range of food and drink should be available at all times (See Appendix 5). Additional guidance for care settings has also been produced by the British Dietetic Association and by the National Association of Care Catering. The timing of meals and snacks throughout the day should be organised to suit the needs of the individual being supported. Some people may need frequent small meals and snacks throughout the day. Some people have particular times of day when their appetite is better, and this will be the best time to offer nutrient-dense items. Consideration should be given to occasions when the day may be different from usual, such as an outing or event, to ensure planning ahead in terms of when, where and what to eat to prevent anxiety or a lack of suitable choices being available.

> Various tools are available to help people plan their meals. Downloadable templates are available from 'Food a Fact of Life' and in the book 'Menu Planning: As Easy as 1, 2, 3' by Pamela McIntosh (see Appendix 2).

Breakfast

Breakfast is an essential meal for two main reasons. Firstly, many breakfast foods are a good source of fibre and other essential nutrients. Secondly, if breakfast is missed, it is more likely that people will be tempted by other less nutritious snack foods later in the day.

Fortified breakfast cereals that are high in fibre, low in salt, sugar and fat can be offered. Examples include porridge, puffed wheat, wheat flakes, wheat bisks, shredded wheat and some mueslis. Look at the labels to choose those that are lower in salt and sugar (See page 128 for details of how to check if foods are high in fat, salt and sugar). Most breakfast cereals can be eaten as finger food or with milk, yoghurt, or fresh or dried fruit. Vegetables can also be served at breakfast (e.g. tinned tomatoes, mushrooms or baked beans). For individuals who have a good appetite in the morning that wanes as the day progresses, breakfast should be viewed as an opportunity to consume a significant amount of energy and other essential nutrients. A range of foods should be offered, rather than just traditional breakfast items.

Packed lunches

People may take a packed lunch when they go to school, visit a daycare centre, college, or other facility, or go on an outing.

It is essential that a packed lunch provides the same variety of foods and nutrients as the meal it replaces. A packed lunch should contain:

- A starchy food. For example, any type of bread: pitta bread, chapatti, crispbreads, rice cakes, or wraps. Choose lower-sodium, higher-fibre breads where available. Pasta salad or a rice 'poke' bowl offers an alternative to keep lunches interesting.
- A protein food, for example, peanut butter, hummus, egg, cheese or chicken.
- One portion of vegetables, for example, raw vegetables or salad.
- One portion of fresh or dried fruit.
- A drink. Water or milk is the best choice.

The quantity of food provided in a packed lunch will depend on the individual's needs, and all the other principles outlined in this report should be considered when planning an appropriate packed lunch. Additional snacks, such as plain popcorn, breadsticks, unsalted nuts, pumpkin or sunflower seeds, rice crackers, or pretzels, could be added occasionally.

Yoghurt or fromage frais provides a good source of calcium. For individuals with higher energy needs, more energy-dense foods may also be appropriate.

School lunches

Most children with learning disabilities will attend school, and some may receive school meals. Schools will be obliged to adhere to the standards for school meals specified by the appropriate Department for Education in the four countries of the UK. The aim of improving school food across the UK is to ensure that all children and young people are offered a range of healthy and tasty food at school, that they learn more about what eating well means in practice, and that those children who are entitled to free school meals

Examples of packed lunches for 5-11 year olds

Egg and cress roll with cucumber sticks, cherry tomatoes, natural yoghurt and blueberries

Chicken and sweetcorn sandwich with pepper sticks, pineapple chunks

> **Snacks should be viewed as mini-meals and should be as varied and nutritious as meals.**

in particular are enabled to meet a significant proportion of their nutritional needs through their school lunch. As schools for children with learning disabilities often cater to a range of complex needs and special diets, it is essential that caterers and other staff in these schools receive tailored training and support to meet these needs and enable them to work in partnership with families and other carers. For children with complex needs and those with autism spectrum disorder, it may be very difficult for support staff to fully involve children in school meals, and staff will require specific training on how to handle eating difficulties. For advice on how to manage faddy and selective eating, see page 119.

Snacks

It is important that nutritious snacks are offered regularly to people who have small appetites and who therefore need to eat frequently or 'little and often', to those who may need to eat a greater amount of calories per day, or to those who are fussy or selective eaters or who are growing rapidly. Snacks should be viewed as mini-meals and should be as varied and nutritious as meals.

For those people with learning disabilities who are unintentionally gaining weight, or who have been advised to lose weight, snacks that are high in fat and sugar (such as confectionery, savoury snacks, sugar-sweetened drinks, cakes, biscuits and ice cream) should be kept to a minimum as these frequently contribute significant extra calories to the diet.

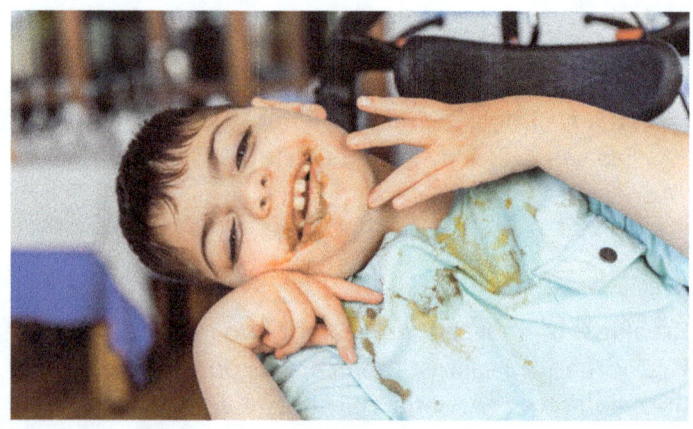

For many people, snack foods are limited to biscuits and crisps, but snacks can and should be varied and planned for. Generally, two snacks per day are appropriate. The best snacks are those that provide essential nutrients without adding lots of salt, fat, and sugar to the diet. Below are some suggestions for good snack choices.

Examples of good snack choices are:

- Fresh fruit such as pears, apple slices, satsumas, bananas, seedless grapes, slices of melon, mango, pineapple, kiwifruit, plums, or berries such as strawberries and raspberries. Choose fruits in season and those that are grown locally, where possible. The fruit from canned fruit in juice can be added to yoghurt or fromage frais.
- Raw vegetables such as peeled carrots, sweet pepper, tomato, cucumber or celery (all well washed) with dips such as hummus, taramasalata, avocado, salsa or Greek yoghurt with chives.
- Unsalted nuts and seeds are a good choice for some people, but should not be given to anyone who has eating difficulties.
- Home-made plain popcorn, home-made oven-baked potato crisps or sweet potato crisps. (To make potato crisps, put thin slices of potato on a lightly greased baking tray and bake in a hot oven.)
- Plain biscuits such as crispbreads, oatcakes, breadsticks, cream crackers, matzos, rice cakes or melba toast. Some of these foods can be high in salt, so choose those that are lower in salt where possible.
- Dairy foods such as cheese or yoghurt.
- Any type of bread (wholemeal or granary if possible); plain scones, crumpets, English muffins, bagels, pitta bread or sandwiches. Look for lower-salt (low-sodium) versions where available.
- Suitable fillings/toppings for sandwiches and toast might be meat (for example, cold roast meats, chicken, cheese, cottage cheese, mashed pilchards, sardines, mackerel, tuna, egg, hummus, roast vegetables, banana, salad or combinations of these.

Eating out and takeaways

Eating out is an integral part of life for many people, offering the opportunity to socialise, meet friends, and take a break from food preparation and cleaning up.

As with the rest of the population, individuals with a learning disability should consider the frequency and variety of meals they eat out or take away within the context of a varied diet. Eating fast food habitually is likely to result in higher intakes of fat, saturated fat, salt, and sugar than recommended, and this is often the case when fast food meals are consumed as snacks rather than meals.

The high energy densities and large portion sizes associated with many fast foods or takeaway meals challenge human appetite control systems and promote 'passive overconsumption' so that regular consumers are likely to accidentally consume too many calories and therefore gain weight.

Takeaways

There is anecdotal evidence that take-away foods are very popular among some people with learning disabilities, particularly where people have greater freedom to choose and shop for their own food. Take-away foods are easy to obtain, the variety of foods on offer is extensive, they can be relatively cheap to buy, and the foods are often very much enjoyed, particularly in social settings, so, understandably, it is tempting for some people to use these outlets regularly. Many foods, including those available in Chinese and Indian restaurants and takeaways, are high in fat and salt. Portion sizes are often very large, and children's portions will be adequate for most adults. Suggestions for healthier takeaway options are provided in the yellow box.

For anyone with eating difficulties, particular care should be taken when ordering takeaway food, especially rice-based dishes, which can cause choking. Individual advice needs to be sought regarding suitable takeaway foods for anyone with swallowing difficulties.

Tips on eating out and takeaways

Indian meals

Good choices: Tandoori chicken, other meats or fish (that is cooked in an oven), chicken or other meat or fish tikka (meat on a skewer without sauce), dry curries, vegetable curries, dahl, channa dahl, plain boiled rice, chapatti or roti bread.

High-fat foods to avoid: Poppadoms and other fried foods such as samosas and onion bhajis, creamy or coconut-based sauces (like korma sauces), fried rices (like pilau rice), and breads that have fat added (like naan bread).

Chinese meals

Good choices: Stir-fries, chicken, vegetable or prawn chop suey, steamed fish, vegetable dishes, boiled noodles and dishes with steamed tofu.

High-fat foods to avoid: Avoid batter (for example, sweet and sour chicken, battered bananas or apple fritters), spring rolls and prawn crackers. Avoid fried rice dishes and fried noodles.

Pizza

Choose thin-crust pizzas and pizzas without cheese in the crust.

Avoid having extra cheese, pepperoni or salami. Add more vegetables or fish toppings instead. Encourage eating a salad with the pizza.

Fish & chip shops

Fish is a good choice, but the batter is high in fat; therefore, eating less or no batter should be encouraged.

Choose small portions of chips. Add vinegar rather than salt. Mushy peas or baked beans are a good accompaniment.

Avoid pies or battered sausage-type products.

Burger bars

Opt for standard rather than 'super-size' options. Choose a plain burger or a veggie burger in a bun with a salad.

Avoid extra cheese or mayonnaise, thick milkshakes, chicken nuggets, or other battered dishes, such as onion rings.

Choose a small portion of French fries and water, sugar-free drinks or small regular drinks.

Drinks

Drinks are essential in the diet to ensure adequate fluid intake. They can also provide an opportunity to supplement the diet with additional nutrients. However, drinking too many sweetened or other soft drinks, particularly between meals, can be damaging to the teeth (see page 98). Drinks which contain sugar can also add calories – but few other nutrients – to the diet.

Providing drinks

It is essential that everyone has access to adequate fluid intake throughout the day. Recommended intakes are shown in the table below. Standard adult cup and mug sizes typically range from 200 to 300ml.

Recommended adequate intakes of water from drinks

	Age	Adeqate water intake from drinks (ml/day)
Infants	7-12 months	640 – 800ml
Children	1-2 years	880 – 960ml
	2-3 years	1040ml
	4-8 years	1280ml
	9-13 years	Boys 1680ml Girls 1520ml
	> 14 years	As adults
Adults including older people		Men: 2000ml Women: 1600ml
Those who are pregnant		As adults + 300ml per day
Those who are lactating		As adults + 600 – 700ml per day

Source: EFSA

Requirements may be higher when someone breathes through their mouth, drools excessively, sweats profusely, is constipated, has loose stools, or has a high fever.

People may be at higher risk of not meeting their fluid needs if they:

- are dependent on others for drinks,
- have difficulty swallowing (dysphagia),
- have diarrhoea and/or vomiting,
- have a high temperature (fever),
- have undertaken strenuous physical activity,
- avoid drinking due to concerns about accessing toilet facilities,
- take certain medications.

We obtain some fluid from the food we eat, but it is vital that drinks are provided regularly as dehydration can lead to headaches, confusion, irritability, tiredness and lack of concentration, as well as constipation and urinary tract infections.
For information on excessive fluid intake, see page 36.

Water

Water quenches thirst and should be the drink of choice between meals when people are thirsty. Free, fresh, chilled tap water should always be offered with meals and regularly throughout the day and should be widely available in any places where people with learning disabilities may live, work or visit.

Providing interesting and colourful insulated cups and bottles for water drinking may encourage some people with learning disabilities to drink more, as may adding a slice of lemon or orange.

Milk

Milk or water, in addition to breast milk, should constitute the majority of drinks given to children aged 1 to 5 years, since milk is safe for teeth and contains other essential nutrients. It is essential to select suitable milks for infants and children, and guidance on this matter should be obtained from a health visitor. When using dairy alternative milks, care should be taken to ensure they are appropriately fortified and unsweetened. Rice milk should be avoided for children under 5.

From the age of 1 year through to adulthood, semi-skimmed milk can be the milk of choice, as it has reduced amounts of fat and saturated fat, whilst providing similar amounts of calcium. Formula milks (including infant formula, follow-on formula, 'growing-up' or other 'toddler' milks) are not required for children aged 1 to 5 years. Skimmed and 1% cows' milk should not be given as a main drink until 5 years of age, but these lower-fat milks can be used in cooking. For individuals who need to gain weight, whole milk may be appropriate.

Soft drinks

There is a wide range of soft drinks available, most of which are sweetened with sugars, sweeteners (such as saccharin or aspartame) and commonly a combination of both. They include:

- squashes and other drinks which need to be diluted
- carbonated soft drinks such as cola or lemonade, and
- fruit drinks, which are drinks that contain a proportion of fruit juice as well as water and some form of sugar and/or sweetener.

Sugary drinks should not be given to children under 5, and should be avoided thereafter, as they contribute to tooth decay and excess weight gain.

Sugary drinks provide additional calories to the diet, and this can be significant over time, since high volumes of soft drinks can often be consumed without impacting appetite. Swapping some or all sugary drinks for water may be particularly helpful if people are trying to maintain their weight or lose weight.

Soft drinks containing sugar can be harmful to everyone's teeth, especially if they are drunk frequently or stay in contact with the teeth for too long. If sugary drinks are given, they should be kept to mealtimes. Soft drinks such as fruit drinks and fruit squashes should not be given at bedtime or during the night, as this practice is highly likely to result in dental decay.

Soft drinks labelled 'low-sugar' or 'no added sugar' may still harm teeth as they often contain some sugar, and they may also be acidic. Any of the following on the label of a soft drink indicates that the drink has sugar added: glucose, glucose syrup, fructose, concentrated fruit juice, sucrose, dextrose, honey, invert sugar, maltose or hydrolysed starch. Sweetened fizzy drinks such as cola or lemonade are both sugary and acidic. The 'diet' versions of these drinks can also be harmful to teeth, even if they do not contain sugar, as the acidity erodes the dental enamel.

Fruit juices

Fruit juices are most beneficial when consumed with meals because, if they are a good source of vitamin C, such as orange juice, this may help the body absorb iron. However, fruit juices have also been shown to be acidic enough to erode dental enamel, so it is best to avoid giving them between meals.

Some fruit juice drinks are available, which contain some fruit juice, with added sugar and water. These can often be high in calories and can be an expensive way to buy fruit juice. 150ml of 100% pure fruit juice counts as one of the 5 fruit and vegetable portions each day and is a better choice. This can be diluted 50:50 with water.

Tea and coffee

Tea and coffee are not recommended as drinks for infants or children, as the tannic acid they contain reduces iron absorption, and due to the caffeine they contain. However, young people and adults may enjoy tea and coffee, as these drinks are an integral part of our culture at social occasions and offer comfort and warmth. While caffeine in tea and coffee has a mild dehydrating effect, this effect is negligible among habitual consumers. It is compensated for by the total amount of fluid in the drink. Sugar added to tea and coffee can damage teeth and contribute to obesity, and everyone should be encouraged to reduce the amount of sugar they use in hot drinks over time. If appropriate, people could consider using sugar alternatives that are less damaging to teeth, such as fructose or sorbitol. However, care must be taken not to consume these in large amounts, as they can cause diarrhoea.

Caffeine

Caffeine is a commonly consumed drug which is not harmful to most people in moderate amounts. Caffeine is commonly found in tea, coffee, cola beverages and chocolate as well as in some pain relievers and energy drinks. In excess, caffeine can cause anxiety, sleep disruption, restlessness, palpitations, dizziness, nausea, diarrhoea and involuntary trembling. Excess caffeine intake can complicate psychiatric diagnosis and can intensify the side effects of medication given for treating mental ill health or interfere with how effective some medicines are.

The safe limit for caffeine intake in adults is suggested at 400mg per day.

Pregnant women are advised to have no more than 200mg of caffeine a day. Typical caffeine contents are shown below.

Cup or mug of instant coffee	75mg/100mg
Can of cola	38mg
Cup or mug of brewed coffee	100mg/140mg
Can of energy drink	80mg
Cup or mug of tea	50mg/70mg
50g bar of plain chocolate	50mg

Source: BDA Food Fact Sheet: Fluid and Hydration

In light of the potential side effects discussed above, the provision of decaffeinated drinks as standard is the preferred option for many.

Herbal and fruit-flavoured teas

Herbal and fruit-flavoured teas can be useful hydrating drinks, making a pleasant change from other hot or cold beverages. Stronger flavours, such as ginger and lemon, liquorice, or peppermint, are often enjoyed by those who have oral hyposensitivity. Chamomile tea is a popular choice for many in the evening before bed and could replace a milky drink for those looking to reduce energy intake. Fruit teas can be brewed, then cooled and served with ice as a refreshing alternative to fruit squash. Green teas do contain caffeine, but decaffeinated versions are available.

Some herbal teas make unsubstantiated claims for health benefits (for example, as a laxative, an anti-diabetes agent, or to aid in weight loss). In most cases, these teas are likely to be harmless; however, some people may drink them in preference to taking appropriate medication. Support staff should be alert to this possibility. Herbal supplements, which may be found in drinks, can interfere with the effectiveness of some medicines (see page 136).

Frozen drinks

People who can swallow safely may be able to manage frozen drinks. These provide a variety of textures, can be fortified to increase their energy content, and can increase fluid intake. For people who find it challenging to handle cups due to tremors or weak muscle tone, frozen drinks such as sorbets or ice pops served in non-edible, easy-to-hold cones may help to promote independence.

Things to remember when planning daily menus
- Include a variety of different foods every day.
- Include at least 5 portions of a variety of fruit and vegetables every day.
- Include a portion of starchy food such as potatoes, bread, rice or pasta at each meal.
- Include good sources of iron and zinc at main meals.
- Regularly include foods or drinks that are sources of calcium.
- Make sure that the food has a variety of textures and colours, looks appealing, and tastes good.
- Make sure that fresh, chilled water is available at and between meals.

For more meal ideas, including recipes and photos to support menu planning, see the accompanying CWT photo resource.

Example Meal Ideas

These meal ideas are examples of the types of foods and their corresponding amounts that, when combined, meet the recommended nutrient intakes for children and adults in a daily menu. In many circumstances, a choice of food at mealtimes is required. These meal ideas may not be suitable or liked by all individuals, and many people will require personalised advice or support on what a suitable diet may be for them, or how best to adjust portion sizes to meet their needs.

1-4 year olds

Breakfast Ideas	Lighter Meal Ideas	Main Meal Ideas	Dessert Ideas
 Eggy Bread with button mushrooms	 Chilli con carne, jacket potato with crème fraîche, tomato & watercress salad	 Cottage Pie, peas and broccoli	 Banana custard
 Cornflakes with raisins, with sliced banana	 Broccoli quiche, mashed potato and baked beans	 Chicken Korma, brown rice and naan bread	 Rice pudding with sultanas
 Porridge and jam, with toasted fruit bread	 Chicken fajitas, salad and sweetcorn salsa	 Chickpea fritters, sweet potato mash and sweetcorn	 Crunchy apple bake

5-11 year olds

Breakfast Ideas	Lighter Meal Ideas	Main Meal Ideas	Dessert Ideas
 Peanut butter and mashed banana sandwich	 Tortilla wrap with chicken and sweetcorn salsa and pepper sticks	 Meatballs in tomato sauce with herb mash and broccoli	Tropical fruit kebab
 Cream cheese bagel with sliced apple	 Baked potato with tuna and sweetcorn filling and salad	 Salmon fish fingers with chunky chips, tomato salsa and salad	 Mini pancakes with strawberries and greek yogurt
 Shredded Wheat with milk and toasted fruit bread.	 Baguette with hummus, carrot and cucumber sticks and dried apricots	 Vegetarian sausages with leek and potato bake	 Fruit Jelly

12-18 year olds

Breakfast Ideas	Lighter Meal Ideas	Main Meal Ideas	Dessert Ideas
 Mexican scrambled egg wrap	 Tomato and avocado bagel with satsuma	 Vegetable curry with lentil dahl and rice	 Pancake with Greek yoghurt and banana
 Beans on toast	 Egg & cress baguette with carrot and pepper sticks	 Tuna and tomato pasta with salad	 Blackberries and custard
 Wheat bisks with milk and orange juice	 Chicken piri piri with savoury rice and salad	 Breaded cod with potato wedges and mushy peas	 Apple rings with crunchy peanut butter

Adults

Breakfast Ideas | Lighter Meal Ideas | Main Meal Ideas | Dessert Ideas

Bagel with scrambled egg, polyunsaturated spread and canned plum tomatoes

Egg and tomato sandwich with low-fat soft cheese on wholemeal bread, served with salad and sliced plum

Chicken and vegetable stir-fry with egg noodles

Baked apple with custard

Toasted bagel with low-salt and low-sugar baked beans

Sardines in tomato sauce on wholemeal toast, with lettuce and tomato & sliced watermelon

Spicy chicken strips, fajita, salsa, sliced pepper and salad

Rice pudding with strawberries

Muesli, semi-skimmed milk, sliced banana and low-fat, low-sugar fruit yogurt

Tomato soup, French bread, oatcakes, ham, carrot, cucumber, tomato and cherries

Poached salmon steak with bubble and squeak and carrots

Baked banana with natural yoghurt and raisins

Other Main Meal Ideas

Vegeburger, jacket potato, salsa and carrot salad

Chickpea curry and rice, spinach curry, chapati

Macaroni cheese with salad

CHAPTER 10 – Menu Planning | 149

How it all fits together – below is an example daily meal plan for an adult on a normal texture diet

Breakfast
Weetbix with raisins and fruit yogurt

Mid-morning
Sliced melon

Lunch
Omlette, oven chips, peas and grilled tomato
Poached pears

Mid-afternoon
Potato farl with soft cheese, blueberries and tea

Evening Meal
Tomato soup and beef roll
Fresh fruit salad

Bedtime
Warm milk

The cost of a good diet

The Food Foundations' Broken Plate report found that, on average, healthier foods are more than twice as expensive per calorie as less healthy foods. Healthier foods have also been increasing in price at twice the rate in the past two years. Alongside the additional cost of purchasing food, the amount of time and resources spent cooking may well be greater for those following a healthier diet. There is little clear information on the cost of food for people with learning disabilities in residential care, or on how much people may typically spend on their food if they live independently. The average amount spent per UK household per week on food and non-alcoholic drinks to be consumed at home in 2022/2023 was £63.50; however, costs per person will vary depending on the number of people in the household.

Sustainability

Concerns about the environmental impact of food travelling long distances, intensive farming, and dwindling stocks of some fish have prompted us to consider more sustainable patterns of eating.

The BDA One Blue Dot project has produced the following nine-point plan for guidance on how to achieve more environmentally sustainable diets:

1. Reductions in red and processed meat, if eaten, to at most 70g per person per day (also recommended by the World Cancer Research Fund).
2. Increasing plant proteins such as beans, nuts, soya and tofu.
3. Only consuming fish from sustainable sources, and from a wider variety of species.
4. Moderating dairy consumption and using fortified alternatives where needed.
5. Focusing on wholegrain, starchy carbohydrate sources.
6. Opting for seasonal, locally sourced vegetables/fruit. Avoiding air-freighted, pre-packed and prepared vegetables/fruit.
7. Reducing consumption of high-fat, sugar, and salt foods.
8. Making tap water and unsweetened tea/coffee the choice for healthy hydration.
9. Reducing food waste, especially of perishable fruit and veg, by choosing tinned/frozen alongside seasonal fresh produce.

Responsibility for food purchasing varies in different settings. Those who are responsible for buying food or helping others shop are encouraged to purchase food that is grown locally and in season. Where possible, people should consider buying fish with the Marine Stewardship Council logo, which ensures it is from a sustainable source.

Food waste is another important issue as this wastes the resources used to grow and transport the food, and food placed in landfill sites will emit methane gas. If significant amounts of food are regularly wasted in a care setting, then an audit of what is wasted and when will be useful.

Reducing the amount of pre-packed food purchased, recycling and composting food packaging and other waste, and growing your own fruit and vegetables where possible can all help reduce global greenhouse gas emissions.

Further information on sustainable eating patterns is available from **BDA One Blue Dot** and **EUFIC**.

Why encourage people to cook?

Many people lack cooking skills, which can be true of both support workers and those they support. Ensuring people have the opportunity to learn these skills, can access adapted recipes, have appropriate kitchen appliances and utensils, and are encouraged to be involved in as much of the food preparation as possible, should be a high priority. Example recipe ideas and cooking skills videos are listed in Appendix 2.

Cooking Connections is a toolkit designed to support carers, healthcare professionals, and organisations in co-designing and co-producing cooking programmes for adults with learning disabilities. The toolkit is available by contacting NHS Dietitian Kathryn Guest at kathryn.guest3@nhs.net.

Some examples of how cooking initiatives have been run successfully are available in the Community Food and Health (Scotland) report 'Cooking up connections: working together to improve food and health for adults with learning disabilities', accessible on the website **https://www.communityfoodandhealth.org.uk/publication-keywords/learning-disabilities.** This website also features helpful information on how to fund and run a community food project.

> Remember that involving someone in cooking activities is not restricted to baking cakes. It is a more useful life skill, and better for long-term health, to be able to make a sandwich or a fruit salad.

Potential benefits of being involved in food preparation:

- May improve appetite.
- Encourages physical activity.
- Encourages a greater variety of food choices.
- Allows people to understand what goes into the foods they eat.
- Helps people understand budgeting and the real additional costs of convenience foods such as takeaways.
- Develops new skills.
- Improves confidence and self-esteem.
- May distract people from less positive behaviours.
- Promotes independence.
- Encourages sociability when people cook and eat together.
- Encourages creativity when thinking about adapting recipes or presenting foods on the plate.

Meeting nutrient-based standards

Some settings may wish to perform a nutritional analysis of their menu cycles to ensure that they meet recommended nutritional intakes for the population group under consideration.

Suitable computer menu planning tools are available for use in various settings; however, a specific tool designed to provide guidance for those who cater to groups of adults with complex needs in residential care settings would be particularly helpful. Menu planning software can be purchased from companies such as Nutmeg@CRBCunninghams or Nutritics.

Menu planners should ensure that any menu analysis software used is based on nutrient values for cooked foods and recipes, and a registered dietitian or registered nutritionist provides that recipe analysis. 'The Nutrition and Hydration Digest: Improving Outcomes through Food and Beverage Services' is another useful reference for anyone involved in planning and delivering appropriate menus within health and social care settings.

Menu fatigue can quickly set in, so menu cycles should be reviewed and updated regularly, based on service user feedback and considering seasonal variations.

References

1. The Food Foundation (2025). *The Broken Plate Report – The state of the nation's food system.* Available at: https://foodfoundation.org.uk/sites/default/files/2025-04/TFF_The%20Broken%20Plate%202025.pdf

2. British Dietetic Association (2024). *The Nutrition and Hydration Digest 3rd Edition.* Available at: https://www.bda.uk.com/practice-and-education/the-nutrition-and-hydration-digest.html

3. Office for National Statistics (ONS) (2024). Family spending in the UK: April 2022 to March 2023. Available at: https://www.ons.gov.uk/peoplepopulationandcommunity/personalandhouseholdfinances/expenditure/bulletins/familyspendingintheuk/april2022tomarch2023

4. Department for Education (2025). *School Food Standards: Resources for Schools.* Available at: https://www.gov.uk/government/publications/school-food-standards-resources-for-schools

5. The European Food Information Council (EUFIC) (2023). *9 practical tips for a healthy and sustainable diet.* Available at: https://www.eufic.org/en/food-production/article/practical-tips-for-a-healthy-and-sustainable-diet

6. British Dietetic Association (2024). *One Blue Dot– the BDA's Environmentally Sustainable Diet Project.* Available at: https://www.bda.uk.com/resource-report/one-blue-dot.html

7. NHS England (2022). *National Standards for Healthcare Food and Drink.* Available at: https://www.england.nhs.uk/long-read/national-standards-for-healthcare-food-and-drink/

8. British Dietetic Association (2022). *Sustainable Diets.* Available at: https://www.bda.uk.com/food-health/your-health/sustainable-diets.html

CHAPTER 11

Special Diets

Special Diets

This chapter explores some of the additional considerations required when planning, purchasing, preparing and serving food to meet the cultural, religious, health, and safety needs of people with learning disabilities.

Please note that diabetic and coeliac diets were discussed in chapters 5 & 6, respectively.

Food for all

Eating together, having special foods, or avoiding specific foods are all intimately related to aspects of people's family lives, as well as their cultural and religious beliefs. It is essential to appreciate the diverse contributions that various cultures and nationalities have made to the diverse range of foods consumed in the UK today. While many people who have settled in the UK still try to preserve some of their traditional food patterns, within each family and for each individual, food choices will be unique, and it is essential to treat everyone as an individual when learning about their food choices and preferences.

Vegetarian diets

Vegetarian diets exclude meat, fish and poultry, as well as certain animal products (e.g., gelatine) and may also exclude dairy products and/or eggs. However, some people may say they are vegetarian but still eat fish (pescatarian), so it is essential to find out what they do and do not eat. Vegetarian diets have been traditionally adopted by many people worldwide, particularly in Asia. Vegetarianism is common among Hindus and some Sikhs as well as among Rastafarians and Seventh-day Adventists. Some people choose to be vegetarian because they believe the diet is healthier, are concerned about the environment, food safety or animal welfare, or because they dislike the taste of meat.

A vegetarian diet can provide all the nutrients needed for good health, and it has been shown that many vegetarians have diets that are lower in fat and saturated fat and higher in complex carbohydrates and fibre. However, it is important not to assume that vegetarian diets are inherently healthy, as some individuals may remove meat from their diet without consuming suitable alternatives. Additionally, it is more difficult to consume sufficient iron and zinc if a good variety of foods is not consumed. Vegetarian diets usually have a high proportion of cereals, and the higher levels of fibre and substances called phytates in cereal foods make it harder for the body to use the iron and zinc in foods.

The body absorbs iron more easily from animal sources, such as meat, than from non-animal sources, such as cereals or vegetables. This means that vegetarians must take extra care to ensure they get enough iron. There is some evidence that vegetarian women in particular have low levels of iron. For advice on iron in the diet, see page 57.

Zinc intakes may also be lower among vegetarians. Eating a good variety of foods ensures that vegetarians obtain an adequate zinc intake. Sources of zinc include fortified breakfast cereals, tofu, nuts, peas, beans and lentils, sesame seeds, milk and cheese.

When cooking for vegetarians:

- Offer suitable protein-rich foods at meals. Avoid over-reliance on cheese-based dishes; ensure that meals based on beans and pulses are included frequently.
- Respect the right of those who avoid meat and fish to have a diet free of these foods by ensuring that separate cooking pots, utensils and cooking oils are used when preparing meat and non-meat dishes.
- Ensure that vegetarians are not given gravies made with meat juices, or soup made with meat stock.
- Avoid ingredients such as gelatine and animal fats (e.g. lard) in foods served to people who wish to avoid these foods (check food labels).

Advice on vegetarian diets can be obtained from the Vegetarian Society (see page 172).

Vegan diets

Vegans generally adopt a diet free of all animal products and will not eat milk, cheese, yoghurt or eggs, as well as meat, poultry and fish. It is possible to eat well as a vegan, but people should always seek advice on how to ensure they obtain the nutrients they need. Vegans need to ensure that they include sources of vitamin B12, Iodine, Selenium, vitamin D and Omega-3 fats in their diet.

Advice on vegan diets can be obtained from the Vegan Society (see page 172), which includes a downloadable version of the Eatwell Guide adapted for vegan diets.

> Adapting menu plans to meet the needs of a group of people with very varied dietary needs can be difficult. It may be useful to seek specialist advice to ensure no one is disadvantaged by the special requirements they need.

Traditional Ethnic & Religious Diets

The racial and cultural backgrounds of people with learning disabilities in the UK, and the people who support them, are hugely diverse. Food choices and practices often play a significant role in shaping people's identity. Embracing diversity is essential for sharing food experiences that consider everyone's needs. Below is a brief introduction to key features of the diet of a selection of cultural groups established in the UK. This is to provide some initial insights into how eating patterns may vary across populations. Many aspects of our lives influence our food choices, and no assumptions can be made about an individual's eating patterns based solely on their ethnic origin.

Religious groups

Hinduism

Many Hindus are lacto-vegetarians. They do not eat meat, fish or eggs. They do not eat animal-derived fats, such as dripping or lard, or any foods that contain animal products, including rennet or gelatin. Milk, yogurt, paneer and butter are permitted as they do not involve the taking of an animal's life. Ghee (clarified butter) and vegetable oils are generally used in cooking. Drinking alcohol is generally discouraged. Those Hindus who do eat meat almost always abstain from eating beef.

Fasting practices vary, with some devout Hindus observing fasting regularly throughout the week and on specific religious days. Festival days will usually involve the preparation and sharing of special foods. Festivals and religious days in the Hindu calendar:

- Mahashivratri – the birthday of Lord Shiva (March)
- Holi (March)
- Ram Navami – the birthday of Lord Rama (April)
- Janmashtami – the birthday of Lord Krishna (August)
- Raksha Bandhan (August)
- Navaratri – nine nights (October)
- Diwali – festival of lights and New Year (October/November)

Islam

Consumption of pork or pork products is forbidden for Muslims. All beef, poultry and lamb must be killed using the Halal method. Any foods containing products from these animals, e.g. gelatine, will be avoided unless proven Halal. Muslims abstain from alcohol, including its use in cooking. Fish with fins and scales are usually acceptable.

Muslims are required to fast from sunrise to sunset during the month of Ramadan. During this time, they will wake early to eat a large meal before sunrise and then break their fast with another large meal after sunset. No food or drink is consumed between these times. Those for whom fasting would be harmful to their health are exempt.

The two major festivals in the muslim calendar are:

- Eid al-Fitr (little Eid) – marking the end of the fasting month of Ramadan
- Eid al-Adha (big Eid) – commemorates the pilgrimage to Mecca

Judaism

Orthodox Jews follow many dietary laws (Kashrut) dating back to the Old Testament. These laws define whether the selection, preparation and consumption of specific foods deem them kosher.

- Animals and birds must be slaughtered in a specific way. The meat must then be salted and soaked in water to remove the blood and render it kosher (permitted). These foods will bear a kosher stamp to indicate their suitability for consumption.
- Only fish with scales and fins are permitted (no shellfish)
- Beef, goat and lamb are permitted in the diet, but pork and pork products are not.
- Meat and poultry must not be cooked or served

with any milk or milk products (e.g. yogurt or cream). These foods must be stored, prepared and served separately, with any utensils involved being washed, dried and stored separately.

- Cooking is not permitted (alongside many other tasks) on the Sabbath (seventh day of the week), which starts at sunset on Friday to nightfall on Saturday. All food preparation will be undertaken in advance.

Important festivals in the Jewish calendar are:

- Rosh Hashanah – New Year (September/October)
- Yom Kippur – the Day of Atonement (September/October)
- Passover – commemorating the exodus of the Jews from Egypt (April)

Jews will fast for 25 hours on Yom Kippur. At Passover, matzo (unleavened bread) is eaten.

Sikhism

Consumption of beef is forbidden in the Sikh diet as the cow is considered a sacred animal. Meat and eggs are usually included in the diet until the Amrit (baptism) ceremony, after which some Sikhs will adopt a lacto-vegetarian diet. Those who do eat meat will not accept halal meat. Jhatka is the preferred method of slaughter. Overconsumption of food is against religious teachings, which warn against greed. Fasting practices may vary.

Festivals in the Sikh calendar include:

- Baisakhi – commemorates the birth of the Khalsa, the Sikh brotherhood (April)
- Diwali – the festival of light (October/November)
- Guru Nanak's Birthday – the founder of Sikhism (November)

Ethnic Groups

South Asian ethnic groups

This includes those who have migrated from areas of Pakistan, India, Bangladesh and Sri Lanka. The vast area from which this community originated means that there is considerable variation in the use of foods and cooking styles, even within the same religious grouping.

Key staples of the diet for many are shown in the following table.

Carbohydrates	Chapattis/roti made from whole wheat flour or rice.
Fats	Ghee, groundnut oil, mustard oil, sesame oil
Fruit and Vegetables	Vegetable curries, occasional salad vegetables, raita/pickles, fresh fruit
Pulses	A major source of protein in the diet
Meat and Fish	Beef is not permitted for those of the Hindu or Sikh faiths. Pork is not permitted for those of the Muslim faith. Fish only feature significantly in the diets of those from Bangladesh or Sri Lanka. Muslims will eat only Halal meat (mainly chicken, mutton and lamb), whilst Hindus and Sikhs are often vegetarian.
Dairy Products	Milk, yogurt and paneer
Eggs	Usually featured in the diet as hard-boiled, fried or as an omelette for Muslims and Sri Lankans.

Shallow frying and deep frying are standard cooking methods within these regions.

African & Caribbean diets

African-Caribbean refers to people of African descent from the many West Indian Islands. Eating patterns will vary considerably across the unique cultures of the different islands, but the foods typically eaten are highly seasoned. Vegetarianism is common amongst Seventh Day Adventists and Rastafarians, and followers of these religions will also avoid stimulants such as alcohol and caffeine.

West African Diets tend to include staples such as cassava, green bananas, yams, plantain and sweet potatoes. One-pot stews are popular. These may consist solely of vegetables or include meat, fish or seafood. Palm oil is often used in cooking. Seeds and nuts are used in cooking and as snacks.

An African & Caribbean Eatwell Guide has been developed by the Diverse Nutrition Association and can be downloaded from their website www.diversenutritionassociation.com

Chinese

The dietary pattern is believed to significantly impact the body's balance and health outcomes in Chinese culture. Altering one's diet to restore balance in the pursuit of wellness can significantly impact people's food habits.

Staple foods in the traditional Chinese diet include rice, wheat dumplings, soups, stews and stir-fries.

Food allergy and food intolerance

A food allergy occurs when the body's immune system reacts abnormally to a specific food. Symptoms can vary widely between individuals and can range from mild to life-threatening. Symptoms typically occur soon after consuming or coming into contact with the food. Common symptoms of a food allergy include:

- **Skin reactions:** Itching, hives (red, raised welts on the skin), eczema (itchy, inflamed skin).
- **Swelling:** Swelling of the lips, tongue, throat, face, or other parts of the body.
- **Respiratory issues:** Runny or stuffy nose, coughing, wheezing, sneezing, shortness of breath, difficulty breathing, chest tightness.
- **Gastrointestinal problems:** Nausea, vomiting, diarrhoea, abdominal pain, stomach cramps.
- **Circulatory symptoms:** Rapid or weak pulse, light-headedness, dizziness, fainting.
- **Anaphylaxis:** A severe, potentially life-threatening reaction, characterised by a drop in blood pressure, loss of consciousness, and difficulty breathing. Anaphylaxis requires immediate treatment with adrenaline and emergency medical attention.

> The 14 most common food allergens which must be labelled on food packaging are: celery, cereals containing gluten, crustaceans (such as crabs and prawns), eggs, fish, lupin, milk, molluscs (such as mussels and oysters), mustard, tree nuts, peanuts, sesame seeds, soya and sulphites.

Food allergies are extremely common, affecting around 6% of adults and 8% of children, and these percentages are rising. They are most commonly seen in the first three years of life. There is no data to suggest that food allergy and intolerance are more prevalent among people with learning disabilities. Food allergies are most likely to occur in children with a family history of allergies such as hay fever, eczema or asthma. Any concerns regarding a food allergy should always be properly explored using validated tests, conducted by a registered healthcare professional such as an immunologist or allergist. Appropriate tests include skin prick tests and IgE antibody blood tests, as well as medically supervised oral food challenges and elimination diets. Reliable diagnosis is essential for preventing reactions, managing symptoms, improving quality of life, avoiding unnecessary dietary restrictions, and ensuring proper support and guidance for individuals living with food allergies.

A true food allergy should always be taken extremely seriously. If someone has a food allergy, it is vital that everyone understands the importance of avoiding contact with those foods that may trigger a serious reaction. It is also crucial that full information on the food allergy is carefully recorded in care plans and communicated to schools, day centres, or other places where the person may visit regularly.
Food intolerance is defined as a reproducible and unpleasant reaction to a specific food ingredient which does not involve the immune system. Examples include lactose intolerance, histamine intolerance, and salicylate sensitivity. Some individuals show reactions to caffeine or to certain food additives. Some people will be able to tolerate specific amounts of a food up to a 'tolerance level' after which they will experience symptoms. Symptoms can occur immediately or may be delayed by several hours and will range in severity and presentation depending on the individual. Some people may also have a food aversion, which causes an unpleasant reaction in the body due to emotional associations with a particular food. People may become convinced that they are sensitive to a food, and this can be encouraged by some popular books and unorthodox practitioners. People with learning disabilities, and their family, friends and support staff, should be discouraged from attempting to restrict the person's diet due to a perceived allergy or intolerance, as this may make it

difficult for them to get all the nutrients they need. This is particularly true if foods such as milk and milk products, or bread and other cereals, are avoided. It is not easy to diagnose food allergies, and food allergy tests sold on the high street or by unqualified practitioners should be avoided.

The provision of allergy-friendly diets has been helped by the increase in availability of 'free from' food ranges in supermarkets in recent years. Allergy UK provides helpful fact sheets on allergies and intolerances, along with an advice line, on their website at allergyuk.org. Useful training on safe handling of food allergens is available for all those involved in food provision at the Food Standards Agency website.

Finger foods

The use of finger foods – foods which are presented to the person in a form that can be eaten easily by hand – is suggested as a way of preserving eating skills and promoting independence for those who have difficulty using utensils or who do not recognise the purpose of cutlery. Finger foods have the advantage of allowing food to be served at room temperature so that people can eat at their own pace. Since spills are minimised, it makes it easier to make an accurate assessment of the amount of food eaten by an individual. It is also suggested that the use of finger foods triggers people's attention and increases their physical involvement and interaction with their meal, which may encourage them to eat more. One possible solution for individuals who struggle to sit still during meals is to provide a bag or pouch they can carry with them. Or, more practically, make sure that food is always available in a readily accessible location. Some examples of finger foods are given on the opposite page. Finger foods should be easy to hold while eating. Some foods, such as breaded chicken or meat, may be too dry for some people to swallow; small, moist finger foods may be most appropriate. Avoid sugary finger foods unless they are part of a finger food meal.

Particular care needs to be taken when planning finger food diets to ensure that all nutrients are included, and advice should be taken if someone has special dietary needs. Finger foods are unlikely to be suitable for most people with swallowing difficulties.

 For more information about finger foods and other special diets, see the National Association of Care Catering. (NACC) publication 'Menu Planning & Dining in Care Homes'.

> **Particuar care needs to be taken when planning finger food diets to ensure that all nutrients are included.**

FINGER FOOD MAIN MEAL
Mini cheese and tomato frittatas with mixed salad and baby potatoes

FINGER FOOD LIGHT MEAL
Meatballs with spicy potato wedges, steamed carrot fingers and tomato salsa

FINGER FOOD SNACK
Toasted crumpet fingers with soft cheese and pineapple chunks

Finger foods

The following are examples of foods which are appropriate as finger foods.

Breads and cereals
Toast
Fingers rolls
Sandwiches
Muffins
Crumpet fingers
Crackers
Eggy bread
Fruit loaf
Teabread
Drop scones
Breakfast cereals
Cereal bars
Chapattis
Wraps
Mini pittas
Won-tons

Beans, pulses, fish, eggs, meat and other protein foods
Frittata slices
Vegetable/soya sausages
Vegetable burgers/ fingers
Quarter hard-boiled eggs
Cheese on toast
Cheese cubes
Fried bean curd cubes
Fish fingers or fishcakes
Fish sticks or crab sticks
Smoked mackerel slices
Chicken fingers from moist breast
Marinated Quorn pieces
Meatballs
Pizza
Quiche
Sliced meat, cut up into pieces
Jamaican patties
Kebab sticks
Tuna, salmon, soft cheese, hummus, pate, etc., on toast or in a sandwich

Vegetables
Carrot sticks or slices
Cooked broccoli spears
Cooked Brussels sprouts
Cooked green beans
Cooked or raw carrot sticks
Chips
Potato waffles
Small or halved new potatoes
Sweet potato wedges or slices
Red or yellow pepper slices
Fried plantain
Fried, crumbed whole mushrooms or raw button mushrooms
Sliced cucumber quartered tomato
Celery sticks
Baby sweetcorn
Vegetable kebabs
Gherkins
Pickled onions
Mange tout
Sweetcorn fitters

Fruit
Banana
Melon
Sliced apple or pear
Strawberries
Grapes
Satsuma segments
Kiwi slices
Pineapple cubes

Snacks
Dried apricots and prunes (stones removed)
Ice cream/frozen yoghurt in cones
Peanut butter sandwiches
Muesli bars
Flapjacks
Marmite on toast
Savoury snacks with dips (e.g. hummus, guacamole, salsa, yogurt and mint)

Example Day Menu – Finger Foods

Breakfast
Hard-boiled egg, buttered wholemeal toast, tomato juice, with tea or coffee

Mid-morning
Apple slices

Lunch
Spicy chicken kebabs with tortilla wrap, yogurt dip and salad leaves

Malt loaf and dried apricots

Mid-afternoon
Toasted teacake with butter and dried prunes

Tea or Coffee

Evening Meal
Thick tomato soup in a cup, cheddar cheese on wholemeal toast and cucumber sticks

Mango wedges and cornflake cakes

Bedtime
Warm milk and sliced banana

Changing food and drink textures

The type and consistency of the food served are very important to ensure that it is both acceptable and safe. There are now internationally recognised descriptors for the texture modification of food and fluids, known as the IDDSI Framework (International Dysphagia Diet Standardisation Initiative) - see the diagram opposite. This framework provides standardised terminology and definitions for all individuals in all care settings who have swallowing difficulties (dysphagia) and is designed for use by caregivers, dietitians, speech and language therapists, food service professionals, or industry to confirm the level at which a food or drink fits in. When texture modification is required, specialist advice should always be sought to ensure that the person's nutrient needs are met and the food is of the correct texture, but some general information is included here on how menus can be adapted.

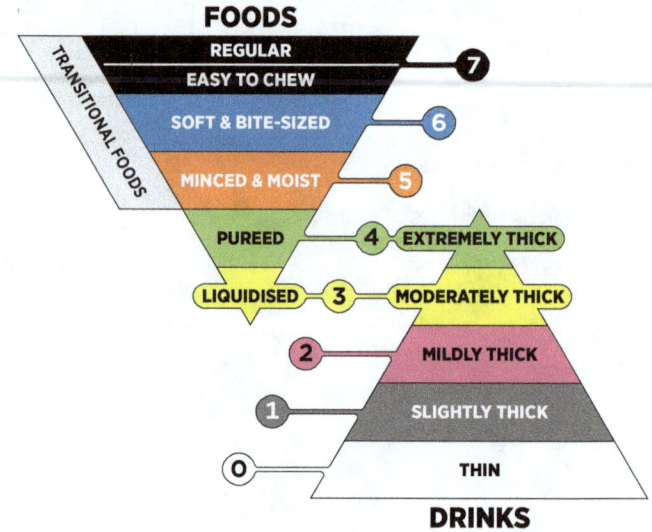

Fluid texture modification

Some people will find it difficult to manage fluids and may require fluids to be thickened. Thin fluids are those such as water, tea, coffee or squash. There are some naturally thick fluids, such as milkshakes or over-the-counter vitamin and mineral-fortified drinks, such as Complan.

For individuals requiring thickened fluid due to dysphagia, a commercial thickener will be necessary to prepare their drinks to the correct consistency (see the box on page 163 for information about thickeners). These are categorised into four different levels of thickness as follows:

Level 1 Slightly thick – Thicker than water. Flows through a straw. Requires a little more effort to drink than thin liquids.

Level 2 Mildly thick – Flows off a spoon. Sippable. Pours quickly from a spoon. Some effort is needed to suck through a straw.

Level 3 Moderately thick – Can be drunk from a cup or via a spoon. Some effort is required to suck through a straw.

Level 4 Extremely thick – Usually taken with a spoon. It can't be drunk from a cup or using a straw. Holds its shape on the spoon and falls off the spoon in a single spoonful.

Food texture modification

The way the texture of food is provided needs to be modified will vary depending on the individual's swallowing difficulty. Descriptors have been designed to categorise food into the five levels listed below:

Level 3 Liquidised – Can be eaten with a spoon or drunk from a cup. It cannot be eaten with a fork as it drips through the prongs. Smooth texture with no bits (lumps, fibres, bits of shell or skin, husk, particles of gristle or bone). No chewing required.

Level 4 Puréed – Usually eaten with a spoon (fork if possible). Does not require chewing. Smooth texture, no lumps. Holds shape on a spoon. Falls off the spoon when tilted. Holds shape on a plate. Not sticky. Liquid must not separate from solid.

Level 5 Minced and Moist – Can be eaten with a fork or spoon. Can be scooped or shaped on a plate. Small lumps are visible in the food (maximum lump size of 4mm). Lumps are easily squashed with the tongue. Minimal chewing required. Food can be easily mashed with just a little pressure from a fork, such as finely mashed fish in a thick, smooth sauce or mashed fruit.

Level 6 Soft and Bite-sized – Can be eaten with a fork or spoon. It can be mashed with a fork or spoon. A knife is not required to cut it. Chewing required. Soft, tender and moist with no separate thin liquid.

Bite-sized pieces no larger than 1.5 cm x 1.5 cm. Food can be mashed with pressure from a fork, e.g. tender meat or soft fruit.

Level 7 Easy to Chew / Regular – Normal everyday foods of soft/tender texture. Any food piece size. Able to move around in the mouth for soft chewing. Can include mixed consistency foods. Does not include hard, tough, chewy, fibrous, stringy, crunchy or crumbly bits, pips, seeds, fibrous parts of fruit, husks or bones.

The requirements of individuals with swallowing difficulties will be highly varied, and specialist advice should always be sought when a texture-modified diet is required. More information on menu planning for special diets can be found in the NACC publication 'Menu Planning & Dining in Care Homes'.

Thickeners and soaking solutions

Numerous commercial products are available that can thicken food and drink, altering their texture. Examples of thickeners currently available include Nutilis Clear, Nutilis powder (Nutricia), Thick & easy (Fresenius), Vitaquick (Vitaflo), Resource Thicken Up Clear (Nestle), Thixo D (Sutherland).

Many of these companies will provide advice and demonstrations on how to use thickeners, use food moulds (which they often provide), and prepare soaking solutions. Soaking solutions can be made from any non-lumpy liquid with thickener added and can be used on foods such as some plain bread, sandwiches, biscuits and cakes to provide a puréed texture item while maintaining the integrity of the food – for example, so that is still looks like a slice of cake.

Before considering puréed diets, advice should be sought from a dietitian and a speech and language therapist to ensure that the appropriate foods and products are used.

Texture Modified Meal providers

Producing nutritionally balanced, varied and palatable texture-modified meals can be time-consuming. Specialist commercial food companies, such as Wiltshire Farm Foods (Apetito), Mrs Gill's Kitchen, Kind Dine, NH Case, and Oakhouse Foods, provide pre-prepared meals in a complete range of food textures that can be purchased for individuals (see table below for more details).

Tips when preparing pureed diets

- Adding liquids to puréed foods dilutes their nutrient content and should be done with care. Most puréed diets will require the addition of high-energy and protein ingredients (for example, extra full-fat milk, cream cheese, polyunsaturated spread, oil, mayonnaise, full-fat yogurt or creme fraiche), but it is important to seek personalised advice for each person about what is appropriate.
- Fruits and vegetables do not need to be, and should not be, overcooked before puréeing, as this will reduce the amount of vitamins present.
- It is vital that puréed food looks attractive. The use of food moulds and food soaking solutions to prepare purées in appropriate shapes can be useful.
- It is important to purée each food separately and, as far as possible, maintain its original colour and taste.
- Puréed foods provide less sensory feedback in the mouth, due to the lack of texture. Ensuring plenty of feedback from strong flavours is usually welcome. Consider adding extra herbs, spices, and other ingredients to ensure the food tastes great.
- Particular care needs to be taken that puréed foods do not become contaminated during preparation. Good food hygiene practice is essential.

Manufacturers of dysphagia meal replacements

Brand	Manufacturer	Range	IDDSI levels	Website
It's Made for You	Oakhouse Foods	Adults	4-6	**Itsmadeforyou.co.uk**
Softer Foods	Wiltshire Farm Foods	Adults	4-6	**Wiltshirefarmfoods.com**
Simply Puree	Simply Food Solutions	Adults & Children	3-6	**Simplypuree.co.uk** (also sold via NHcase.com/special-diets)
Mrs Gill's	Mr Gill's Kitchen	Adults	3-6	**Mrgills.co.uk**

Level 4 Breakfast
Wheat bisk purée with shredless marmalade and stewed apple purée.

Level 6 Lunch
Chopped ravioli in butternut squash sauce.

Level 5 Breakfast
Scrambled pancakes soaked in maple syrup served with Greek yogurt.

Level 4 Dinner
Cheese soufflé purée with mashed potato purée and creamy broccoli purée.

Level 6 Breakfast
Porridge with chopped canned prunes in juice

Level 5 Dinner
Minced broccoli rice and tofu.

Level 4 Lunch
Fish in parsley sauce purée with sweet potato purée and leek purée.

Level 6 Dinner
Pea and mint risotto.

Level 5 Lunch
Creamy chicken and vegetable soup with pesto mash.

Level 6 Dinner
Flaked fish in parsley sauce with mashed sweet potato and creamed spinach.

Examples of high-risk foods that may need to be avoided if a texture-modified diet is required

Always seek professional advice

Stringy, fibrous textures: Pineapple, runner beans, celery, rhubarb, and steak.

Vegetable and fruit skins: Baked beans, broad beans, black eyed beans, soya beans, grapes, peas, sweetcorn, and apples with peel.

Mixed consistency foods: Minestrone soup or cereals that do not blend with milk, e.g., muesli, mince with thin gravy.

Crunchy foods: Toast, dry biscuits, crisps, popcorn, flaky pastry, raw carrot, raw apple.

Crispy foods: Crackling, dry cereal, crispy bacon.

Crumbly items: Pie crusts, bread crusts, cakes, or dry biscuits, crumble topping, and scones.

Chewy foods: Marshmallows, chewy sweets or toffees, cheese chunks, chew bars, breakfast bars, chewing gum, chewy meat, e.g. crispy duck, cooked hard cheese, e.g. cheddar.

Hard foods: Boiled sweets, toffees, nuts or seeds, raw vegetables, hard crusty bread rolls.

Floppy Texture: Lettuce, cucumber, baby spinach leaves.

Husk: Sweetcorn, bran, bread with grains or seeds.

Sticky / Gummy foods: Nut butters, sticky rice.

Round or long foods: Whole grapes, sausages.

Foods containing bone or gristle.

Foods with a variety of textures: Hamburger, hotdog, pizza, spaghetti with meatballs, sandwich.

Juicy foods: Watermelon.

Adapted from Complete IDDSI framework detailed definitions 2.0 2019

Example Day Menu for an adult on Level 4 pureed texture

Breakfast
Egg purée and creamy mushroom sauce, soaked buttered toast, thickened vegetable juice with tea or coffee

Mid-morning
Thickened creamy chicken soup purée, thickened milky drink

Lunch
Salmon pâté purée, mashed potato purée, beetroot purée
Gooseberry fool (strained)

Mid-afternoon
Macaroni cheese purée and puréed can of tomatoes

Evening Meal
Spaghetti Bolognaise purée with pea and carrot purée
Stewed plum purée with custard

Bedtime
Thickened milky drink

CHAPTER 11 – Special Diets | 165

References

1. Food Standards Agency (2021). *Food allergy and intolerance.* Available at: https://www.food.gov.uk/safety-hygiene/food-allergy-and-intolerance

2. Peters, R.L., Krawiec, M., et al. (2021). Update on food allergy. *Pediatric Allergy and Immunology,* 32(4), pp.647–657. https://doi.org/10.1111/pai.13443

3. Sicherer, S.H. and Sampson, H.A. (2018). Food allergy: A review and Update on epidemiology, pathogenesis, diagnosis, prevention, and Management. *The Journal of Allergy and Clinical Immunology,* 141(1), pp.41–58. https://doi.org/10.1016/j.jaci.2017.11.003

4. The British Society for Allergy & Clinical Immunology (BSACI) (2021). Available at: **https://www.bsaci.org/**

5. British Dietetic Association (2021). *Food Allergy Testing Food Fact Sheet.* Available at: **https://www.bda.uk.com/resource/food-allergy-intolerance-testing.html**

6. Abdelhamid, A., Bunn, D., Copley, M., et al. (2016). Effectiveness of interventions to directly support food and drink intake in people with dementia: systematic review and meta-analysis. *BMC Geriatrics,* 16(1). **https://doi.org/10.1186/s12877-016-0196-3**

7. The International Dysphagia Diet Standardisation Initiative Framework (IDDSI) (2024). Available at: **https://www.iddsi.org/standards/framework**

8. European Food Safety Authority (EFSA) (2010). Scientific Opinion on Dietary Reference Values for water. EFSA Journal, 8(3). **https://doi.org/10.2903/j.efsa.2010.1459**

9. British Dietetic Association (2020). *Fluid (water and drinks).* Available at: **https://www.bda.uk.com/resource/fluid-water-drinks.html**

10. Ruxton, C.H. and Hart, V.A. (2011). Black tea is not significantly different from water in the maintenance of normal hydration in human subjects: results from a randomised controlled trial. *British Journal of Nutrition,* 106(4), pp.588–595. **https://doi.org/10.1017/s0007114511000456**

Good sources of Nutrients (based on average adult servings)

	Good (>30% RI)		Source of (15-30% RI)	
Vitamin A	■ Liver* ■ Liver Pâté* ■ Liver sausage ■ Carrots	■ Spinach ■ Sweet potatoes ■ Canteloupe Melon	■ Mango ■ Canned apricots ■ Margarine ■ Butter	■ Cheese ■ Kidney ■ Kale ■ Eggs
Vitamin A	■ Herrings ■ Mackerel ■ Roe ■ Sardines	■ Trout ■ Fresh tuna ■ Salmon ■ Eggs	■ Fortified breakfast cereals ■ Fortified Yoghurts ■ Liver Pâté*	■ Margarine ■ Fortified Malted drinks
B Vitamins – Thiamin	■ Potatoes ■ Pork, bacon and ham		■ Fortified breakfast cereals ■ White or Wholemeal bread ■ Yeast extract ■ Currant buns ■ Nuts	■ Peas ■ Oranges ■ Liver* ■ Malted drinks
Riboflavin	■ Liver* ■ Kidney ■ Quorn	■ Milk ■ Eggs	■ Malted drinks ■ Lean meat or poultry ■ Yogurt	■ Almonds ■ Fortified breakfast cereals
Niacin	■ Salmon ■ Tuna ■ Sardines ■ Herrings ■ Chicken	■ Liver* ■ Bacon ■ Kidneys ■ Lean meat	■ Brown rice ■ Wholemeal bread ■ Nuts (especially peanuts) ■ Peanut Butter	■ Fortified breakfast cereals ■ Liver sausage ■ Yeast extract
Vitamin B6	■ Chicken ■ Bran flakes		■ Bananas ■ White fish ■ Pork ■ Tuna	■ Avocado ■ Fortified breakfast cereals
Vitamin B12	■ Liver* ■ Kidney ■ Oily fish ■ White fish ■ Red Meat ■ Turkey ■ Bacon and sausage	■ Eggs ■ Milk ■ Cheese ■ Bran Flakes ■ Some plant based milks ■ Nori seaweed	■ Pork ■ Marmite	
Folate	■ Liver* ■ Kidney ■ Spinach ■ Broccoli ■ Yeast extract ■ Brussels sprouts	■ Cabbage ■ Asparagus ■ Runner beans ■ Cauliflower ■ Wheat bisks ■ Orange	■ Most fortified breakfast cereals eg. Cornflakes ■ Beef ■ Parsnip ■ Potatoes ■ Ackee ■ Peanuts	■ Wholemeal Bread ■ Green leafy salads ■ Peas ■ Chickpeas ■ Kidney beans ■ Avocado

* As these foods can contain high levels of vitamin A, it is suggested that they are not eaten more than once a week. Anyone who is pregnant should avoid eating liver and liver pâté (and avoid dietary supplements which contain vitamin A), as very high intakes may damage the foetus.

	Good (>30% RI)		Source of (15-30% RI)	
Vitamin C	■ Blackcurrants ■ Orange (and orange juice) ■ Strawberries ■ Guava, Kiwi fruit ■ Mango, Pineapple ■ Grapefruit ■ Spring Greens	■ Green and red peppers ■ Satsuma, Peaches ■ Broccoli, Cabbage ■ Cauliflower ■ Brussels sprouts ■ Potatoes	■ Peas ■ Watercress ■ Spinach ■ Tomato ■ Ackee	
Iron	■ Liver* ■ Kidney ■ Liver Pâté* ■ Wheat bisks		■ Fortified breakfast cereals ■ Corned beef ■ Sardines ■ Soya beans and Edamame beans	■ Spring greens ■ Quinoa
Calcium	■ Sardines ■ Cheese ■ Tofu ■ Yoghurt	■ Milk ■ Soya drink fortified with calcium	■ Green leafy vegetables	
Zinc	■ Liver* ■ Lean lamb ■ Corned beef		■ Ham ■ Poultry ■ Canned Sardines	■ Kidney ■ Cheese ■ Wholegrain bread
	High Fibre (more than 6g per 100g)		Source of (more than 3g per 100g)	
Fibre	■ Wholegrain or wholewheat breakfast cereals eg bran flakes, wheat bisks, shreddies, shredded wheat, sultana bran ■ Puffed wheat cereal ■ Dried figs ■ Wholemeal bread	■ Chick peas ■ Muesli ■ Kidney beans ■ Lentils ■ Broad beans ■ Quorn ■ Chia seeds ■ Dried dates ■ Quinoa ■ Flaxseeds / linseeds	■ Brown bread ■ White bread with added fibre ■ Wholemeal pasta ■ Baked beans ■ Blackberries ■ Prunes ■ Dried apricots ■ Fresh or frozen peas ■ Sweetcorn ■ Broccoli	■ Brussels sprouts ■ Humous ■ Canned peas ■ Edamame beans ■ Sweet potato ■ Cabbage ■ Carrots ■ Almonds ■ Sunflower seeds ■ Potato crisps

* Liver and liver pâté are very rich in vitamin A, and it is recommended that these foods be consumed no more than once a week.

APPENDIX 1 – Good sources of Nutrients

Resources
Organisations

There are many organisations which offer help and support related to specific learning disabilities, and we are unable to list them all here. General information and advice on learning disability issues, specific learning disabilities and on local organisations can be obtained from Mencap (see contact details on page 169).

Age UK
T: 0800678 1602
E: contact@ageuk.org.uk
www.ageuk.org.uk

Allergy UK
T: 01322 619898
E: info@allergyuk.org
www.allergyuk.org

Alzheimer's Society
T: 0333 150 3456
www.alzheimers.org.uk

Association for Real Change (ARC)
T: 01246 555043
E: contact.us@arcuk.org.uk
www.arcuk.org.uk

ARC Northern Ireland
T: 028 9038 0960
E: arc.ni@arcuk.org.uk
www.arcuk.org.uk

ARC Scotland
T: 0131 663 4444
E: arc.scotland@arcuk.org.uk
www.arcscotland.org.uk

Asthma + Lung UK
Helpline: 0300 222 5800
E: helpline@asthmaandlung.org.uk
www.asthmaandlung.org.uk

Beat Eating Disorders
(formerly the Eating Disorders Association)
T: 0300 123 3355
E: help@beateatingdisorders.org.uk
www.beateatingdisorders.org.uk

British Dietetic Association
T: 0121 200 8080
E: info@bda.uk.com
www.bda.uk.com

British Heart Foundation
T: 0300 330 3322
E: heretohelp@bhf.org.uk
www.bhf.org.uk

British Institute for Learning Disability (BILD)
T: 0121 415 6960
E: enquiries@bild.org.uk
www.bild.org.uk

British Nutrition Foundation
T: 020 7557 7930
www.nutrition.org.uk

British Society for Special Care Dentistry
(Formerly the British Society for Disability and Oral Health)
T: 01302 578 838
E: info@bsscd.org.uk
www.bsscd.org/specialcaredentistry

Care Quality Commission
T: 03000 616161
E: enquiries@cqc.org.uk
www.cqc.org.uk

Care Rights UK
(Formerly known as The Relatives and Residents Association)
Helpline: 0207 359 8148
E: team@carerightsuk.org
www.carerightsuk.org

Carers UK
T: 020 7378 4999
E: info@carersuk.org
www.carersuk.org

Cerebral Palsy UK
E: info@cerebralpalsy.org.uk
www.cerebralpalsy.org.uk

Change
T: 0113 244 060
E: info@changepeople.org
www.changepeople.co.uk

Chartered Institute of Environmental Health
T: 020 7827 5800
www.cieh.org

Coeliac UK
T: 0333 332 2033
www.coeliac.org.uk

Coram Family and Childcare
(Formerly known as Daycare Trust)
T: 020 7239 7535
E: info@coramfamilyandchildcare.org.uk
www.coramfamilyandchildcare.org.uk

Department of Health and Social Care
T: 0300 790 4007
E: dhsc.publicenquiries@dhsc.gov.uk
www.gov.uk/government/organisations/department-of-health-and-social-care

Dementia UK
T: 0800 888 6678
E: helpline@dementiauk.org
www.dementiauk.org

Diabetes UK
T: 0345 123 2399
E: helpline@diabetes.org.uk
www.diabetes.org.uk

Disability Rights Commission
DRC Helpline
T: 08457 622 633
Textphone: 08457 622 644
www.drc.org.uk

The Diverse Nutrition Association
E: info@diversenutritionassociation.com
www.diversenutritionassociation.com

Down's Syndrome Association
T: 0333 1212 300
E: info@downs-syndrome.org.uk
www.downs-syndrome.org.uk

Down's Syndrome Scotland
T: 0300 030 2121
E: info@dsscotland.org.uk
www.dsscotland.org.uk

The Elfrida Society
T: 020 7359 7443
E: elfrida@elfrida.com
www.elfrida.com

Enable
T: 0300 0200 101
E: enabledirect@enable.org.uk
www.enable.org.uk

FAIR (Family Advice and Information Resource)
T: 0131 622 1962
E: fair@fairadvice.org.uk
www.fairadvice.org.uk

Foetal Alcohol Spectrum Disorder Network
(Formerly known as Foetal Alcohol Syndrome Aware UK)
T: 07743 380163
E: fasdnetwork@mail.com
www.fasdnetwork.org

Food Standards Agency
T: 0330 332 7149
www.food.gov.uk

Foundation for People with Learning Disabilities
E: fpld@fpld.org.uk
www.learningdisabilities.org.uk

The Fragile X Society
T: 01371875100
E: info@fragilex.org.uk
www.fragilex.org.uk

Freelance Dietitians
www.bda.uk.com/find-a-dietian

Headway
T: 0808 800 2244
E: helpline@headway.org.uk
www.headway.org.uk

Hospital Caterers Association
E: HCA@lansdownepublishing.com
E: NatSecretary@hospitalcaterers.org
www.hospitalcaterers.org

Klinefelter's Association
T: 0300 111 4748
www.ksa-uk.net

Mencap
T: 020 7454 0454
www.mencap.org.uk

Mental Health Foundation
T: 020 7803 1100
E: info@mentalhealth.org.uk
www.mentalhealth.org.uk

MIND
Mind info line: 0300 123 3393
E: info@mind.org.uk
www.mind.org.uk

National Association of Care Catering
T: 08707 480 180
E: info@thenacc.co.uk
www.thenacc.co.uk

National Autistic Society
T: 0207 833 2299
www.autism.org.uk

National Network of Parent Carer Forums
(Formerly known as the National Family Carer Network)
www.nnpcf.org.uk

National Institute for Health and Clinical Excellence (NICE)
E: nice@nice.org.uk
www.nice.org.uk

The National Society for Epilepsy
T: 01494 601 300
Helpline: 01481 601 400
E: helpline@epilepsysociety.org.uk
www.epilepsysociety.org.uk

National Society Phenylketonuria
T: 0303 0401090
E: info@nspku.org
www.nspku.org

NHS 111
(Formerly known as NHS Direct)
T: 111
www.111.nhs.uk

Nutrition Society
T: 020 7602 0228
E: office@nutritionsociety.org
www.nutritionsociety.org

PAMIS (Promoting a more inclusive society)
T: 03308 181081
E: info@pamis.org.uk
www.pamis.org.uk

Prader-Willi Syndrome Association
T: 01332365676
E: admin@pwsa.co.uk
www.pwsa.co.uk

Public Health Scotland
(Formerly known as NHS Health Scotland)
T: 0345 646 0238
www.healthscotland.scot

ResCare
T: 07789416604
E: office@rescare.org.uk
www.rescare.org.uk

Rett UK
T: 01582 798911
E: support@rettuk.org
www.rettuk.org

Royal College of Nursing (RCN)
T: 0345 772 6100
E: rcnfoundation@rcn.org.uk
www.rcn.org.uk

Royal College of Occupational Therapists
T: 020 3141 4600
E: hello@rcot.co.uk
www.rcot.co.uk

Royal College of Paediatrics and Child Health
T: 020 7092 6000
E: enquiries@rcpch.ac.uk
www.rcpch.ac.uk

Royal College of Psychiatrists
T: 020 8618 4020
E: pss@rcpsych.ac.uk
www.rcpsych.ac.uk

Royal College of Speech and Language Therapists
T: 020 7378 1200
E: info@rcslt.org
www.rcslt.org

The Royal Society of Public Health
T: 020 7265 7300
E: info@rsph.org.uk
www.rsph.org.uk

SCOPE
Helpline: 0808 800 3333
E: helpline@scope.org.uk
www.scope.org.uk

Scottish Consortium for Learning Disability
T: 0141 248 3733
E: admin@scld.co.uk
www.scld.org.uk

SENSE
T: 0300 330 9250
E: info@sense.org.uk
www.sense.org.uk

Thrive
T: 0118 988 5688
E: info@thrive.org.uk
www.thrive.org.uk

Tuberous Sclerosis Association
T: 0808 801 0700
E: support@tuberous-sclerosis.org
www.tuberous-sclerosis.org

Turner Syndrome Support Society
T: 0141 952 8006
E: turner.syndrome@tss.org.uk
www.tss.org.uk

Turning Point
T: 020 7481 7600
www.turning-point.co.uk

United Response
T: 01803 868550
E: info@unitedresponse.org.uk
www.unitedresponse.org.uk

Vegan Society
T: 0121 523 1730
E: info@vegansociety.com
www.vegansociety.com

Vegetarian Society
T: 0161 925 2000
E: hello@vegsoc.org
www.vegsoc.org

Resources

Recipes and Cookbooks

BBC
This resource offers a variety of recipes and includes some helpful videos on food preparation techniques (e.g., chopping an onion).
www.bbc.co.uk/food

Care to Cook – accessible recipes
www.caretocook.co.uk/accessible-recipes

Cook As You Are – By Ruby Tandoh
117 accessible, affordable, non-aspirational recipes, helping you find ways of cooking (and enjoying it!) no matter your budget, skill or the state of your kitchen.
www.goodreads.com/book/show/56646769-cook-as-you-are

Eileen's Kitchen Table
These text-free cookbooks contain simple, economical & nutritious recipes that are presented to the user through a series of photographs. Each recipe includes a detachable shopping list.
www.eileenskitchentable.ie/cookbooks

EyUp! in partnership with the SWYPT
This charity sells easy-read Cook and Eat recipe books, depending on the size of the meal, as well as for baking.
www.eyupcharity.org/shop

Focus on Undernutrition App
A free app available to download from the Google Play Store and the Apple App Store. Includes downloadable resources, recipe cards, masterclasses and videos from the Health Kitchen.

Food – a Fact of Life
Accessible recipes and videos
www.foodafactoflife.org.uk/pupils-with-additional-needs/recipes-and-videos/

Widget Symbol Resource Packs – Food
A selection of easy read recipes to download.
www.widgit.com/resources/lifeskills/food/index.htm

Eating well: resources for family, friends, support staff and health professionals

British Dietetic Association
This resource features food fact sheets related to specific conditions, providing dietary suggestions.
www.bda.uk.com/food-health/food-facts/all-food-fact-sheets.html

Food – A Fact of Life
This website provides cooking skills videos, educational resources and interactive games, run by the British Nutrition Foundation, with a specific section for those with additional needs.
www.foodafactoflife.org.uk

Healthier Families *(Previously Change4Life)*
Easy ways to eat well and move more. It includes colourful and straightforward recipe ideas, quizzes, and a sugar scanner app.
www.nhs.uk/healthier-families

Healthy Eating Healthy Living pack – Scottish Commission for People with Learning Disabilities
A training pack designed to encourage healthy eating as a way of life for people with learning disabilities. The pack provides all the materials needed to run a course on Healthy Eating and Healthy Living, teaching participants the knowledge and skills required to eat a healthy and balanced diet.
www.scld.org.uk/healthy-eating-healthy-living-pack

Me at Mealtimes
A leaflet designed to support conversations around mealtimes for those who are finding managing meals difficult.
www.wwl.nhs.uk/media/.leaflets/5ffd5b58b83a54.88594120.pdf

Menu Planning: As Easy as 1, 2, 3 by Pamela McIntosh
A practical resource for individuals with learning disabilities to use with their supporters to plan a healthy eating menu.
www.amazon.co.uk/Menu-Planning-Easy-Pamela-McIntosh/dp/1908993561

PEACE
PEACE is a Pathway for Eating Disorders and Autism developed from Clinical Experience. This pathway supports autistic people suffering from an eating disorder, their loved ones and their clinicians.
www.peacepathway.org

Replica Food
Life-sized food models and replicas.
www.replica.co.uk

Talking Mats
Eating and Drinking themed visual resource for food-related conversations and decision-making.
www.talkingmats.com

Games and activities – Healthy eating games are available from educational resource suppliers such as www.sensorywise.co.uk and www.tts-group.co.uk

Eating well: resources for people with learning disabilities

A Picture of Health
This resource uses easy-to-read fact sheets on healthy eating.
www.apictureofhealth.southwest.nhs.uk/healthy-life-styles/diet

Books Beyond Words – co-created word-free picture stories for people with learning disabilities. Titles available include:
- Cooking with friends
- Getting on with Type 1 Diabetes
- Getting on with Type 2 Diabetes
- Looking After My Heart
- Moving More and Feeling Good
- Rose Gets in Shape
- The Trouble with Poo

www.booksbeyondwords.co.uk

Easy Health
Easy read health information (leaflets and videos) about common health conditions.
www.easyhealth.org.uk/pages/easy-read-health-leaflets-and-films

Eatwell Plate
The Eatwell Guide illustrates the recommended proportions of food groups in our overall diet to achieve a healthy, balanced diet.
www.nhs.uk/live-well/eat-well/the-eatwell-guide/
An interactive version is available at https://fss-eatwellguide.scot/

Marianne's Plate (Previously Healthy Portion Plate)
This is a 10" melamine plate showing portion sizes of each food group and weight. It has pictorial and empty versions, making it easy to understand.
www.mariannesplate.com/

A Healthier Me – Mencap
A downloadable resource pack to help start your journey to making healthier choices. It includes healthy eating information, activities, recipes and a meal planner.
www.mencap.org.uk/ahealthierme

NHS Food Scanner App – Download the free app and start making healthier choices today. Available for download from the Apple App Store or Google Play Store.

Poobusters Constipation Video – NHS Derbyshire Healthcare
This is an accessible video for people with a Learning Disability, to facilitate conversation around constipation and what to do about it.
www.youtube.com/watch?v=R16WY6MLBBU

See and Eat
SEE & EAT books each showcase a different vegetable's journey from farm to fork. The website includes a link to Mole's Veggie Adventure, a free nutritional education app.
www.seeandeat.org

Oral Health & Dysphagia

British Society for Special Care Dentistry
Guidelines for Oral Health Care for People with Learning Disabilities.
www.bsscd.org/specialcaredentistry/

Leicestershire Partnership eating and drinking risk assessment
A single-page risk assessment tool with space for recommendations pertaining to each identified risk.
https://webarchive.nationalarchives.gov.uk/ukgwa/20160831135534/http://www.improvinghealthandlives.org.uk/adjustments/index.php?adjustment=375

Mouthcare assessment and mouthcare plan – Public Health Wales
www.phw.nhs.wales/services-and-teams/dental-public-health/gwen-am-byth/mouthcare-assessment-and-mouthcare-plan/

Mouthcare for children with swallowing problems – All Wales Special Interest Group
www.sigwales.org/wp-content/uploads/dysphagia-child-mouthcare-booklet3.pdf

Mouthcare Matters
Website from Health Education England which includes a Mouthcare Recording and Assessment Tool alongside factsheets on topics such as:
- Supporting people with a neuro-disability to maintain good oral health
- Cleaning the mouth of an adult with a neuro-disability
- Dry mouth in adults with a neuro-disability
- Lip and tongue biting in people with a neuro-disability
- Oral Hypersensitivity
- Reduced saliva control in adults with a neuro-disability (drooling)
- Care-resistant behaviour towards mouth care in people with a neuro-disability
- Safe Oral Suctioning in Adults with a Neuro-disability
- Denture care for adults with a neuro-disability

www.mouthcarematters.hee.nhs.uk/links-resources/neuro-disability-resources/index.html

Swallowing difficulties
Website designed to provide a source of information for prescribing and administering medicines to patients with dysphagia.
www.swallowingdifficulties.com

Recipe Ideas for those with dysphagia
Available from:

Nutilis – www.nutricia.co.uk/patients-carers/recipes.html

Oak House – www.oakhouse-kitchen.com/dysphagia-recipe-hub/

Premier Foods - www.hospitalcaterers.org/media/2153/international_dysphagia_diet_standards.pdf

Videofluoroscopy
This easy-read booklet explains what a videofluoroscopy is. A consent form is also included.
https://webarchive.nationalarchives.gov.uk/ukgwa/20160704190734/https://www.improvinghealthandlives.org.uk/adjustments/index.php?adjustment=382

Suppliers of specialist eating and drinking equipment, thickeners and soaking solutions for puréed diets

Ableworld
www.ableworld.co.uk

Healthcare Pro
www.healthcarepro.co.uk

Living Made Easy
www.livingmadeeasy.org.uk

Neater
www.neater.co.uk

Nottingham Rehab Supplies (NRS)
www.nrs-uk.co.uk

Nutilis: Nutricia Clinical Care
www.nutricia.co.uk

Thick & Easy: Fresenius Kabi Ltd
www.fresenius-kabi.co.uk

Vitaflo: Nestle Health Science
www.vitaflo.co.uk

Special diets and conditions

Books

Can't Eat, Won't Eat – Dietary Difficulties and Autistic Spectrum Disorders
B Legge (2002)
Published by Jessica Kingsley. ISBN 978 18533029745.

Helping Your Child with Extreme Picky Eating: A Step-by-Step Guide for Overcoming Selective Eating, Food Aversion, and Feeding Disorders
K Rowell (2015)
Published by New Harbinger. ISBN 10 162625110X

The Fun with Food Programme: Therapeutic Intervention for Children with Aversion to Oral Feeding
A McCurtin (2017)
Published by Speedmark Publishing Ltd. ISBN 13 978 0 86388 5662.

The Allergy-Free Family Cookbook: 100 delicious recipes free from dairy, eggs, peanuts, tree nuts, soya, gluten, sesame and shellfish
F Heggie (2015)
Published by Orion. ISBN 10 1409155811

Digital

Diabetes UK – Resources and tools to improve care for people with diabetes and a learning disability.
www.diabetes.org.uk/for-professionals/improving-care/good-practice/for-people-with-learning-disability

Gluten Free Food Checker App – free to download for members of Coeliac UK.

Nutritional screening

MUST tool
The MUST tool is widely used in community settings by health professionals to determine nutritional status.
www.bapen.org.uk

SANSI Tool
A validated Nutritional screening tool (SANSI), which can be used as an alternative to the MUST tool, to ensure the additional nutritional risks prevalent in mental health settings can be identified.
www.stah.org/assets/SANSI-Paper-version-2025.pdf

The Patients Association Nutrition Checklist
The Checklist helps patients, families, and staff working in health and social care identify the potential risk of undernutrition in adults, and provides signposting to information and sources of help to those likely to be at risk.
There are two versions of the checklist: one for use by patients and their families, and the other for healthcare professionals, social care staff, and volunteers supporting them.
www.patients-association.org.uk/patients-association-nutrition-checklist-toolkit

The Nutrition Wheel
Providing an interactive version of the tool mentioned above, the Nutrition Wheel is a wipeable tool designed for use by supporters working with older people. It aims to identify people at risk of malnutrition through having a conversation. For people at risk, it also guides the supporter to provide straightforward advice and signposting to help the older person improve their nutrition.
www.malnutritiontaskforce.org.uk/nutrition-wheel

For local screening tools, talk with your hospital or community dietitian, who can recommend suitable tools to use.

Hydration

National Hydration Association
www.malnutritiontaskforce.org.uk/national-hydration-association

Pregnancy, breastfeeding, children and families

www.healthystart.nhs.uk
www.nhs.uk/start-for-life/
www.firststepsnutrition.org
www.nhs.uk/healthier-families/

Catering and menu planning

Catering for Health and Care (Northern Ireland)
www.food.gov.uk/business-guidance/nutritional-standards-for-catering-in-health-and-social-care

BDA Digest
Produced by the British Dietetic Association, this resource provides expert knowledge and support for all involved in the provision of food and drink services in healthcare.
www.bda.uk.com/practice-and-education/the-nutrition-and-hydration-digest.html
www.bda.uk.com/practice-and-education/mental-health-learning-disability-inpatients.html

Training Provision

Challenging Weight Stigma Learning Hub - Public Health Scotland
https://learning.publichealthscotland.scot/course/view.php?id=622

Diabetes
https://cpd.diabetes.org.uk/

Focus on Undernutrition
Dietetic-led online training for care staff and caterers in care homes. Topics include management of undernutrition, dysphagia, menu planning and special diets.
https://training.focusonundernutrition.co.uk/

Healthy Weight – NHS England online training at E-learning for health.
'Supporting healthy weight in an adult with a learning disability'
www.e-lfh.org.uk/programmes/supporting-healthy-weight-in-an-adult-with-a-learning-disability

Weight Monitoring Chart

Name: ....

Date of birth: .... Height: ....

How is this person weighed? (hoist/wheelchair scales/in slippers/before breakfast, etc.): ....
....

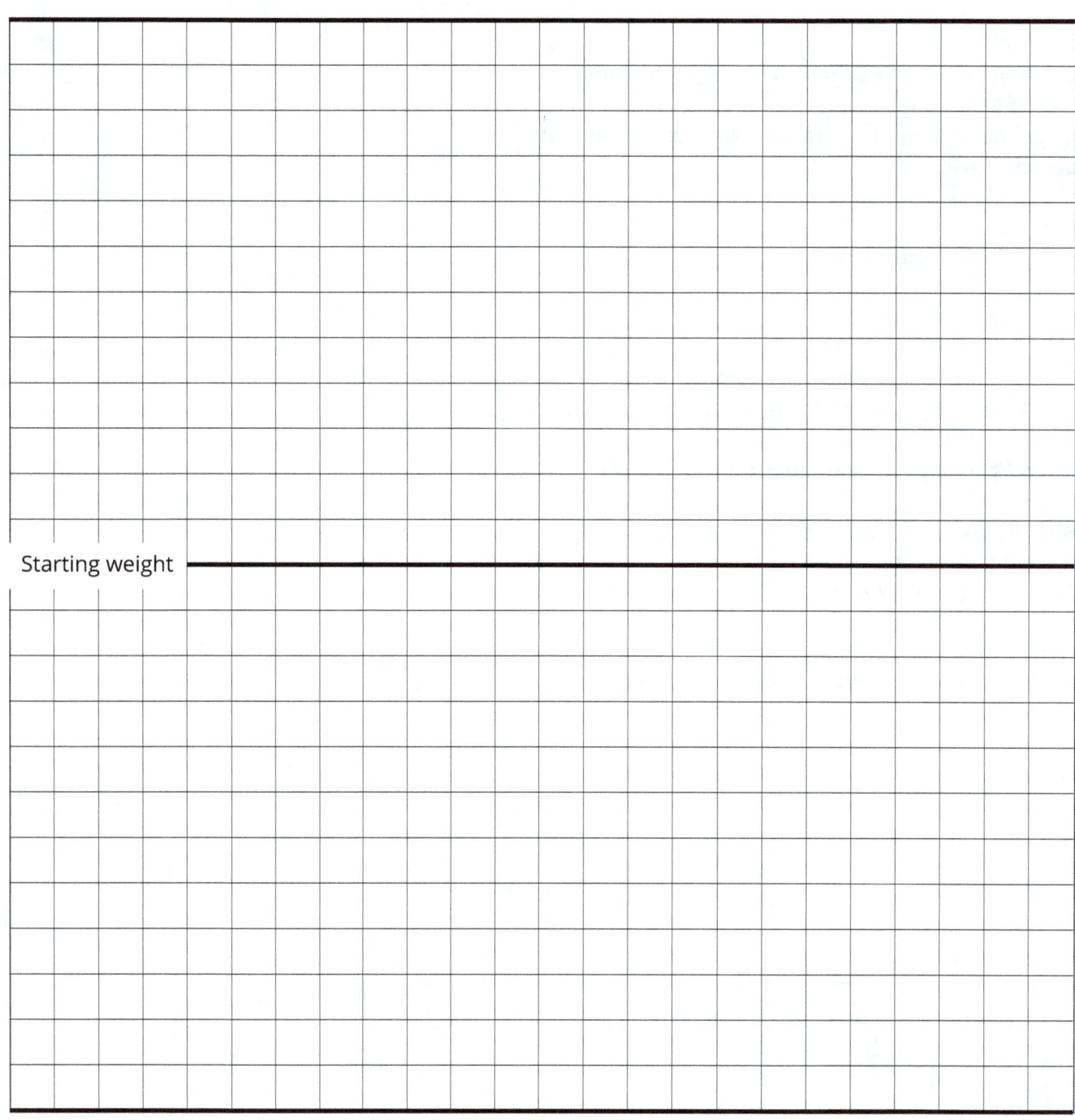

178 | APPENDIX 3 – Weight Monitoring Chart

Food, Fluid, Bowel & Symptom Chart

Name: ....

Date:	**Food** Include portion size, type, and brand. *Document food offered and what was eaten*	**Drink** Include amount, type and brand. *Document fluids offered and what was drunk*	**Behaviours** e.g. rubbing sides of tummy, crying, screaming.	**Bowels** e.g. type / hard, soft, watery. Amount: large/medium/small/smear **Symptoms** e.g. eczema, reflux, vomiting.
Breakfast				
Mid-morning				
Lunch				
Mid-afternoon				
Evening Meal				
Supper				

Health and Social Care Act 2008 (Regulated Activities) Regulations 2014: Regulation 14: Meeting nutritional and hydration needs

The regulation in full

14. –

1. The nutritional and hydration needs of service users must be met.
2. Paragraph (1) applies where –
   a. care or treatment involves –
      the provision of accommodation by the service provider, or an overnight stay for the service user on premises used by the service for the purposes of carrying on a regulated activity, or
   b. the meeting of the nutritional or hydration needs of service users is part of the arrangements made for the provision of care or treatment by the service provider.
3. But paragraph (1) does not apply to the extent that the meeting of such nutritional or hydration needs would –
   a. result in a breach of regulation 11, or
   b. not be in the service user's best interests.
4. For the purposes of paragraph (1), "nutritional and hydration needs" means –
   a. receipt by a service user of suitable and nutritious food and hydration which is adequate to sustain life and good health,
   b. receipt by a service user of parenteral nutrition and dietary supplements when prescribed by a health care professional,
   c. the meeting of any reasonable requirements of a service user for food and hydration arising from the service user's preferences or their religious or cultural background, and
   d. if necessary, support for a service user to eat or drink.
5. Section 4 of the 2005 Act (best interests) applies for the purposes of determining the best interests of a service user who is 16 or over under this regulation as it applies for the purposes of that Act.

Guidance for the implementation of this regulation from the Care Quality Commission (CQC):

This sets out the guidance that providers must have regard to against the relevant component of the regulation.

14(1) The nutritional and hydration needs of service users must be met.

Guidance on 14(1)

- Providers must include people's nutrition and hydration needs when they make an initial assessment of their care, treatment and support needs and in the ongoing review of these. The assessment and review should include risks related to people's nutritional and hydration needs.
- Providers should have a food and drink strategy that addresses the nutritional needs of people using the service.

14(2) Paragraph 1 applies where –

(a) care or treatment involves –

the provision of accommodation by the service provider, or

an overnight stay for the service user on premises used by the service for the purposes of carrying on a regulated activity, or

(b) the meeting of the nutritional or hydration needs of service users is part of the arrangements made for the provision of care or treatment by the service provider.

Guidance on 14(2)

- Providers must meet people's nutrition or hydration needs wherever an overnight stay is provided as part of the regulated activity or where nutrition or hydration are provided as part of the arrangements made for the person using the service.

14(3) But paragraph (1) does not apply to the extent that the meeting of such nutritional or hydration needs would –

(a) result in a breach of regulation 11, or

(b) not be in the service user's best interests.

Guidance on 14(3)

- Providers must follow people's consent wishes if they refuse nutrition and hydration unless a best interests decision has been made under the Mental Capacity Act 2005. Other forms of authority, such as advance decisions, should also be taken into account.

- CQC recognises that some services may vary the way they apply this regulation to take account of people's assessed needs and wishes. This includes specialist eating disorder services and some palliative care or end-of-life situations.

14(4) For the purposes of paragraph (1), "nutritional and hydration needs" means –

14(4)(a) receipt by a service user of suitable and nutritious food and hydration which is adequate to sustain life and good health,

Guidance on 14(4)(a)

- Nutrition and hydration assessments must be carried out by people with the required skills and knowledge. The assessments should follow nationally recognised guidance and identify, as a minimum:

- requirements to sustain life, support the agreed care and treatment, and support ongoing good health,

- dietary intolerances, allergies, and medication contraindications, and

- how to support people's good health, including the level of support needed, timing of meals, and the provision of appropriate and sufficient quantities of food and drink.

- Nutrition and hydration needs should be regularly reviewed during the course of care and treatment, and any changes in people's needs should be responded to in good time.

- A variety of nutritious, appetising food should be available to meet people's needs and be served at an appropriate temperature. When a person lacks capacity, they must have prompts, encouragement and help to eat as appropriate.

- Where a person is assessed as needing a specific diet, this must be provided in line with that assessment. Nutritional and hydration intake should be monitored and recorded to prevent unnecessary dehydration, weight loss or weight gain. Action must be taken without delay to address any concerns.

- Staff must follow the most up-to-date nutrition and hydration assessment for each person and take appropriate action if people are not eating and drinking in line with their assessed needs.

- Staff should know how to determine whether specialist nutritional advice is required and how to access and follow it.

- Water must be available and accessible to people at all times. Other drinks should be made available periodically throughout the day and night, and people should be encouraged and supported to drink.

- Arrangements should be made for people to receive their meals at a different time if they are absent or asleep when their meals are served.

- Snacks or other food should be available between meals for those who prefer to eat 'little and often'.

14(4)(b) receipt by a service user of parenteral nutrition and dietary supplements when prescribed by a health care professional,

Guidance on 14(4)(b)

- Providers must have systems to make sure that people using the service receive their prescribed parenteral nutrition and dietary supplements at the specified times.

- Parenteral nutrition and dietary supplements must only be administered by appropriately qualified, skilled, competent and experienced staff.

14(4)(c) the meeting of any reasonable requirements of a service user for food and hydration arising from the service user's preferences or their religious or cultural background, and

Guidance on 14(4)(c)

- People should be able to make choices about their diet.

- People's religious and cultural needs must be identified in their nutrition and hydration assessment, and these needs must be met. If there are any clinical contraindications or risks posed because of any of these requirements, these should be discussed with the person to allow them to make informed choices about their requirements.

- When a person has specific dietary requirements relating to moral or ethical beliefs, such as vegetarianism, these requirements must be fully considered and met. Every effort should be made to meet people's preferences, including preference about what time meals are served, where they are served and the quantity.

14(4)(d) if necessary, support for a service user to eat or drink

Guidance on 14(4)(d)

- People's food must be placed within their reach and presented in a way that is easy to eat, such as liquidised or finger foods where appropriate.

- Food must be served and maintained at the right temperature for the whole mealtime.

- People should be encouraged to eat and drink independently. They should receive appropriate support, which may include encouragement as well as physical support, when they need it.

- People must have appropriate equipment or tools to help them eat and drink independently.

- Each person who requires support should have enough time to enable them to take adequate nutrition and hydration to sustain life and good health.

References

1. UK Government (2014). *The Health and Social Care Act 2008 (Regulated Activities) Regulations 2014.* Available at: https://www.legislation.gov.uk/ukdsi/2014/9780111117613/regulation/14

2. Care Quality Commission (2025) *Regulations for service providers and managers: relevant guidance.* Available at: https://www.cqc.org.uk/guidance-providers/regulations-enforcement/regulations-service-providers-managers-relevant-guidance

An example of a Mental Capacity Assessment to determine Josie's capacity to make her own, unsupported decisions in relation to eating and health

What is the decision to be made?
Does Josie have the capacity to make decisions about what she eats with an understanding of how this affects her health?

What has happened to cause you to question capacity?
Josie has diabetes and a heart condition. Josie has gained 1.5 stone / 9.7kg / 8.6% body weight between February and June, increasing BMI to 42.4.

Due to having a BMI in the obesity classification 3 range, as well as being diagnosed with diabetes and a heart condition, there is a significant risk to short-term and long-term health and mobility.

Josie continues to eat a lot of snacks and large meals high in fat and sugar. It has been unclear if these are unwise choices which Josie has the capacity to make, or whether Josie lacks the capacity to decide whether to eat well to manage her health.

Information – detail the information being given to the patient on which you will base the capacity assessment.
Several sessions have taken place with Josie to look at easy-read/accessible education about her health conditions and healthy eating. Pictorial information has been used in the sessions and includes body size, physical activity, food groups, portion sizes, menu planning, healthy snacks, and food shopping. This education has been used to support Josie in developing knowledge, enabling her to eat a balanced diet and manage her diabetes and heart condition.

All information was provided in a pictorial format, and a Talking Mats-style method was used for part of the assessment. Josie was asked to look at and discuss 2-3 pictures at a time, which ensured that the information was delivered in manageable chunks. The language was simplified to assist understanding. Parts were repeated, and breaks were given to support processing. Prompts were used throughout to help focus on the tasks. Josie was asked intermittently if she was happy to continue with the assessment, to which she agreed. Indeed, Josie appeared relaxed and seemed to enjoy the assessment.

Detail the support provided to help the patient make an informed decision for themselves.
These sessions have taken place in Josie's home, where she feels relaxed, and Josie has been supported by people close to her whom she trusts. The sessions took place at a time of day that is optimal for Josie, and distractions were limited within the environment. Her Speech and Language Therapist communication assessment was used to ensure that information was delivered in a person-centred way.

Can she understand the information?
Yes ☐ No ✓
Give details below.
No. Josie could not understand salient information about what she eats and how it affects her diabetes or heart condition. Josie was asked questions such as "How does your eating affect your weight? How does your weight affect your diabetes and heart condition? What will happen if you don't change the way you eat today, this year, in a few years' time?"

When looking at pictures, Josie could not differentiate between varied body sizes, food groups, or portion sizes. She was unable to plan meals or identify healthy snacks.

Can she retain the information for long enough to make a decision?
Yes ☐ No ✓
Give details below.
No. Josie was unable to retain the information throughout the sessions. Additionally, after one session, Josie helped herself to some crisps. When asked if she thought crisps were good or bad for her diabetes and heart condition, she replied "good".

Can she use or weigh up the information to make a decision?
Yes ☐ No ✓
Give details below.
No. Although Josie expressed that an apple was healthy and chocolate was unhealthy, she did not demonstrate an ability to use this information in a

decision-making process. She could not weigh up the pros and cons of making a change or not making a change.

Can she communicate her decision by any means?
Yes ✓ No ☐
Give details below.
Yes. Josie is a good verbal communicator with a good range of vocabulary.

Is she unable to make this decision? (i.e. not able to do one of the above)
Yes ✓ No ☐

Does she have an impairment/disturbance of her mind/brain (not necessarily a mental disorder) Yes ✓ No ☐
What is the impairment?
Josie has a mild/moderate learning disability, which impacts her cognition and ability to make decisions.

Is the inability to make this decision because of the impairment or disturbance of functioning of her mind or brain
Yes ✓ No ☐
Explain why you think this is.
Josie's learning disability is impacting her ability to make decisions related to changing her diet to manage her health.

Does she lack capacity in relation to this decision?
Yes ✓ No ☐

Sample Food/Nutrition Policy

Depending on where and how you work, your food policy might look something like the sample food policy below:

Nutrition Policy for House 4

1. We will review our menus regularly and involve all service users in designing them.
2. We will ensure that everyone involved in cooking for service users is confident in preparing a range of nutritious options.
3. We will commit to role modelling healthy eating habits. This will include not drinking sugary or fizzy drinks between meals and selecting snacks from our designated snack list.
4. We will ensure that planned activities are not food-orientated. Where possible staff will engage in activities with the person they are supporting. Regular opportunities for engaging in physical activity will be provided in line with current recommendations for good health.
5. We will speak with friends and family to discuss provision of treats and gifts that support the health of the people in our care.
6. We will ensure all people in our care have a mental capacity assessment in relation to diet, health and weight completed and stored as part of their care planning.

Height Conversion Chart

Feet	Inches	Metres
4	0	1.22
4	1	1.24
4	2	1.27
4	3	1.30
4	4	1.32
4	5	1.35
4	6	1.37
4	7	1.40
4	8	1.42
4	9	1.45
4	10	1.47
4	11	1.50
5	0	1.52
5	1	1.55
5	2	1.57
5	3	1.60
5	4	1.63
5	5	1.65
5	6	1.68
5	7	1.70
5	8	1.73
5	9	1.75
5	10	1.78
5	11	1.80
6	0	1.83
6	1	1.85
6	2	1.88
6	3	1.91
6	4	1.93
6	5	1.96
6	6	1.98

Weight Conversion Chart

st lb	kg	st lb	kg	st lb	kg	st lb	kg	st lb	kg	st lb	kg
2 0	12.7	5 0	31.8	8 0	50.8	11 0	69.9	14 0	88.9	17 0	108.0
2 1	13.2	5 1	32.2	8 1	51.3	11 1	70.3	14 1	89.4	17 1	108.4
2 2	13.6	5 2	32.7	8 2	51.7	11 2	70.8	14 2	89.8	17 2	108.9
2 3	14.1	5 3	33.1	8 3	52.2	11 3	71.2	14 3	90.3	17 3	109.3
2 4	14.5	5 4	33.6	8 4	52.6	11 4	71.7	14 4	90.7	17 4	109.8
2 5	15.0	5 5	34.0	8 5	53.1	11 5	72.1	14 5	91.2	17 5	110.2
2 6	15.4	5 6	34.5	8 6	53.5	11 6	72.6	14 6	91.6	17 6	110.7
2 7	15.9	5 7	34.9	8 7	54.0	11 7	73.0	14 7	92.1	17 7	111.1
2 8	16.3	5 8	35.4	8 8	54.4	11 8	73.5	14 8	92.5	17 8	111.6
2 9	16.8	5 9	35.8	8 9	54.9	11 9	73.9	14 9	93.0	17 9	112.0
2 10	17.2	5 10	36.3	8 10	55.3	11 10	74.4	14 10	93.4	17 10	112.5
2 11	17.7	5 11	36.7	8 11	55.6	11 11	74.8	14 11	93.9	17 11	112.9
2 12	18.1	5 12	37.2	8 12	56.2	11 12	75.3	14 12	94.3	17 12	113.4
2 13	18.6	5 13	37.6	8 13	56.7	11 13	75.8	14 13	94.8	17 13	113.9
3 0	19.1	6 0	36.1	9 0	57.2	12 0	76.2	15 0	95.3	18 0	114.3
3 1	19.5	6 1	38.6	9 1	57.6	12 1	76.7	15 1	95.7	18 1	114.8
3 2	20.0	6 2	39.0	9 2	58.1	12 2	77.1	15 2	96.2	18 2	115.2
3 3	20.4	6 3	39.5	9 3	58.5	12 3	77.6	15 3	96.6	18 3	115.7
3 4	20.9	6 4	39.9	9 4	59.0	12 4	78.0	15 4	97.1	18 4	116.1
3 5	21.3	6 5	40.4	9 5	59.4	12 5	78.5	15 5	97.5	18 5	116.6
3 6	21.8	6 6	40.8	9 6	59.9	12 6	78.9	15 6	98.0	18 6	117.0
3 7	22.2	6 7	41.3	9 7	60.3	12 7	79.4	15 7	98.4	18 7	117.5
3 8	22.7	6 8	41.7	9 8	60.8	12 8	79.8	15 8	98.9	18 8	117.9
3 9	23.1	6 9	42.2	9 9	61.2	12 9	80.1	15 9	99.3	18 9	118.4
3 10	23.6	6 10	42.6	9 10	61.7	12 10	80.7	15 10	99.8	18 10	118.8
3 11	24.0	6 11	43.1	9 11	62.1	12 11	81.2	15 11	100.2	18 11	119.3
3 12	24.5	6 12	43.5	9 12	62.6	12 12	81.6	15 12	100.7	18 12	119.7
3 13	24.9	6 13	44.0	9 13	63.0	12 13	82.1	15 13	101.2	18 13	120.2
4 0	25.4	7 0	44.5	9 0	63.5	13 0	82.6	16 0	101.6	19 0	120.7
4 1	25.9	7 1	44.9	9 1	64.0	13 1	83.0	16 1	102.1	19 1	121.1
4 2	26.3	7 2	45.4	9 2	64.9	13 2	83.5	16 2	102.5	19 2	121.6
4 3	26.8	7 3	45.8	9 3	65.3	13 3	83.9	16 3	103.0	19 3	122.0
4 4	27.2	7 4	46.3	9 4	65.3	13 4	84.4	16 4	103.4	19 4	122.5
4 5	27.7	7 5	46.7	9 5	65.8	13 5	84.8	16 5	103.9	19 5	122.9
4 6	28.1	7 6	47.2	9 6	66.2	13 6	85.3	16 6	104.3	19 6	123.4
4 7	28.6	7 7	47.6	9 7	66.7	13 7	85.7	16 7	104.8	19 7	123.8
4 8	29.0	7 8	48.1	9 8	67.1	13 8	86.2	16 8	105.2	19 8	124.3
4 9	29.5	7 9	48.5	9 9	67.6	13 9	86.6	16 9	105.7	19 9	124.7
4 10	29.9	7 10	49.0	9 10	68.0	13 10	87.1	16 10	106.1	19 10	125.2
4 11	30.4	7 11	49.4	9 11	68.5	13 11	87.5	16 11	106.6	19 11	125.5
4 12	30.8	7 12	49.9	9 12	68.9	13 12	88.0	16 12	107.0	19 12	126.0
4 13	31.3	7 13	50.3	9 13	69.4	13 13	88.5	16 13	107.5	19 13	126.5
										20 00	127.0

Index

A
Activity 17, 67, 77, 83, 85, 94, 114
ADHD 33, 38, 40
Advocacy 16, 106, 108
Aids to eating 117
Alcohol 29, 60, 69
Allergies 20, 111
Annual health check 15, 93, 113
Anorexia nervosa 32
Antipsychotic medication 38
Appetite: insatiable 36
ARFID 32
ASD 33, 40, 119
Aspiration 35, 97
Attention deficit hyperactivity disorder 33, 38, 40
Autistic spectrum disorder 33, 40, 119
Avoidant restrictive food intake disorder 32

B
Behaviour:
    at mealtimes 122
    impact of diet on 39
    binge eating 32
BMI 75
Body mass index 75
Body weight 18, 74, 83, 187
Bone disorders 21, 61
Bowel management plan 21, 94
Bowel monitoring 21, 92
Breakfast 139
Breastfeeding 70
Bruxism 36, 122
Bulimia nervosa 32

C
Caffeine 69, 144
Calcium 21, 58, 133, 169
Calories 50, 62, 84
Cancer 52, 82, 130, 132
Capacity 19, 78, 81 105
Carbohydrates 52, 129
Care standards 19, 105, 139, 180
Causes of learning disabilities 28
Cerebral palsy 28, 74, 92

Chart:
    weight monitoring chart 76, 178
    bowel monitoring 179
Children 67, 140, 143, 146, 147, 148
Choice: food choice 108
Choking 35, 97, 119, 142
Cholesterol 38, 53, 61
CLDT 74, 112, 113
Coeliac disease 96
Coffee 144
Colours: artificial food colours 40
Commissioning 15
Community learning disability nurse 113
Community learning disability team 74, 112, 113
Congenital hypothyroidism 28, 31
Constipation 21, 38, 53, 76, 92
Coronary heart disease 61, 81, 130
Cost of a good diet 151

D
Dairy products 54, 133, 143
Day services 27
Dehydration 57, 60
Dementia 29, 32, 38
Dental health 22, 79, 98, 122
Diabetes 38, 81
Diarrhoea 38, 96
Dietitian 33, 74, 79, 94, 112, 113, 136, 163
Down's syndrome 28, 71, 74, 80, 92, 96
Drinks 17, 142
Drooling 36, 122
Drugs 37, 39, 61
    for constipation 95
    for mental illness 38
Dyspepsia 35
Dysphagia 21, 35, 97

E
Eating disorders 32
Eating environment 77, 107
Eating out 142
Eatwell guide 49
End of life 71
Energy (calories) 50

Epilepsy 31, 38
Erosion: tooth erosion 99
Ethnic groups 75, 156
Excessive drinking 36, 123
Exercise 17, 67, 77, 83, 85, 94

F
Faddy eating 119
Family: involving family 19, 109, 110
Fat (in the diet) 51, 128, 134
Fetal alcohol syndrome 29
Fibre 53, 61, 93, 169
Finger foods 19, 66, 159, 160
Fish 39, 40, 51, 131
Fish-oil supplements 39, 40
Fluid 17, 59, 143
    excessive fluid intake 36, 123
    fluid and constipation 92
Folate 56, 168
Food allergy 20, 111, 158
Food fortification 78
Food hygiene 20, 111
Food intolerance 20, 96, 158
Food labels 128
Food refusal 21, 22, 32, 120
Food supplements 78
Fragile X syndrome 29
Fruit 130
Fruit juice 130, 144

G
Gardening 114
Gastrointestinal disorders 92
Gastro-oesophageal reflux disease 35, 119
gastrostomy 18, 78
gluten free 40, 96
glycaemic index 53
GORD 35, 119
grinding teeth 36, 122
growth charts 74

H
Health action plan 16, 113
Health professionals 112
Heart disease 61, 81, 130
Helping people to eat 106, 117, 119

Herbal supplements 136
Hinduism 156
Horticulture 114
Hygiene: food hygiene 20, 111
Hyperphagia 36
Hypothyroidism 28, 31

I

IDDSI:
    guidelines 162
    levels 162
Immune function 63
Impact of diet on behaviour 39
Independence in eating 19, 117
Independent Mental Capacity Advocates 106
Indigestion 35
Infants 66
Infections 63, 97
Intolerance to food 20, 96, 158
Iron 57, 155, 169
Islam 156

J

Judaism 156

K

Ketogenic diet 31, 40
Klinefelters' syndrome 29

L

Labels: food labels 128
Laxatives 95
Learning disability:
    definition 26
    impact on eating and drinking 34
    impact on everyday life 27
    impact on health 31
    prevalence 26
Learning: impact of diet on 39

M

Malnutrition 76
Meal ideas 146
Mealtimes 107
Meat 131, 132
Medication reviews 39, 98, 120
Medicines 37, 61
    for constipation 92, 95
    reviews 39, 98, 120
Menopause 70
Mental Capacity Act 19, 105, 106, 108
Mental capacity assessment 20, 106, 111, 183
Mental health 31
Menu planning 139, 145, 152
Menus 145, 150, 161, 164
Milk 133, 143
Minerals 40, 57, 169
Mouth sensitivity 121

N

Nausea 38, 121
Neurofibromatosis 29
Niacin 56, 167
Nutrients: sources of 52, 167
Nutrition support 18, 62, 78
Nutritional status 18, 74
Nutritionist 111, 113

O

Obesity 70, 79
Occupational therapist 112, 117, 118, 121
Oily fish 39, 40, 61, 69, 131
Older adults 70
Omega-3 fats 39, 40, 51, 52
Oral health 22, 98
Organisational culture 110
Osteoporosis 61
OT 112, 117, 118, 121
Overweight 64, 79

P

Packed lunches 139
Parenteral nutrition 79
Parents with learning disabilities 27, 70
PEG 79
Phenylketonuria 30
Physical activity 17, 67, 77, 83, 85, 94
Physiotherapist 113, 118
Pica 35, 123
PKU 30
Policy 15, 20, 110
Polydipsia 36
Polyphagia 36
Polyunsaturated fat 52
Positioning for eating and drinking 118
Posture 37
Prader-Willi syndrome 30, 36, 74, 80
Pregnancy 69
Prematurity 30
Probiotics 96
Protein 54, 131
Psychologist 113
Puréed diets 162
PWS 30, 36, 74, 80

R

Refusal of food 32
Regurgitation 36
Residential care 27
Respite care 27
Rett syndrome 30
Rewards: using food as a reward 111
Riboflavin 56, 167
Rights and responsibilities 15, 105, 106, 108, 110, 113, 180
Rumination 36

S

Safety: food safety 111
Salt 128, 135
Saturated fat 51, 128
School lunches 140
Selective eating 37, 119
Sensitivity: mouth sensitivity 121
Sensory considerations 33, 34, 37, 84, 93, 98, 108
Sikhism 157

SLT 78, 79, 97, 112, 121, 163
Snacks 140
Soaking solutions 163
Social workers 16, 113
Sodium 58, 128
Soft drinks 144
Sources of nutrients 55, 167
Speech and language therapist 78, 79, 97, 112, 121, 163
Standards
    for care homes 19, 105, 180
    for domiciliary care 19, 105, 180
Stanols and sterols 61
Starch 52, 53, 129
Sugars 52, 53, 98, 128, 134
Supplements 21
    for children 68
    for pregnant women 69
    of vitamin D 21, 39, 62, 69
    of Omega-3 39
Sustainability 131, 151
Swallowing difficulties 21, 38, 97
Sweeteners 99

T

Take-away meals 142
Tea 144, 145
Teenagers 68
Teeth 98
Texture of food 162
Thiamin 56, 167
Thickeners 163
Thyroid disorders 31
Tooth erosion 99
Toothbrushing 22, 98, 100, 101
Training 16, 110, 114
Trans fats 51
Treats 111
Tuberous sclerosis 30
Turner syndrome 30, 96
Type 2 diabetes 81

U

Underweight 74, 76
Unsaturated fats 51, 52

V

Vegan diets 155
Vegetables 54, 130
Vegetarian diets 155
Vitamin A 55, 69, 167
Vitamin B12 56, 168
Vitamin B6 56, 168
Vitamin C 57, 168
Vitamin D 21, 39, 55, 61, 62, 67, 69, 167
Vitamin E 55
Vitamin K 55
Vitamin supplements 21, 40, 62, 67, 69, 136
Vitamins 54, 167
    for children 68
    for pregnant women 69
Vomiting 38, 121

W

Waist measurements 75
Water 59, 143
Weaning 66
Weight:
    management 82, 84
    monitoring 18, 76, 187

Z

Zinc 58, 155, 169

www.ingramcontent.com/pod-product-compliance
Lightning Source LLC
Chambersburg PA
CBHW080411300426
44113CB00015B/2472